NORTH AMERICAN POSTMODERN PASTORAL

THE

Arcadia

AHSAHTA PRESS BOISE, IDAHO 2012

Project

JOSHUA COREY AND G. C. WALDREP, EDITORS

NORTH AMERICAN

POSTMODERN PASTORAL

THE NEW SERIES #48

Ahsahta Press, Boise State University, Boise, Idaho 83725-1525

ahsahtapress.org arcadiaproject.net

Design by Quemadura Printed in Canada

Library of Congress Cataloging-in-Publication Data

The Arcadia project : North American postmodern pastoral /
edited by Joshua Corey and G. C. Waldrep.

p. cm. — (The new series ; 48)

ISBN 978-1-934103-29-6 (pbk. : alk. paper) —

ISBN 1-934103-29-2 (pbk. : alk. paper)

1. Pastoral poetry, American. 2. American poetry—
21st century. 3. Experimental poetry, American.

I. Corey, Joshua. II. Waldrep, George Calvin, 1968–

PS593.P37A73 2012

811'.608—dc23

2012015630

This publication was made possible in part by
a grant from the National Endowment for the Arts.

ART WORKS.
arts.gov

TEXTUAL ECOLOGIES

NECRO/PASTORAL

Introduction

A media spews representation but we are our own |
description. —BRENDA IIJIMA

As I write this, a man in a green Volkswagen convertible drives by at a stately pace, a potted Japanese maple perched in the passenger seat next to him climbing nearly to the height of the stoplight. The light turns green and he, it, they, roll slowly away, almost unremarked by the other customers huddled round their laptops at this sidewalk café. It is a little allegory of ecological desire, the desire to take nature with us, to integrate it into the roadways and networks of the modern. The red maple in the green Volkswagen: a baroquely indeterminate image of pastoral as adaptable vehicle for our fantasies, a vehicle that we should not and cannot discard (since there is no "outside" to ideology) but for which we must discover new pathways and destinations. Yesterday, torrential rains and flooding, the temperature barely above sixty degrees; today at the café it's past ninety, just tolerable in the breezy shade. With the advent of global climate change, weather becomes historical: that most simple and immediate refuge from uncomfortable topics, the tentative ambient glue between persons otherwise unlike, talking about the weather has become thoroughly humanized, politicized, totalized. So "nature" becomes what the pastoral always already was: a charged ideological fantasy that is not *only* ideological, but a structural reality nine-tenths buried in the unconscious of society, sending us messages in the form of symptoms we name tsunamis, snowstorms, extinctions, asthma. What can strangers talk about now except this fact of strange weather that puts an end to strangers, that makes us, literally and experientially, uncomfortable neighbors cheek-by-jowl in the favela we've made of the world?

For the present, we in North America continue to live on a precariously familiar Earth—to breathe more or less clean air, to swim in more or less clean waters, to picnic under oaks and maples in leaf, to chase deer out of our gardens, to sort the recycling, to go for hikes on trails, to meditate in deserts, to eat fruit out of season, to wait in line at drive-thrus, to listen to mash-ups on our iPods, to read avant-garde poetry printed on unrecycled paper, to sing the praises of green consumership on our blogs, to brag about our hybrid car's gas mileage, to buy clothes made in Bangladesh from Target, to dine at locavore vegan raw-food restaurants, and to dress our babies in organic cotton onesies. We are living in Arcadia: that bubble riding atop the tidal forces of history that the American soldiers in Vietnam referred to as being "back in the world." Like the arcades of Walter Benjamin, this Arcadia is a virtual paradise: a phantasmagoria of commodities, an archive of sentimental objects called "trees," "birds," and "landscapes" as obsolete and gnomically significant as books of stamps, electric typewriters, or Polaroid photographs. Behind our imperial Arcadia's gauzy curtains terrible things stand only half-concealed—sweatshops, toxic dumps, depleted uranium, drone strikes, the violence administered by oil companies and other gigantic, seemingly unaccountable corporations—but we keep the curtains drawn, peeping only occasionally with prurient horrified interest at oil-soaked pelicans or Spielbergian dioramas of Manhattan under water. We are like Virgil's shepherds on the brink of their violent dispossession, or like Adam and Eve had they been able to see the fratricide that awaited them in the land east of Eden—yet we go on picking at that apple tree until it's bare.

What comes after the end of the world as we knew it, as the evidence for human-caused climate change mounts in direct proportion to the political will to deny it? As the green world transforms itself ineluctably into an archive of genomes ripe for exploitation by biotech firms, or preserved against ultimate disaster in the Svalbard Global Seed Vault in northernmost Norway? In the face of what Bill McKibben has called "the end of nature" and the beginning of life on "the tough new planet" of "Eaarth"?[1]

The contemporary versions of pastoral presented in this anthology are indeed

1. "The world hasn't ended, but the world as we know it has—even if we don't quite know it yet." Bill McKibben, *Eaarth: Making a Life on a Tough New Planet.* New York: Times Books, 2010: 2.

Eaarthly, combating cynicism, apathy, and despair with their fierce commitment to the intersections of the present tense with the boundaries of historical and ecological knowledge. This volume is hardly intended as a call to conscience or a referendum on environmental policy or to wave the red (or even the green) flag of revolution. We are all too conscious of the likelihood of preaching, to the choir or otherwise. Instead, this book is a call to imagination—not to the imagination of dire futures, but to the interruptions of poetry. These interruptions—breaks in the mediated dreamscape of images passively consumed (a dreamscape in which "nature" plays a dominant and even oppressive role)—are also connections, recalling readers to life as it is lived in diverse human and animal bodies, in particular biomes and cityscapes, attuned to intimations of the mortality of everything.

"We want the creative faculty to imagine that which we know."[2] In spite of the massive accumulations of data, in spite of the efforts of activists and scientists and documentarians and poets, real knowledge about our situation, our crisis—the deep-down knowing of bodies in relation—continues to elude us. Reality as we know it is no longer the perceptual, tactile, Baconian world of grasses and trees, shepherds and sheep. Ours is a virtual world of overlapping simulacra in which the very concept of "nature" is challenged, denatured, filtered, and reborn. The pastoral itself is one of our culture's oldest and most enduring simulacra, a virtuality to which we can effect temporary escapes from the frenzy of modern life. So often we are urged to put down that iPhone and take a walk in the woods, light out for the territory, live deliberately, stockpile canned goods, and then return rested and ready to the fray. But like any simulation, pastoral contains with it a kernel of critical negativity that, when properly activated by poet and reader, promises to put us in touch with the reality, or realities, of our contested world.

To write the postmodern pastoral poem is to write from consciousness of this ultimate yet elusive reality, to be a digital native with dirt between one's toes. These

2. "We want the creative faculty to imagine that which we know; we want the generous impulse to act that which we imagine; we want the poetry of life: our calculations have outrun conception; we have eaten more than we can digest." Percy Bysshe Shelley, "A Defence of Poetry" in *The Major Works*, edited by Zachary Leader (Oxford University Press, 2003): 695.

poets are flaneurs in the country, naturalists in the city, zoologists in the suburbs. They do not use language to paint pictures of a natural world that is "out there" somewhere; after Language poetry, words and syntax, like the pastoral itself, form a hybrid terrain of human and nonhuman elements to be negotiated and explored. Certain tendencies are discernible in the work presented here, all of it first published after 1995. Dan Beachy-Quick, Sarah Gridley, and Brian Teare are among those younger poets intent on pursuing and transforming the legacy of American Transcendentalism, mining the nineteenth century for patterns of perception and insistence that can sustain the twenty-first. Another diverse group that includes Brenda Hillman, Evelyn Reilly, and Marcella Durand infuse their version of pastoral with attentiveness to social textures and capital flows; as Durand puts it in "HPOME 1," "in menagerie do we drift / a generation of motor oil and dusks spent whiling away / the opacities." Still other poets are harder to place—and it would be a disservice to the thorny individuality of their work to try—but are broadly engaged in the task of negotiating local powers by mapping the permeable border between the self and non-self, the I and its environment. C.S. Giscombe's prose poems from his book *Prairie Style* deal with some of the ways in which the African American experience has changed and been changed by its interactions with the social and physical landscapes of the Midwest. Rob Fitterman's abrasive and funny writing confronts a landscape that has been thoroughly branded, erased, and inscribed by pop culture. Lisa Robertson, whose long preoccupation with the pastoral has made her one of the most innovative thinkers and writers on the subject, explores the strangely gendered set of norms, wishes, and fears mobilized by pastoral, a zone negotiated by architecture, activism, and weather reports. And Juliana Spahr's long poem "Gentle Now, Don't Add to Heartache" is a new classic of the genre, employing a Whitman-esque catalog of "whirligig beetle larva, hickory, sparrow, caddisfly larva, fluted shell, horse chestnut, wartyback, white heelsplitter, larch" and much else to generate a powerful accumulative argument for empathy, including empathy toward the solipsistic all-consuming "I" that Rimbaud taught us is really an Other, an environment in its own right.

Speaking for myself, I wanted this anthology to stand in the light of Frank O'Hara's claim in "Meditations in an Emergency": "I can't even enjoy a blade of grass unless there's a subway handy or a record store or some sign that people do not totally *regret* life." The blade of grass, the record store: necessary inclusions to the Arcadias of these poems (though the grass may be engineered by Monsanto, though the record store may be an MP3-blog or the CD rack at WalMart). Postmodern pastoral retains certain allegiances to the lyric and individual subjectivity while insisting on the reality of a world whose objects are all equally natural and therefore equally unnatural. Celebrity websites and abandoned factories and *telenovelas* and the New Jersey Turnpike are all eligible objects of postmodern pastoral's dialectical nostalgia, sites in which the human and the unhuman mix and collide, as much as in any mountain peak or jungle or wetland.

Because this is an anthology of poems, its primary orientation, its allegiance, must be to the aesthetic, to the movements of language and the imagination. Yet as the ecocritic Kate Soper has remarked, "it is not language that has a hole in its ozone layer";[3] imagining "the good life," or its betrayal, has a clear relation to the actual suffering world. Postmodern pastoral offers a means of mapping the shifting terrain of that world while maintaining its ethical consciousness that the map must never be mistaken for the territory.

If it is to be not altogether delusional and vain, an anthology such as this one must be a living and motile assemblage of our best hopes for what poems can be: vessels of attention to the world and to language, attention at its most intense. To be present, with/in the world, with/in words, in active relation to the living (and dying) environment—that is the ordinary utopianism practiced by these extraordinary poems.

Joshua Corey LAKE FOREST, ILLINOIS OCTOBER 2011

3. Kate Soper, *What is Nature?* (Oxford: Blackwell Publishers, 1995): 151.

PART ONE

NEW TRANSCENDENTALISMS

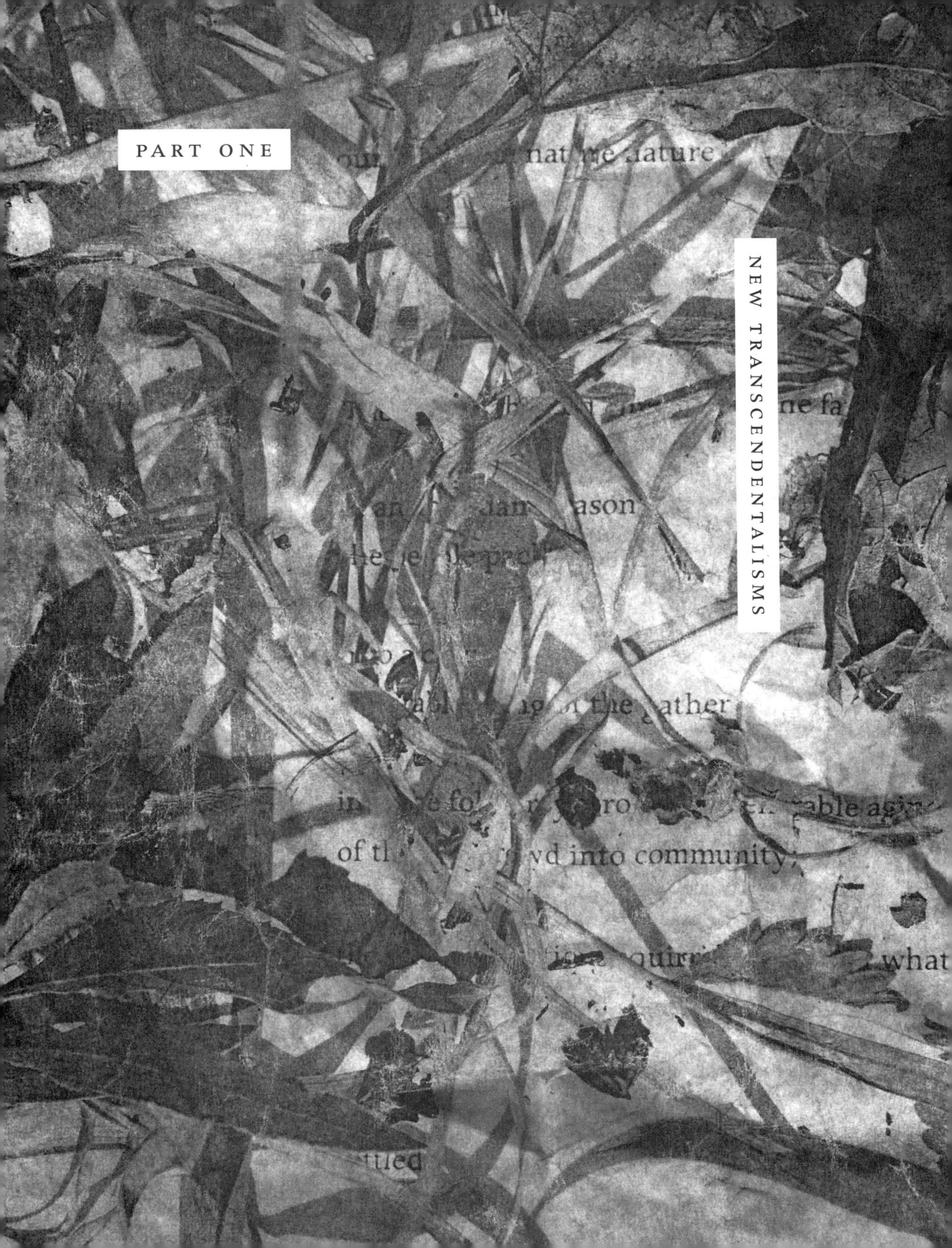

Brent Cunningham

FROM **Bird & Forest**

PRINCIPLE OF THE FOREST

The forest has no principle to begin with. If we decide to have our bird stand for human speech, the forest will grow an auditory canal, a middle ear, a cochlea. If we prefer our bird to be the soul, the forest will leaden and concretize itself.

An empty background for the bird's traversal, set with obstacles to be navigated: isn't this the principle?

Maybe two days go by without another thought. The mind is away at some foreign war. When it returns, its doubts are subsumed by its newest idea.

The forest waits, indifferent to fluctuations, intent on its own existence. It outlasts human fantasies, even those which continue for years.

I can't remember exactly when words stopped pleasing me. I knew about this death only in the way a graveyard knows about a war. What was it I wanted from writing? To produce texts that expressed something?

They wait for nothing, these forests, certainly not for the birds that fly through them. Neither are they distraught when the birds exit their borders.

For the living, patience is only yet another desire to see if life is supportable. Being what they are, humans must endure long periods that contain scarcely any astonishments, as texts must endure them.

But in that composite called forest, life is supportable wherever it exists. Therefore humans travel out to spend time in its sanctuary, hoping to absorb this principle.

Even when a forest burns up, its trees do not panic. And this is also true when that smaller flame, the bird, sweeps through its branches.

It *cannot be* that contradictions should matter. So says the forest.

PRINCIPLE OF THE BIRD

It flaps, chirps, flutters. It jerks, twits its head, takes off, returns, hops a bit, at each stage nullifying its former self. A manic, dissatisfied creature with a 5-note song.

Only the enclosure permits the bird to exist. It flies from one end of the construction to the other. Never mind its eating, mating, migrating, masturbating, or how it might account for itself. Could any of these have driven it into the forest? But this is not the question.

The bird enters the forest; it is introduced. It doesn't think, but uses the machine of instinct buried in its flesh, a device wrapped in an assembly.

By a curious process this combination is not inhuman.

Tragic feathery thing! Trying to know everything at once, to convey and remember at once, when the limit is so obvious.

When the creature can't contain anymore, it flies off, into the trees, as a pursuant, to start again its questions.

NOTES ON THE TWO PRINCIPLES
Note 1

Partway through my plans for the future, I found myself in the bewilderment and confusion of a forest. Why these examples of sound? Why take it all so personally?

The forest had hardly enfolded our hero; it would be a long traversal. He sat down on one of those fallen romantic logs. And soon: grew distracted and hungry.

Wandering in circles, he falls into a ditch, bitter, violent, alienated, exhausted. Staring up at the canopy, the sickness runs its course. Who was I actually so furious with? With expression? With the inherited language?

Actually the forest is rather beautiful from this new perspective. Its leaves break up the light; its silence is remarkable; not even a bird cries out. A rare affection for humanity washes over the hero.

Today, after all, was only one day, and this was only one small distraction on the way to something large and various. At times my purposes must become obscure to myself—it's only natural! Why Goethe himself once said . . .

Reason or not, the branches do not evaporate, the distant tremor, the noise.

Note 2

Were the leaves of this forest deciduous? Was it winter? Was it night?

Always sneaking behind the curtain!

Well, then: a summer forest, in sunlight. Discomfort made the trees to grow. Thick bark, flat leaves, a few ferns.

Note 3

The bird pecks at the fruit.
The seed drops to the soil.
The forest springs up.

Outside of the forest, you find: you weren't outside.

The fighting, the aggravation, the unhappiness: what does it matter if you lived on the earth, doing whatever was necessary.

The fighting, the aggravation, the unhappiness: what does it matter since you lived on the earth, doing whatever was necessary.

Note 4

Every tree is not every other tree. The floor is separate from the canopy, while the ferns are a certain roughness. Whatever is bequeathed a single word will slide down a funnel to the general.

The writer divides; the reader assembles. Meanwhile the government defends itself.

Note 5

It's sunny outside the forest, in the human world, but between people there is mis-understanding. And not only between them.

Everything the bird knows is stored in its blood, feathers, and nerves. Thus has it solved the difficult problem of transmission.

Everything no matter what must be desanctified. Then, again, desanctified. Then, again, desanctified.

Writing has only solved the problem of mute human blood. But logic goes into your mind, possessing it, until you are free.

Note 6

—Is he really just sitting there, in his small room, in his chair, doing nothing?

—His mind is turning over. Sometimes he smokes.

the mind and words in the mind a landscape also

"words are signs for natural facts"

facts of shagbark hickory some ash tallest sycamore thickets of
bladdernut its seed pods Jane Colden's "boxes" which rattle in the wind clutter the
ground after wind and rain
redbud corrugated hackberry and everywhere multiflora everywhere seedlings
of everything

facts and the fact of water

deer in the landscape in twos and threes sometimes in greater numbers
though this is not a deer-park privileged place of
privilege for an old family paid for by an old family's old money

the mind and clutter of words in the mind

some of which begin which begin with the
same fatal letter

to make a division draw a fine line slash and slashes to cut through the clutter

keep apart bring closer

the white deer is a fact most secret fact in the landscape what the landscape keeps
to itself
what's kept hidden kept hushed held back in the mind first and
last fact and after some of which

closer
the true the truth the true animal body a little closer.

Brenda Hillman

The Vowels Pass by in English

—& the owl drops flowers
from its eyes [*Dentaria californica*]—
the raceme, the stubbed stem lands straight
in the woods— as the ancients do;
on a hazel branch, a cocoon
hoists itself . . . with a worm's mind—;

i-eee is released in winter
as humans hold bones to the fire—
they were there a long time,
(interpreting the dead loves
as meaning seeped through the cracks
of centuries held by everyone—);

the ocean rises by inches —when
the wave withdraws, plovers pick evidence
from married footprints as the lyric does,
or sanity . . . Luminescent creatures
sink red in the sand—
for they have swallowed . . . all 3 sunsets!

& the vowels pass by in English,
　the ruined banisters of the A, a bridle-
ring of the O, the saddle of the U
　　brought from the underworld;
i had to negotiate with devils
　to retrieve even this much
from the language of the colonizers—

Cascadia

Prior to 130 million years ago much of California lay beneath ocean waters.
It was bordered on the east by the mainland of North America and on the
west by a land mass known as Cascadia. —ROBERT DURRENBERGER,
Elements of California Geography

In the search for the search

During the experiments with wheels

Holiday Inn   After the scripted caverns

When what had been attached

Lompoc   Was no longer attached

After choosing the type of building

hydrangea   In which no one has died

We recalled a land or condition

one of those   Whose shape was formal

teeth bedspreads   Formality gave pleasure

A shadow's shadow dragged it

Back to the sea of eyes

most natives   A poem floats inside its margins

They are death and birth receding

say Lom-poke   Beauty is not an impasse

Better not to blame

The loved one for a slip

made glad   God had a slip of not existing

All girls are an island

Capri Motel   Those trucks on 101 with reclining

Ojai   Decals of flame and smoke

The willless breath outshocked her

                    In Chualar a boy threw up

an under-
                    Behind a case of Coke

            In the search for the east to admire

nevered spider &
                    After reconsidering which was west

                    In an era of not singing

                    At the school of lyric abstraction

    pre-Naugahyde
                    The skin of an unthought is thought

                    After kissing Los Angeles once

chair
                    The landmass known as Cascadia

                    His parents pick strawberries for us

                    The I caused flagrant slipping

marbleized
                    Sing sank sunk in the Something-ocene

        sidetable
                    Earth started out loose

                    Pretty loose   just debris

a shape-shaped
            California motels sometimes have

                    Colonial type scallops in the moulding

    inner courtyard
                    The boy must have been hot

                    The business of margins waiting

Country Inn
                    What must Drake have thought

and Suites
                    When he strolled past the bankruptcy office

                    Marigolds on the boardwalk

        Costa Mesa
                    The back of a poem is brighter

                    Than the back of a painting

                    Osiris rode a ferris wheel

                    Ophelia rollerbladed

couch having
                    Syntax is the understudy for infinity

            They don't know what caused Cascadia

        its horizon
                    As the arrangements became larger

                    The lyric had become depressed

remote
                    Abalone chips in the sidewalk

control

There were little mirrors in his spine
As he threw up

teabag

Do you still love the sentence
Aristotle's four causes of change
Formal Material Efficient Final
And what of the warbler latitudes
And what of the unknown where
The inexhaustible plays against form

Four Points

A compass went south of crazy
Missions indicated by green squares
The skin of a thought is a thought

Saint

Torn earth is better than conquerors

Monica

His parents pick strawberries for us
He picks strawberries for us
On where Cascadia slid

to sing   and

We found a glassy spot to be assembled
A merging subverts the categories

to conceal

Some words shouldn't marry
Consider flow for example
And the unmarried rocks
In the east for the search to admire
We spoke the stuttering the slurred
Spiky poplars near Atascadero

Motel 6

Rose to protect the empty
Some moths live only two hours
Formal cause means definition

Lost Hills

Means ask your friend in the blue shirt
Why Cascadia's hair is noisy
In issues of representation

dandelion seed

He threw up from being sick

cream   When the land mass had slid under
                                   After a feathered response
          shower   Water running in the motel
                                   To get the being stained out
Fame   The immortal precedes the left margin
                                   A million pagers not working
     corrugated wind   A satellite had turned left
                                   Into a round-sided life
Best Western   A truck turned left at the Pacific
     Village   Inn   A sofa-unit in its flat-bed
                                   A line is a unit of attention
Fresno   California's lines so separate
                                   The dirt was heard chip-chipping
our girl such a   Silicon A forbidden wren
                          The second cause of change said the search
Neo-Platonist   Material cause   what it's made of
                                   The Countess of Tripoli listened
     song not   Don't try to get the stain out
                                   The red made you live faster
          a   No longer eating strawberries
                                   He had another call coming in
thought   Nestled down in the paisley pattern
                                   The island proposed a merger
     Then did   Half-moon Dewy and the Secret Julys
                                   Cascadia didn't merge it floated
                                   His song survived his supply
                          She peeled back the skin of meaning
                                   Change has four causes slid Aristotle
La Quinta Inn   The boy hardly bent throwing up
Redding   He had little mirrors in his spine

Material cause means why

nun-colored   Because of what

All boys are an island

channel-changer   In issues of representation

Had a pretty good head on her shoulders

magpie   His head   made up of singing

Loss of meaning is made up

nunning by   Of two things loss and meaning

Phenomenal accuracy as a moral stance

Kildeer love the really shitty fields

Near the missile-testing site in Lompoc

They run past drought tolerant gardens

The talk of the town

Radisson   Shirley flies a plane in that one

Nail City Bravo Pizza Taco Loco

San Diego   The beyond sang the anti-lyric

His parents pick strawberries for us

He picks strawberries   For us

To will   World champion Nafta unacceptable stain

The cloud of unknowing knew

the future panicked   In the search for the C in Cascadia

She felt chastened by angularity

Credit unions offering farm credit

anti-song   Damselflies over ferrous chloride

The land mass coddled the sea trench

They turned right into the argument

Switching to de-caf was the problem

Cercamon and Peire Cardenal

post-Naugahyde   Material cause what it's made of

truth   Fat-free chocolate envelope

I'll be good mama you can come out

In heaven we'll be recognized

The left had a fear of margins

Some moths live only two hours

Country Inn
And Suites   From flying low in the fields

The face-shaped vault of infinity

Powerbar   Her address was mad at her

It wasn't just the not singing

I laughed or   We anguished it up and released it

Whatever gets old and scaly

it cried   Baja snapped off at Malibu

Which rhymes with pale blue

Tattoos on the backs of nymphettes

We could have been happy sooner

Californians aren't good at merging

Ellis Motel   Little mirrors in his spine

Cascadia didn't merge it floated

Tulelake   Why did the chicken cross the ocean

Get someone to help you do it

A poem touches its margins gently

Twelve=the waltz × 4 causes

Formica   The scrub jay cracks seeds for hazel

kitchenette   Thought it was Charlie knocking

We'll eat no more strawberries

She thought envelopes are fattening

after the owl   Her letters arrived unsealed

In the trench for the east to admire

In one motel was a gooey spirit

true   Read *The Highwayman* as children

Black-haired woman tied up

Naugahyde   Shoots herself to warn him

They'll write in the noir of heaven

The Ojai mountains near Jane's house

Quiet as the soul of Because

Too much earth for each strawberry

The little seeds get stuck in your teeth

On earth they will be noticed

And all the human themes

In recognized it will be heaven

The final cause of change said Aristotle

The reason to which things tend

Quality Inn   The beyond is made of the beyond

She had a face lift on her hands

Space prone punctuation driven

The change didn't sink it floated

You of missing cities

The island sang right in slow motion

bath gel   They'd call this their great lost love

But the cliff knows

Where to find the ocean

Executive Inn   People think poets make poems

Poems make poems lying down

shower cap   The final cause the Goddish reason

There's a song that sang all night

There were mirrors in his spine

He bowed like California

Todos los dios estan una isla

This accidental May

Didn't fear the right margin

Country Inn   The reason to which things hover

                                    In the next millennium

                                    Don't wake your sleeping brother

                    In the earth for the search

And Suites   After considering which was west

                                    They came upon a piece of land

shoe cloth under   It had fragments in its spine

                                    It had everything you wanted

        soap   In the tablets on which it was written

                                    There's a space that sings all night

little soap   Not knowing the lyric was broken

                                    The sun looking pretty strange

                                    Lying down on the 101 it floated

        little   You want to or you don't

soap   Want to change but you'll change

Gustaf Sobin
Under the Bright Orchards

. . . ink's for the
phosphorous white eyelets, for sprinkling the
pages with
blown
phonemes. a counterworld, you'd

called it: an erratic calligraphy
of
hatched shadows (*was what*
had brought us, carried us, in dark drafts, across
the
vaporous landscapes of the
rigorously

pre-
scribed). a squiggle, then, for the
first hornet, pale
tracery

for the rush, clustering, of
bud. does it curl, will it catch? wrap us, this
very instant, in the
folds of our

own dictation? here, here's
a
dash, and there, the scooped hull of some sudden
imperative. drags, now,
in deep loops, our

hearts under, holds us in the
spell of
its running numbers. rocks, walls, the laddered
light: what the knuckles,
a-

lone, substantiate. passage, a passage, at
last, through the blanched
im-

measurable.
yes, here, in a shiver of
blossoms, gloss of
winds, draws us—in
the
hollow coil of our own dark scribbles—past.

Pastoral

. . . was the way the fingers lay limp, supine,
over the coils of that
pillowed
bone. pastoral, a
plate glazed in the high flame of the

hal-
lucinatory. what's
there, quite suddenly, isn't: doors, windows,
furnishings, no, no more than the
night in the dim

floating cabochon of
its

stars. through the
least
whispers, now, would rise, gaze as the
languorous mirror
grew turgid. for it's that, that vitreous clay
you'd prod, moulding as you did the slick
facets of

fixation. here, but only
for that

feigned perdition, that mock
succumbing. here against the abeyant immensity of

no-
where, yes,
no-
where's once again, would

follow the line of a single finger as the finger it-
self—indolent prop—teased you past the
bulk of your

very
viscera. hump of

flowers on the
far
side of all history: yes, here, here's the hills and
here, the body's

lost botany. breathe it. yes, breathe that
red-
olent portrait before the
portrait it-
self
gets hissed into the hard shower of so
                                many constituent cells.

Joshua Harmon

Inscape

Held a flat thornback. Even, a rather,
the untended gizmo: imply less
tree than tried, surfeit of surmised
selves: torn. Withers atop a weather
within, a name says a saw was.
There is thin and thin to think of it,
divisions part hidden, subduals
of sway: slash of branch, swing of twig,
sworn-off spoke, straw of year, scuff, part:
broke in the brake. So hover, hull, hear:
such bang-up schisms, radar letters
to what leaves. Green bolts in hills' heat: nub
and quick, windy and wracked, pulls a slip:
a furl limns tips split, a sleaving, slift.

*

Ten leaves amidden mast the hammering
yaws. Ware wind their color: florid stipple,
trebly grain. Frisky linens, these, bough-banked
or sun-maimed, unroomed, yare: don't call me
woodsome, wish of dust-deer risen, ghostly
continuance: so bereft, bypass spells,

curl. Willing undoes wanting, mazer than me.
Fettle the unlasted, embered other
in rash of burnt furze: flapper, a forethought,
bloom of timing to feaze percussive
memory. Airy swap, camlet cloak, go:
it isn't want of finish that fetches
fiery loft, shivering glaze in full dusk:
may fables of enclosure wish otherwise.

Sally Keith
The Action of a Man

He shot the man who took his wife.
Muybridge did.
Whiskey, whiskey & smoke, smoke—
Outermost edge of the burning, burning sun—
What does one do at the end of the day

To soothe oneself? From the museum
Seventeen miles to the ancient lake,
Home to sea monkeys, brine shrimp &
Bacteria that blooms. Of the Pleistocene
The lake once covered up

Entire states. From any direction
The sculpture is a spiral in shape.
& How many tons of stone did it take?
How many boxes breaking up light?
Mud, salt crystals, rocks, water . . .

North, North by East, Northeast by North . . .
Weaving large baskets out of reeds
Sent for from San Francisco
The Cantonese, as in the deep Yangtze
Canyons, lowered themselves down

To blow out the rock. For the train itself,
For its speed, for steam, for the movement
Of steam rising off, early motion photographers
Held understandable intrigue.
To see that exhibit take the elevator down

Four flights, go out the front door
Turn right two times and cross the bridge.
It was an economy class rental, an Aveo,
Entirely white. It was instantaneous:
He shot him dead who took his wife.

*

I was there that day without a phone.
From blood comes blow and bloom,
Etymologically. The wind blew.
The water was said to be red. The wind
Sounded loudest from the bluff where I sat

Blowing inside the pelican wings, air
Sifting stone. Unfulfilled
Was Asa Whitney's lifelong dream
To see the tracks span the coasts.
Occidental was the famous horse's name

Muybridge photographed for Stanford.
To get to the gallery the bridge
You have to cross is called the Taft,
Northwest, Washington, D.C.
To get shellac, to coat the coils

Sketched on the record, for the gramophone,
First you had to find the bug:
You punctured the bug to get the dye.
Shellac as slang, is to beat or thrash.
The work was unusually dangerous

Requiring the men to tamp black powder
Into the holes, shallow in the rock face,
Find a light for the fuse despite
The strong wind. "Celestials"
They called the Cantonese

Because of the other world in which
They believed. Where does one go
To eat around here? At the end of the day
What does one do to soothe oneself?
I would have called. That much I know.

                    *

The edges of the lake don't seem to move.
This was my first observation, apart from
The sculpture, Smithson's, the *Jetty*
Pressed down into the salt, the crystals
Of salt framing the shape. "Lake"

According to Dürer was the best for red.
According to Chesterton *Red is the most joyful*
And dreadful thing in the physical universe. . . .
He took whatever kind of transportation
He could get: wagon, train, or else, a boat.

He shot him dead. Whiskey & smoke.
Whiskey for the railroad gangs, smoke
Signals in the distant hills, threads of
Smoke rising from the cigarettes.
The directions I sent you are from my house.

Mud, salt crystals, rocks water . . .
South, South by West, Southwest . . .
The mountains look as though they broke.
The black shadow casts across the flat
Of the earth, convincing me, again

Motion starts somewhere else. It wasn't
That the waterfall most interested him
(Muybridge) but the steam, movement
Of steam rising off. You can see it
In his photographs, a tesseract.

Shrubs hold up at right angles.
A yellow bird is dead in the fresh oil slick.
I just thought somehow we would keep in touch.
Etymologically, lake once referred to linen
And crimson, lake as in to leach, to like.

*

Says the voice in the film circling the sculpture
Mud, salt crystals, rocks, water . . .
Southwest by West, West by South, West . . .
Press your thumb into the sea.
Drop the rock in the palm of your hand.

Cubes of salt have attached to the black basalt.
Saltbush, Fivehorn, Smotherweed, Little Sagebrush.
The man shouts to his wife across the lake—
Salt crusting the surface lets you walk out on top of it—
There are mice living in the oil drum, all rusted out.

(I don't know whether to believe him or not.)
Beside the jetty, an abandoned mining camp.
I should have brought the phone.
What kind of walls are there, holding together
The parts of the heart? How many spirals

Hide inside the brain as we know it *wider than*
The sky. The horizon shakes as the camera pans.
This place reminds me of the moon.
Mud, salt crystals, rocks, water . . .
On the doorknob he must not notice his hand.

The hand stretches out through the open space.
In the opening of the doors, the hand centers itself.
To the chest of the other, the hand aligns,
To the heart. He got the news and couldn't stop.
Evaporation

Is the only way for a pluvial lake
To escape. "You burn me"
Is Anne Carson's translation of Sappho
Fragment #38. I didn't know what was next.
My idea of sculpture says Carl Andre *is a road.*

*

The name of the bridge is the Taft.
The largest concrete bridge in the world
In 1907: a miracle of compression &
Exceedingly rare, designed by
The famous railroad bridge engineer

George S. Morrison. From 55,000
Cubic yards of concrete, left to cure
On the ground below for a year, seven
Roman arches have been hoisted up
& Filled in with tiers of airy spandrels.

That a horse lifts all four of its hooves
In full gallop was the achievement
Of the photograph. I first saw it,
Smithson's *Spiral Jetty*, a tiny fern head
Pressed down into a crimson wash,

In the series of aerial photographs.
David Maisel shot them from a helicopter.
From a helicopter (helix for spiral in Greek)
Smithson who had finished the *Jetty*,
Having arranged for dump trucks to haul

The heavy basalt, who had marked
The diagonal line of the spiral
With a string, lost his life
In Texas surveying a prospective
Site. I would have called.

I cannot stop myself from thinking this.
The pace of the car is painfully slow
& I worry the washed out gravel road
Will give me a flat. It is pink at dusk.
I cross the bridge returning home.

*

Connecting the coast, to see the tracks
Was Whitney's lifelong dream. It was
James Howden, the British chemist, who
Made better the blowing out of rock for tracks.
With nitroglyceride less oil was needed.

It expedited work by half. Even the clearing
Of smoke was quick. After the trial and not
Acquitted, Muybridge left. There is no possible
Frame by frame explanation. Mountains,
The Medoc-Indian War, acrobats, coffee

Cultivation, San Francisco streets, bird flight:
These are some other examples of
Muybridge photographs. Smithson's
Sculpture, once under water, is back.
You can walk out on top of it. The bacteria

Blooms brighter in late summer than now
& none of my photographs will show it.
I walked to the center and back. I walked
Between the rings where the water is
White, the color of milk, from the salt.

The bottom felt like broken glass.
No phone, but two bottles of water
From the gift shop where you can find
Postcards showing the famous photograph:
Jupiter meeting *No. 119,* the engineers

Wearing similar hats, their fingers almost
Touching, rising smoke. It is just before
The champagne toasts, the shots around
Of whiskey, the sending of the telegraph:
At last the continent connects.

Bin Ramke
A Measured Narrowness

The hare's breath trembled the
leaf before the teeth devoured
narrowness of space between
hungers. Wretched rabbit.
A minuscule mind mattering
is a thing, is a smallness
of thing this lovely evening
when we sit on stones and
light creases the grasses before
us. Parkland. Seasons. A thing
called cognitive dysmetria applies
so every rabbit reduces—distinguish
hare from rabbit, light from
even lighter. Hispid Hare with
her little leverets bounding.
The leporid, or so
I imagine, is under this turf
with altricial babies, worrying.
What we call them,
Lagomorphs, part of the world.
Who says it, and why, and whether
"matter" means to make into
world what was only mind before:

orography, hill writing, makes clouds;
makes clouds rain. The little molecules
rabbitly rattling down the tin roof;
but the rabbits are safe in their holes
and the hares are faster than lightning,
and the writers all rigor and rightness.

Forrest Gander
Edge-Lit Scene

Turns to her, then,　　　　　　　　　from the northern
oriole taking a dust　　　　　　　　bath. It is her voice
unseats him. Years　　　　　　　　it will take
　　to thread himself back　　　　　　　　into the dull wood.

Two spider bikes lean　　　　　　　　against the Dairy Dream,
their shadows, toward evening,　　　　　　an aftertenderness
　　she sees and aches.

With children, they grow　　　　　　　　more involved,
　　more isolate,　　　　　　like grazing animals, vaguely
aware of the other.

And something small slips　　　　　　from them, murmur rising
above a crowd's silence　　　　　　during the performance.

It is their performance. Like hens they fill　　rooms with their voices
not because the egg,　　　in passing out, hurts them.
Because the place has been made　　　　　　empty within.

When they tithe their attention,　　the thing itself
is incomprehensible. They think　　they have swallowed
　　stones for each other. They think　　　　they are blocked
　　by their sacrifices,　　　　suffocating

in a dark shaft.　　　　　　Who can say
　　they will hit again　　　that gorgeous galena ore
which is emotion,　　　the fact of emotion?

Escaped Trees
of Lynchburg

Mostly, they live disagreeably   amid volleys of far-off barking
and a chalk lake, spring-fed,   clear. Watercress and wild
celery in the current   undulate. Trees, the central figures
of their own originality,   come bare down the slope
to bathe.   Sudden raptus in the land,
arborescing.   The poplar
and its reflection   are disturbing, like twins.

The trees live disagreeably,   secreting
chemicals that attract   parasitic wasps
when caterpillars start   to strip the leaves.
February sap rose   from woodpecker holes.
Surreptitiously deft,   willows speed in their lingering,
all together and insolent,   acoustic nodes on their branches
sough a neuter language.

Each topos is seeded   by a loop of tendril.
In mud around the lake   horsefly larvae, partly buried,
pierce the bellies of young toads,   suck them dry. The present
is the unknown, a development   without resemblance. A small
inflorescence of blue   mist from stills
precarious on upward slopes   will condense the cow-smell
and hold it to the hills   like a shadow cast in space.

Winter tits hovered,   dipped their beaks into sap
at the icicle's tip.   The lark arborescing, that secret
neuter language,   and no one to decipher
the concealed from the given.

Merrill Gilfillan

FROM **Ten Carbonated Warblers**

FOR O. MESSIAEN

1.

This is your chance
to sit back and sing

half hidden against the sky—
being
BLUE-WINGED

2.

I say Black Holes
perform something easy
voluptuously misunderstood

Immaculate conception maybe

Tincture of tincture

Houses   On the hills!

TENNESSEE
                or NASHVILLE

        3.

    Stop the car
where

BLACKBURNIANS
                    are

        5.

    Physique unique
at all seasons

A voice in the street
at your feet

Dark eyes go to . . .
Anna Moffo

    BLACK-THROATED BLUE

6.

Memorable village
without roosters
whose dogs bark at dawn

Memorable men in fields
looking up

Pockets full of
say
CAPE MAY

8.

O
Open fire

Who cultivates
the master tick

Between the rows
of geology's sense
of time

PALM   PINE

Eleni Sikelianos

ODE: To My Peoplery, Little Trees

Nothing binds
a community like cats catching flies
like spending money at the corner store
money binds many birds
a community, handing out cigarettes
lighting matches with shaky hands
soda pop binds, and wine   There are no
trees here oh no, no trees
diminishing trees I miss you
where did you go in the crystal dark, disappearing
into Brooklyn's arches like an infinity   infidelities   untrivial trees tippling

over secretly into when no telephone poles exist, satellites orbing, toppling into
radar sound when no one was watching barely-there trees
birth little trees, have a little nose, are hiding
in the sidewalks of this city   They
please help the consequent trees trying to get more significant
eat cigarette butts, drink wine, have big eyeballs
So there they are in their jackets
"Someone should open a way for them through the ice"

Trees

        think of snow

   They

        know duration

The Russians are not apologizing to them
The Mexicans are burning them
The Americans—there are no
good Americans

There is an invisible tree
in your pocket, your book or in your purse, it's invincible
Trees still do
a newspaper or two.
There are ghost trees in your subway and buslines, at Bergen Street,
plus real trees at the green pit that is Morningside Park

No, that's a python, this is a bog with trees beyond the Pillars of Hercules
In the laws of less-and-less, trees confine to one sex what
in humans can profitably be done by two Who-
     soever has been initiated into the mysteries
   of Kabeiri knows what I mean:

      O thou thouest of trees' throat and frogs forsake being for sale

unto saplings; trees, like movies and dinosaurs their bodies are getting bigger
   their brains, small

Smaller, you are sitting on a chair that used to be a tree   I cannot explain this
   as metonymy

the eyes of my people, so those on stars
of trees, trees
What you breathe!

Maiden doctor fix this tree
its chichis and choners
moghuls and trees. Gen
                    X is

            better than trees. dead fishes
        in dead seas
        tanks of everything poison! I banish you from rivers and trees for I feel
all hysterical for trees.
The Niger gum's tired, "la woods" is

another way to say "little tree" traveling with stars in a
folding landscape, falling R
yea deep in paralysis the blue goal is no howlitzer, Gum Shoe,
            abuse the scene
            by rotting a weed
            in it: you is
            the weed. No, no
            it's me, a
            minor tree, her
how early around the ears, There was
a tiny tree. All she heard was inserted
On that scaffolding, with the aid of ropes, infinitesimal trees
move up and down the faces of buildings

The Most Beautiful Theorems of the Theory of Animals, Numbers

No john can exceed the mellow
bath of one square root

of the light the insects form
in the tints & forms of the sleeves of trees. And in the fits,
the dark, and the dark

starling turns
the whole startling

head into the mouth,
head,
night,
flesh. If
Massachusetts
Carolina Ohio could walk
& talk I would tell them : rain

is made
of places trading
with the flesh. What is flesh

through the bush

of far pines & eternal
sky? Congress

of asters, polymers, free
to start carbons, cars.
The jewel is strange, Animal, shaved

by slip-
knots, gulf-

lightning, radiation. Therefore shall I unsex my dress
rising up like an antelope, bending

down like a pear? Ocelli, ovipositor, in my dreams of affixing
the glittering twigs

back to their sticks I did conceive
of the bathing forms and sleeves of
conscious-
ness.

T. Zachary Cotler
Ångström Zion

1 m, nervous system: the Orphic
archetype sings to some women, who lead
a pain-colored calf under unsheathed
axon willows. One of the women dies
away through cirques of bony lime, till she
stops feeling him feeling women hear him.

10 cm, spinal section: in the heartwood
of a world-tree, fibers bundle into braids
of braided necklaces of runes for which
the Odin type gives up an eye. He reads,
dendrochronologically, potential for apocalypse
in radially and vertically stacked disks.

2 mm, network: these leaves' veins are red
and lapis, signifying that *the Sovereign Lord says*
I will stretch out my hand against Edom and kill its men
and their animals, and approximately a billion
leaves receive the signal, and the calf
screams like a woman dreaming birthing a calf.

100 μm, neuron: light and water metaphors
collect on the somatic surface of a leaf.
In membranous arrays of nights and days,

the motion of the women in the pain
song is drops and flashes, dots and dashes,
propagating backward into memory.

20 nm, synapse: an icosahedral synagogue
of light inside a water drop, the last receptor
of a fraction of the women's and their animal's
reflections as the song goes out of range. They think this is
the last night or day. The drop shatters on the edge
of a leaf theoretically trembling with chaos.

1 Å, ion: in the void in Norse
known as *Ginnungagup*, in Greek, *Kaos*,
in Hebrew, *Tohu VaBohu*, a cow licks salty ice,
rasps open channels in the surface, until the leaf-
crowned head of a Eurydicean type surfaces. The face
cries. It is made of astonishingly long numbers.

Jane Wong
FROM **Sea of Trees**

"Whether my bark went down at sea—" —EMILY DICKINSON

Pitch. A plum, a sweet   planet. Pitch an arrow
over the missing apple. Tree of magnesium. An ounce
of truce is heavier than a storm. To lose my struggle, my

hat to wind. Shrunken, forgoing morning and marrow.
Slumped, still, the feathers off—I: an already loosened
jar. Sparring, not: Chronos, you great little monarch of

great little death. Wings of thorn, ocean of pine, tassels,
timeless rot. Here bends the ocean trench, bound in yarn,
your all-in-all consuming watch. Wash, a photograph in

reverse does not repeat. The curse of good deeds: the day
rises and demands another.   Drawing circles in a lake, in
a spoon reflecting on empty. Pocket-less, pointless, the owls

no longer turning to look at what is happening: the point
of a mountain sharpening in a sky I cannot shut out.

*

Ring of lilies, ring of rust   the darkening sun:
eclipsed corrosion. Rise at once, master of forget-me-
nots, master of polished armor. Ardor, a coachman

leaves me his horse, weeping. The heart in fog, in hooves
he can only see lightning. The signal of atmosphere in
atrophy. Blue waste, this cold liver of a sky. The horse

sleeping like a house with a painted door. I sleep in
rafters, in early drafts, bird drift. To ask to enter.
You can stop a stair, still an hour in glass. Gloss,

the jeweled mane reflecting. How you dare to knock
through— I flew to   a higher point: safety
in trees, in any number of branches, blight. I made

a splint out of a mirror, a guard out of a nestling. My
little army of little beaks: tearing the sun inside, out.

          *

Hunt in hiding, in hives of orange   spoil.
Hunt, Chronos, you great sleeping bear. Growl
in paws. Snout of rose   smash. Bind my

hands around a hollow so there is no hurry, no
harrowed field to empty in. I empty out: star of
ash. I begin as a tree and a tree begins as table

to set down a fork, a knife.   Cut, hemispheres
fall from left to right. Ruin of orbit, the correct
answer is what   is time. The hush of bread

gone to spoil. Or, lying on a park bench until
the grass grows over. Call it moss mouth, cricket
of the lungs. When a man coughs, he coughs to

be alone. Talking is no longer an option, no longer
a corner of sea to flee to. My alibi full of coral.

Sarah Gridley
Anatomy

Nerves upon the tops of trees. An otter makes lightning circles in her tank, confusing our sense of humors. In the leaves of a light- or shade-loving plant you are always heading deeper outside. Outside is a watering hole big as your eye. Tonight it will come back in to your body, a storm with windows never closed. If it holds a knife inside the dream, you will tell it your story in every sense. Of your dog who barks up every tree, of each experience working free of the bones. A cooled and exploded star lives in your palm. The expensive thought turns black on its surface.

Edifice

In the river's comprehensive reflection stand the tall, thin men who taught me Latin. Rumpled and shining, they smile at one another and exchange congenial handshakes. When I am always older in their repetition, the days seem more and more analogous. A silver, edgeless river cools off the only sun. Light coats the high tuition. The long hand of the clock sticks, spasms, resumes. I am called on. I am sight-reading a description of Dido's Carthage. Light climbs the Latin. This could be stalling or stopping for time; this could be feeling among the honeycombs in which space holds time compressed. Outside a city below all cities, I am holding my heart to the river. I am passing my hand above a single bee. Above ambiguous castings of the sun, its thistle, silt and favor.

Father

You say to verify is not, by any means, to bring to light. I point to silver granules left behind on a tenable surface of then. You see silver in the word emulsion. I see a milky light, almonds crushed in water. You cross yourself and list in threes. I say *grain* inside and think whatever happens. Was it anonymity or truth when early photographers wrote in place of signatures, *Sol fecit*: The sun made it. One seed, all its allied grasses. Brain before mind—someone conducts its restlessness in the low light between the singular and collective singular. Tell me the truth. Or say it is hidden. I said to soothe once meant to verify. You ask what is the negative. Is it love or music pulling whiskey from light. The one or the many things left on our tongues.

Some of What Shines

- is the ambient world, a bustle of light outpacing you, some, a slip-knot you thought was real, red streak of the black gloss capping the drumming bird-skull. Some of what shines is bison skulls, a pyramid pile we ground to bonemeal. Here is the corn in steady rows, there the eliding hurry of train-light. Gloaming is another word for ghost, a coast of earth and moon, and haunted, a silhouette roaming the long house of conscience.

- is the sinking feeling. Look: you are only just becoming yourself.

- is the earth itself. Earth, a period looped in moon, thoughtful in what it in turn encircles. Much of what shines is below valuation though the story of earnings works to attract you. Where loblolly pines line up in the no longer cultivated field, select needles loosening in the lower ranks of shade, a red cockaded woodpecker dines on the cones.

- is a lake alone. Though only baring the physical, a mirror once rooted with miracle.

FROM Half Sick of Shadows

Who is this?
And what is here?

Not a branch
or a star

but a flower named
for its deep-toothed leaves.

Not for the wide-bright florets—
sepals soft enough and light

to loft each shell containing seed—
up to twenty thousand

ovaries
dispersed on breeze

Mei-mei Berssenbrugge
Glitter

I.

A wood violet has bloomed, when I come back from my walk in early spring.

I stop to welcome it, cooing, walking around it, not as if I were floating, but the surface of the world circled unfurling petals.

Person and violet with so little in common my voice reveals as a resonance of unmanifest identity.

The violet looking back, loses objectivity and enters the expansion of recognized things.

You could say our identities reach out to encompass the forest environment, like telepathy: a moment opens space by rendering it transparent in intensified consciousness.

Others embrace weather and wild land as means to the suprasensible, in violets an emotional desire for spring light: glitter, the mirror.

Connection, often the form emotion takes, appears to me as a visual image.

2.

Thoughts are sent out by one rock informing other rocks as to the nature of its changing environment, the angle of sun and temperatures cooling as night falls, and even its (loosely called) emotional tone changes, the appearance of a person walking, who's not appropriately empathic.

Thoughts meet and merge with other thoughts sent out, say, from foliage and other entities.

I tell you, your own thoughts and words can appear to inhabitants of other systems like stars and planets to us.

Intensities of thought, light and shadow between us, contain memories coiled, one within the other, through which I travel to you, and yet are beautifully undetermined.

For what you say to me is not finished within my thought or memory, but you grow within my memory and change, the way a shadow extends as light passes over it in Akashic emptiness.

You grow through what I have to say to you, as a tree grows up through space, then what I have to say changes.

That's why we need the identity of our physical forms.

Here, we don't know what's behind physical stars and planets.

3.

The tree encompasses its changing form, while ego, my self of physical experience, looks in the past for something to recognize.

Flexibility would be the key word to another, since the experience is plastic, carrying a larger identity.

When he looks into my eyes, she said, I see adoration that makes me feel wonderful.

Then, I can do things.

Here we mean sun, alteration, myself are actions, the culture of Tibet disappearing, a thousand hopes of David Foster Wallace.

Imbalance between identity's attempt to maintain and intrinsic drives results in an exquisite by-product, consciousness of self, so richly creating reality, which seems plastic, but continues like a light beam, an endless series of beams.

Creativity breaks through identity, and my awareness flows through transparency as spontaneous synchronous phenomena experienced with others today.

Its changing light and weather spectacles are fantastically aesthetic.

4.

The moment it sees me, the violet grows more deeply purple and luminous to me.

Its looking collapses violet frequency into a violet in the world, cohering attention and feeling.

What I perceive as a flower in woods may be the shadow of a flower-being's action in fairyland, a transcendent domain of potentia.

The transparency I imagine moving through is being through, not actually seen or touched, not the buzzing of a million invisible bees.

What you call feeling, like connective tissue or vibrating lines between us, represents this vitality, and I prefer the term vitality to time.

In fairyland, all violets are simultaneous.

Camille Dungy

Her mother sings warning of the new world

You will know the place
when the children run paler
        and their mother's breasts
                are high
                with quelled milk.

                Do not let yourself love
the man who boasts he planted each blade of the sod you admire.

        The grass is from England, and each steer
it markets is worth more than the life of hands
whose work is to bury then raise what this Englishman takes
        for his own.

He will feed you well.

                        At rest in his lounge
you will taste the juice of sapodilla
        and crushed cherries.

He will feed you well.

        For this quenching,
women will forgo sleep while you dream—netted
and cool—on the white yield he allots to your body.

Elizabeth Robinson
Crossing

What one wants is a way to get across the terrain without leaving it. The story of human life, at this moment in history, is the story of the combustion engine, of the motor's bass clef below a line of thought, the shimmer of hot air in the foreground when it warps upward from the highway.

It's now possible that most of the world's population lives in semi-arid climates. Not so far back, there was the dream of the arable. A shock of greenness besieges the nostrils and lips of a child who has never sniffed it before.

How does one break up the day into increments of hours, time having become more artificial than ever, as the road claims its own number and keeps going on? Lakes, on the way, also look phony—desperate outsized puddles. Ansel Adams's photograph of the moonrise over Hernandez, New Mexico: image cutting through memory. Lunar liquid—the only real cure for thirst.

A town whose name in English means "burnt." All the way across the continent, there's a mark on the vinyl ceiling where a shaken can of root beer spurted up and made a stain. One dreams of grinding a hole through the floor of the car so as to watch space moving underneath, but that bit of sugar water on the ceiling stays still. It's as though obedience makes a bargain with movement. Whatever year seat belts became a standard part of car hardware.

Some decades later, a woman's mother sends her a box of rocks, each wrapped carefully in a Kleenex. They make no sense at all. Like an arm, extended out of the car window: the skin burns but can't record where the sun was when it hit. What follows. The woman feels silly throwing the almost-unused Kleenexes away, but heaves the rocks in a single unburdening into her backyard: Oregon coast, Arizona desert, Connecticut woods, Maine island.

Nothing induces sleep or thought like the steadiness of an engine. The sound of a Navajo radio spot for Kentucky Fried Chicken. Car passengers cruise past wordless at the scene of a huge and orange car fire. At the state line, the girl riding shotgun leans forward, puts her hand on the dash, in order to cross the border first.

Amarillo is both ugly and full of pollen. All the way through the town, the motor chugs its correct pronunciation: ah-mah-ree-yo. The driver sniffs. Rumor has it that when Georgia O'Keeffe lived there, she took her paints and drove so far out of town, she could only get back by waiting for nightfall and following the lights back.

They also say that when it got too hot, she crawled under her car to lie in its shade. So the engine's a tether to the lightsource, its own umbrella, the convection between the bare road and an ambivalent compass. Before air conditioning was standard, one had other ways to carry environment, like its own sheen on the skin.

Date milkshakes at a desert convenience store. Postcard of the world's largest nickel from one of the Dakotas. One could spend almost an entire day saying nothing, except the occasional: we need gas; let's stop so I can pee.

Outside Las Vegas, a man climbs from his car, back sodden with sweat, the perforated skinprint of the car's plastic seat embossed on his shirt. His daughter buys a postcard with a roadrunner on it. And a tacky pink backscratcher shaped like a cartoon hand. Frequently, in hours that follow, she leans forward in the seat, eyes up at the speeding-past sky, the plastic fingers on the backscratcher scraping up and down her spine.

Oni Buchanan
No Blue Morpho

I wanted
the Blue Morpho
to anoint me
with his fragility
I was in his presence
in the tent
of butterflies
he did not land
on me though I stood
very still for a long
time very still
with my arm
extended like a thin
resilient branch
buoyant curious respectful
a pliant limb I thought
venturing into the scented air
of blossoms and delicate
curling offshoots
a graceful arc of tender
branch but he did not
land on me I tried
to look succulent I
imagined myself
exuding fragrance

and the lobes of my ears
ripened taut with
the redolent essence
of honeysuckle
but no Blue Morpho
came to alight upon
my shoulder and unfurl
his slender tongue
toward the delicate
curve the rosy curve
no Blue Morpho
alighted upon me
that day beneath
the butterfly canopy
the air was
mixed part saturated
warmth fertile humidity
part the cries of a caged
canary part the effervescent
sound of evaporating
mist from the cascades
of a man-made waterfall
I stood very still hoping
to be mistaken
for something more
beautiful more luxuriant
luminous tropical a fragrant
possibility but no
Blue Morpho anointed me
with his delicate foot

no Blue Morpho landed
momentarily on my
outstretched arm to
breathe his shimmery
wings and launch
again no Blue
Morpho drew a curve
in air that rested
on my shoulder for
a solitary point
instead in my
perfect concentrated
stillness I heard
for the first
time the microtones
of wing scales drifting
softly and invisibly
through the heated air
microscopic motes of
color-fashioned dust
descending through the
perfumed air
as various butterflies
brushed imperceptibly by
the scales
accidentally sounding
as they fell the
air itself brushed
their sound I
overheard that nearly

imperceptible symphonic

grid that map of tones

within the satiated air

that net of sounds

that caught me in its

webbing that fell

from wingtips delicacies

dropped by the

Blue Morpho as he

flew on in unerring

loops his joy

beamed elsewhere

nonintersecting beacon

Aaron McCollough
[*log*—a mild vision]

I . 0 — HIMSELF

that's okay   letting go some bees today
the old man kept in slatted wooden crates
obtaining to the husbandry of bees—
a bluish white in places where the paint
has been repainted (the new color
skimmed milk as one dips rags in kerosene
at an impasse)—and expecting the worst

triggering some smoke then running behind
the rusty boiler
                        to admit confusion
as a wedge (the wedge we have is painted
a flaking red, misshapen at the face)

must admit not knowing what to do
                        and so confusion

the soul has had enough   meaning
    the wait
                the genius of this place is "was":
the same rose blows . . . nothing changed but the hives

and this is america!
. . . the bees stealing out and in . . .

1.1 — WALT

that's okay, wedge   and over here, sleepy
with the humming of the bees / with industry /
admit a tablet to prevent confusion
then proceed   proceed
proceed with hacking at the privet root

the task at hand: planting twenty hemlocks
measuring the room between and burying
the soily bulbs   evergreens over years
they grow and overgrow

      and they are like your bees

1.0 — HIMSELF

then i will sing to make the work feel swift
my love is less afraid   at night i sleep
and less and less afraid   i may yet come
to love the world beyond my bed   beyond

      my love

1.2 — A RUBE

eros by any

the same rose blows

can't do better than that

than   a toast

a toast to thanatos?

    I . 3 — W . C . BRYANT & (A RUBE)

the solemn brood   (what of such love?)
of care plod on   (where learned?)
and each one as before   (to what may love be girded?)
will chase his favorite phantom

    I . 0 — HIMSELF

(remember what to let) some letting go
the privet lies unhedged, and we're
defenseless so between the hedges   and okay

she has come to work
and I have come to work

shall i describe her precision against my berserk:
      with a piece of fruit
        the roots
        the

and she loves to rest   my love is precise

if the day is full of troops

                        returning

the day is full of fear

where all must move their homes

          with which fear

we comply and move

1.4—HIS WILL & HIS LOVE:

> *evry will desires purity w/o turba int   powr xtends   holds in subjexion*
> *(less it escape fromt)   therefore the weak doth run and seek the limit,*
> *hidden in mystery, sought by all creatures*

love: not confused but out of control. good:
        to labor is not to love: though loving
        and leave the weeds   no ugliness in plantain
        nor beauty in grass   don't dare distinguish
        the green from the green   not sisyphus flower
        from narcissus from wandering jew

will sings of devices and a positive love:

                posits a love:

Melissa Kwasny

Talk to the Golden Birches

Peppered with mold and myrrh, clawed like cloud-strips, they grow in the copse on the hill. The first one I found, lying on its side, the next half-covered with moss. Gilt, *adjective*, their colors of gold. Gilt, laid on the surface. Gilt, *young female swine.* There is a surprise in every forest, many etymologies to cross, and directions, not paths to decide on. Satyr, black mushroom, sticking its foot out of the grave. Tree fungi, so stiff they won't tear off. Before the hieroglyph was deciphered, it was thought of as a language not to be read but *revealed*. One had to be initiated to understand it. To pick through the litter at its feet. To tip the cereal bowl of breakfast stars. Emissaries, but of what? The river is wind-pocked. The leaves brew a tea exactly the same color as this bark—metallic, like tin snipped and roughed up. "Where did November come from?" How old is the soul? Our dear exotic companion. Marked by public tragedy—those who locked hands and fell from the towers—and the private—those who looked away.

Talk to the Water Dipper

I hear it fall and then its shuffling in the un-burnt paper of the last fire. Do you have a story about a chimney and a bird? Because here I am in a forest, and it is just before dark. I am afraid to open the door. The woman who has lost her memory says that she doesn't like it here, that there is no one or no place to visit. She wishes the furniture weren't an art piece. She wishes she weren't always bored. *Is there a higher power / there is a higher power* reads the plinth of the sculpture on the path, but to me it is too simple a question / answer. In the life of the water dipper, this was probably the only time it would be inside the house of a human, which must appear like a giant trap with upper reaches. Everything must seem square and, thus, wrong. No fly throughs. No under-things and bridges. Nothing to eat either, all jar. But it must have liked the stove door that opened of its own accord to a world beyond all previous measure. What did I mean there? Not in the way it does, mimicking the stream. A myth, but that's the rub, something's got to turn into something else. A myth: the water dipper, the mossed cottage trees, the tin man, the rose, etc.

The Butterfly Conservatory

The colored lights they are always stringing. The placemats they set. How I stay past an initial shyness at my own delight. A Large White dies, bodiless, a papyrus with fading ink. Nothing dies with less evidence of rot. When the scrolls were found at Qumran, there were forty copies of the Psalms. Eight lines in each stanza, read from right to left. What it must have felt like to recognize one had discovered this famous text, perhaps in its original form. They carry their prayer books, their portable shrines, the ones that depict their battles with the wind. A written language is one with trap doors to fall through. When I talk to myself, they open, too. A butterfly suddenly becomes impatient in its shroud, the one that resembles a gray leaf. The one that is imitating a raindrop. Could any of us mark the moment we realized we were unhappy? Could we mark the moment we wanted out? In the house of the butterflies, there is a glass case. In it, the pupae of hundreds. Monarchs strung like jade earrings across the wire threads. Painted Ladies like drying seaweed or straw. Please, don't let me hurt anyone today. *Who will make me to lie down in green pastures. Who will prepare a table before me.*

Laura Moriarty
Plumas

Flashing jay. Stellar. Wings and body. Sky. Lake. Blue vase. Ultra. Deep night. Stratosphere. Ink.

The roof blue. The trees black.

Cloudy though still warm.

A discordant chorus.

Fowl.

Chimera. A fox. Stunned by light.

At dusk a man fishes for trout.

Lamplight. Kimono. Night again.

Day again. Goose quill.

We write.

Down and feathers. Inland beach. We read.

About symmetry about

Sound.

Spoon against cup. Toast.

Surface choppy. Husband. Thought.

People sleep in rented boats.

Geese on the beach. Grass and clover.

There is a storm. The lake is audible. The rain sweeps from the west. Our boat seems.

The memory of something. The waves were gold. I dream I know someone. But there is no point in knowing.

Reading about the city in the country. At night.

The air is filled with the sound of a piper.

Writing.

The city of those thinking about the city.

Up here they are a deep.

Afternoon sleeping. Blue.

The cell receives information in material form.

Time of day. Storm.

Coffee. Notebook.

"The very concept of a form, with an internal self-'reflection' or duplicate of itself as its defining characteristic—the concept, in other words, of symmetry with its constitutive dualisms (reflectional symmetry and rotational symmetry, asymmetry as itself determined by symmetry and so on)—implies a circumscribed space: a body with contours and boundaries."

A book with a sky on it. *The Production of Space*. Lefebvre.

Or song.

"The casket is empty
Abandon ye all hope
They ran off with the money
And left us with the rope."

The Pogues.

The blue dishes we bring from home.

Goose. Geese.

Leaves among them. A small one with a loud song.

Osprey.

Sleep before diving.

We sleep or walk.

Thick with flowers.

The blue dock.

When we move
The objects have a new arrangement
But are the thoughts
We recognize in them
What "we"
"And as for me" (from a song)
And as for me
Not knowing

Summer seems dark though the days are long. The brightness is flooded with an absence of memory and obsession. There are questions.

Unasked. We get ready to go but don't go.

Questions about possibility.

A single and occasional cloud of butterflies in the heat of the day. Goose down.

Noon and wind.

What we are
When most (unconsciously)
The same is a remembered
Song from a movie of a book
About memory A part
Altered to fit the music
When we play (ourselves)

Cabaret

I have you then.

A jar of wings.

Two clowns in a canoe.

A blackbird shaking the bright body. Black and blue. Yellow.

Left shaking. Wings.

Black and white lake. Night.

My sleeping. Rented.

Seen from a chair in the corner.

Love.

Bucks Lake, Plumas County, May 1992

Brian Teare
Transcendental Grammar Crown

I had no Monarch in my life, and cannot rule myself,
and when I try to organize—my little Force explodes—
  —E.D. TO HIGGINSON

I gazed long. I saw how mutability & unchangeableness were united.
  —FULLER, *Summer on the Lakes*

But we would rather believe that music is beyond any analogy with word language . . .
  —IVES, *Essays Before a Sonata*

You cannot hear music & noise at the same time. We avoid all the calamities that may
occur in a lower sphere by abiding perpetually in a higher. —THOREAU, *Journals*

Health, south wind, books, old trees, a boat, a friend. —EMERSON, *Journals*

The leap from matter
(*Idealism*)

abstraction   lays waste

to day   ox-eye knodding

roadside   can't help

but fail touch   if the real

must be monument   to a systemic thinking   —it's not   that we don't

cotton to optimism   just   from the local   purview   it looks like rain   :

when we're in bed   & eavesward   thunder tumbles   to shake the panes

we think about   oiling

our boots   —which is

to say   to be our body is sticky   hurt fir   white-green lichen   the fawn's

brown sides   shot through with spots   like pastured asters   we walk in

skin   & salamanders exactly   the orange of old pine   & still we love

our minds   *do* seem clearer   the way quartz tricks a window   into earth

*

Our minds do seem
(*Rain Guide*)

unending silver gilding   whose color   surface

doesn't suffer   like light's   clarifies outline   :

lily   bell   yellow   yarrow   vetch   white

violet   lace   crown   —what happens is

syntax   color-

less   texture

clamor   dress

—wanting nothing   for a sentence   to make

noise sense   we went   earward to wear

appearance   a noun   a page   a field

guided to wildflowers   —is lips   is hooded

is ends in spikes   purple

paired leaves   a square

stem   :   hello   hairy skullcap

                    *

Hello
(*Ives*)

—interval   from felt

to string   a struck

ear's   the soul's seat

set ringing   —easy

                    now   song   has a few rights   can break

                    a law   if it likes   if our ear veers   hymnward

                    it won't wear   no ribbon   to match its voice

—intellect is never

a whole   soul

finds things there

          —must a song   always

          be a song

          some

          in this book   can't be sung

    *

This book can't be sung
(*Reading Walden*)

—solitude   self-definition   :   pure

nationalism!   beans in a row   & a year

to hoe them   heroic vatic stance struck mock

epic   all ironic to trick the mind   into seeing

America   a masculine parable   a second-growth

forest   to walk there   an easy wilderness   vernacular

apples   your grammar so declarative   it *is*

a government   —prophetic voice   come

closer   bring your certitude   so we can pinch

it to pith   force it   to the far wrong side

of moribund bachelorhood   we are stunned blood

we are inherited citizen dualism   we must begin

to ring   must in your ears   rebuttal   stuffed

with spirit   your whole ruddy skin   stung with it

*

Inherited citizen dualism
(*Field Poetics*)

doubt   entered the field

in the form of a body

always   grass at edge

calf-high   then rising

as heat   midday does

waist-length

　　　　—transcendent   reason   :   mind forsaking

matter it finds   impossible questions

　　　　　　　　　　to consider   —roots

　　　　　　　　　　cool   green   below

　　　　　　　　　　browning stems   it

　　　　　　　　　　didn't want to   eat

　　　　　　　　　　our mouth   intended

                    to tangle   is not

                    mind   it's never

                    wanted   for order

          *

                    Our mouth is not mind
                         (*E.D.*)

you will never forgive us

for we never visit   sick

with god-longing   livid

fever   reeling   bestial

need sends us on all fours   in the field   where heat

ends mid-stem   spectrum's very heaven   boils above

hawkweed & birdsfoot   trefoil & a roil   of inflorescence

—doubt   a terrible field

to live in   whose laws

are made by a god

without cause or qualities

were we to cry out   lord   our voice   the wrong season

for milkweed   it's the only thing   to come home to is

what scatters   what's always going away

        *

What's

(—)

as saint

is slant

to pain

storm   norm numb null

thorn   pressed to thumb

as wait

is pain's

time's

plait

in all's

stall   what becomes

of becoming

fear

nadir of feeling

*

Of feeling
(*Sonnet*)

—no monument   no moment   no human

passion   just spider's fiber   cantilevered

thing   hedged   best guess   a net

to register   the transparency   identity

becomes   its minimal matter   fragile

—and then what   plaint & wait   as if

your whole life   a pattern of spectacular

aptitude   for disappointment   your

intelligence   a broken wing   a bird

feigns   to distract the hunt   from kill

—it's useless   to reduce gesture   further dear

form   :   are you reason   are you even feeling   :   fail better

   *

Fail better
(*Thoreauvian*)

—solstice brings the field

to its knees   yarrow

flax   vetch   heavy

estival air a gall of pollen

—& aren't you novice   again in lit   Euclidean gilt

shadows to true   each natural fact   toward more

radical matter   :   a robe of rhetoric   auric eulalia

—to angle praise   fodder the color of how you felt

as a child   pure Bible-light   ochre smoke & ivory

vellum pages   cut stems   sweet   —taller now

than grass   you can't

but muster   nothing

longing a rope you'd use

to haul it all   other-wise

       *

Other-wise
(*Grasses Parable*)

—to have been built bent

to bear witness   to have

been thin-stemmed   spined

like a mind   to have said

—it's true   we saw the grasses   turned snake

flesh   fall crept cribs of cryptic ribs   we wished

it was a dream   but the fields   went weird & left

—was it a dream   at forest's edge   we watched

dark arc over the fields   how trees begin to lean

at that hour over   their own shadows   & the voice

called the grasses   back

by name   —timothy

bent   orchard   hair

poverty   sweet vernal   come

*

Sweet vernal
(*"The Over-Soul"*)

above   the canopy creaks

wood on wood   exactly

the sound   of docks

on the lakes of our childhood

& wind   :   water walking

awkwardly on top of itself   toward shore   —the problem with solitude is

each fact is twice   :   once ours once   its own   :   & so vision   is question

& response   is also twice   sight besets the trees   that are memory also

& wind   water that touched shore so long ago   it washes up here   above

—you said the soul   knows only

the soul   sight seems our own

& doesn't   why a lake sound

high in the trees   why the smell

of hay   sweeter than seeing

　　　*

Vision is question
(*Ives : July 4th*)

afternoon encumbered

by thunder   birches

turned dirty   curvy

piss-yellow stormlight

& someone singing   behind the trees' screen   *a place in the soul*

　　　　　　　　　　　　　　　　all made of tunes   of long ago

　　"a certain

　　　　　　　　　　　　　　　　—but it is hard   to love

　　kind of ecstasy"

　　　　　　　　　　　　　　　　old men's   sentimental

　　　　　　　　　　　　　　　　off-key singing   even

when beauty   moved them   as it moves us   to watch fire

works in wartime   eerie green

                                        "but they sing

mimetic   sound of missiles

                                        in my soul"

whistling   bitter smoke

smothers the field   a song our fathers loved : *Shall we   gather at the river?*

        *

The field a song
(*Leaving New England*)

in the field   we dream

west   how poppies tip

toward orange   *heliotropic*

a word yellow   edge a furl

        fragrant   —to say good-bye   is specific

                        as the node where grass branches   & stem

intends   *inflorescence*   a word we love

where it clusters   fuzz   most modest

of blossoms   green timothy sheathed

of a sudden   in yellow   —we lie

on our backs   a view   framed by grass

& light rises   three times   the owl

sounds round   as a nest   :   the very

air crows thwart   their throats upon

*

The very air
(*Faith Reason*)

but we tire   of spirit   sight

striving always   for elsewhere as we are

so much   among phenomena   God

        loses luster   where we are local only   inured

to detail   starting small   with grasses

        flowers then trees   we don't know   nor rocks

days   to recite the names   of them all

        seems heaven enough   to us   because what is

language that   "categories of thought

        embodied in individual living forms"   thread through us

& things equally   —matter   a sidereal charity

        & doesn't it bract   doesn't it sepal & send seed splitting sheath

into soil   doesn't our flesh   the very fossils   tremble bedrock

    *

Fossils tremble
(*Matter Gap*)

it's easier   to walk now

through grammar   colonial stone

wall fallen   to gaps   on soft needle

plush   sprung rust rot so acid

nothing else can grow   —you would know   is it soul the fern

interrupts itself   to reproduce   it is easier   to ask now

if grammar better follows nature   to die in cycle   than culture

in ruin   the gaps are different   aren't they   —but neither

better explains   how to say

anything   where to put each word

so it lives differently   in relation

to the real   as it dies   what is it

to be   the leap from matter

to a transcendental   grammar

Tony Tost
Kept

Mother memory, or memory daimon, thick heart of the tree, running in place.

All the endings, who is my keeper, a change of seasons, my shirt in the tree.

A severity of care, the offering story, a gallery of beginnings, the begging can end.

A recall of leaves, a seed of seasons, nighttime tree-climbing, shadows enlarged.

Treetops stop swaying, the breeze still stinging, a sweat of moonlight, transit grasped.

Each word a circle, the end was saying, running on her hands, a memory squall.

What remains unknown, an image keeping, the wind is stacking, a tap of beaks.

And mothers buried, and as their weeping, again the plow, back into the grain.

A split of branches, a flame is circles, kept silent and awaited, the pulse of a tree.

Great fire of image, the alone unloaded, waft and whipping, the message is mind.

Each passage writes it, the popular emotions, a pitch of polis, the crept are called.

Greek days gather, a mouth in the middle, moths in a puddle, a leak of sublime.

Feeding on guilt, an epic breathing, a law of feeling, image shitting its rule.

Strategic suffering, each victory quaking, a cooling board bending, this mural of smoke.

The child and chisel, a tide of shadows, the scenes are mirrors, a shiver of pines.

O breeze of berries, forgive the living, what moon I'm milking, drinking the links.

Like a large tree humming, my insides floating, can't I call you, flickers in the throat.

To frame the faceless, in the drone and darkness, according to another, devoured by light.

Remember the future, a chance to name it, from flower to flower, by talon and beak.

What were the ballads, my children hunt them, Shelley and Milton, the lands of my youth.

Adam Strauss
No Fathers Without Mothers

[Dear teacher

[   ] Please let's

[   ] Now plait

[   ] Wreathes

By the [   ]

Sea my [   ]

Hearing grieves [   ]

For father [   ]

[   ] Lost at [   ]

[   ] Here is [   ]

[   ] Pink under-lit clouds [   ]

[   ] Lumen

Upwelled [   ]

[   ] Father's tilling shines

Others
Necessary

The middle
[Of to]

Led me [soul]
[A]lied—
Elm mile [you]
Died

The [wrong way
By yew ewes
Were all bray
Sluice

Was] me
[Unheady]

"The Wild Carrot Taking the Field by Force"

The   goal is to   create
A flexible structure—
Don't call it   chaos. Rose

Stem   rips a hem of his—
Rakes skin: a tender swarm
Of atoms are rose   hips

Hip to the   field of   hops
Where it's likely neither
I nor   you will have been.

I see more of the world
In words than another
Way. You   don't have to put

On the red light. A pool
Of wild water in
Sunny woods and I'd be

Happy—no: my view can't
Withstand   walking through: I'll
Take the fen—all my   loves.

Timothy Donnelly
In His Tree

They are untold: the advantages of entangling
oneself completely in a place like this, up and beyond
all chance of discovery, here where *untold* means
not *in the dark*, but *numberless, numberless* not
without number, but *many*—and if I sit in the dark
now and wait without number, the difference is

I do it voluntarily. Not the way the yellow leaf
is chased by another but the way the word *yellow*
can be drawn by hand through the same pond
air and then across an open page. Here the one keeps
evolving into the next, like listening into seeing
thin layer after layer of nacre affix to (to whelm)

the body fastened to sleep in the heart of a pearl.
All afternoon a feeling needed to be described to me
before I knew what I felt. The very terms of this
predicament had disqualified me from the honest
work of that description—prior to my knowledge of
how could I describe a thing?—while the whole

burden of assigning the work to a desk not my own
promised nothing but to deepen the predicament's
bite in my perception, and having watched hours
and even days turn out largely perceptual in the end
I would observe at this crossing no fast distinction
between seeming to be worse and actual worseness.

But an object absorptive of all my attention, a thing
outfitted with otherworldly fire, set to consume
more than I could ever feed it, might so completely
overtake the mind that there would be no room
available for feeling and therefore neither cause
nor way to describe what just wasn't there. And so

I set out to find that thing, drawn down by an under-
water instinct true to the warp and weft of a small
false deafness, locked deep in the blue-green private
compartment broken up into shifts and strung in
accordance to the wiles of arachnid light, a light too
truant from its source to reflect a compact back

with fidelity: the sun its half-remembered lozenge
trapped among the birch. Everywhere suddenly
rivalingly glinting like a new place to contemplate.
Cobbled paths linked by garden bridges arched
over the pond's narrows and ambled on to unusable
amphitheaters brightened by mats of continuous

aquatic vegetation: primarily macrophytic algae
fringed in eelgrass, coontail, and the American lotus
rising a child's height above the water's surface.
Suspended in the air on a firm stalk the enormous
round leaves shaped into bluish, soft-sided cups;
if floating, into plates; if emergent, they were as yet

unopened scrolls, a history of the pond's bottom
unnoticeably written on them. Portions of the lotus
interknit beneath the surface provided habitats
for invertebrates not visible from bridges: cryptic
rotifers and hydras, the larval and the nymph
incarnations of mosquitoes, beetles, damsel- and dragon-

flies fast as horses as adults, but in their youth
sustenance for numberless fish, amphibians, reptiles
and all the fervid waterfowl whose bills plunge
upward and down with untold destructiveness.
And I could tear my eyes from none of this, probably
because the mind kept seeing more than an eye

or kept wanting to, detecting in what it landed on
what it didn't see but knew, sensing the relation
between things present and between present things
and those remembered or supposed: humanity
in the park's stonework, messages raveled in
long bolts of music stampeding from the ancient

calliope at the heart of the carousel, and the future
bound in decay. A lost past beating in sago palm,
the hagiography of red caladium, and the resistance
to deterministic thoughts on identity implicit in
ten skipjacks convulsing from the shallows at once.
Always a stuntlike communiqué in the loop-the-

loop in which wind blows a paper cup across macadam,
deep in a mushroom, and in 108 sunflower faces
turned to face the setting sun, its diameter spanning
108 times that of the earth, here where we in turn
invest in 108 feelings: the first 36 pertaining to the past,
as many again to the present, and as many again

trailing off into the future, each coruscating dimly
as daystars, or as stars at night through exhaust, each
known by its own appellation, each with a unique
list of probable causes, cures, and a prolix description
reworked as history determines what we can feel.
All afternoon a feeling needed to be described to me

but the wording only veered it nearer to the word.
Or even just to check on it would change the way I felt.
Furthermore it constantly underwent self-started
evolutions I pretty much never managed to observe:
fluctuating on like a soft shifting mass, yielding
instantly to pressure and engulfing any object senseless

enough to have trusted in its surface, incorporating
whatever it can into the grand amalgam of itself
discovering itself and finding everything perfectly
indispensable and pointless as the rowboat comparison
builds for the landlocked hydrophobe in all of us.
Nothing terrestrial could be equal to a force like this.

No leathery general could ascertain its stratagem
squinting through binoculars across the scorched sands.
The TV might be getting warm, but police hounds
can't track it down because it smells like everything.
To surrender to it means you taste its invincibility
deliquescing in your dune-dry mouth, its properties

becoming yours, as when vigilant in a cherry tree
one converts into the branches, the drooping downy-
undersided leaves, the frail umbrella-like flowers
and impending fruit, until you forget what you were
watching for to begin with, the need to know now
culminating not in dominance, not control, but liberty.

Karla Kelsey
Vantage of Landscape & Soft Motion

I.

& so turning in departure the dock dipped & the world turned on its side until
months later I looked to the future of zinc set against rust, oscillation & char seen
through a claude-glass with a green tint & whitecaps whipped by the current

& breeze

of if I. But if I

am in & through the window & the summer storm, walking through heat-

heavy lilac

to crouch under the holly tree, departure composed in the view from the dock
drawn in nettle & air as inside the shelter of my body we fall, particles of sand

& salt

among water-

vented pollen

dispersed by image & breeze. This discord saturates with the seen-through-a glass,
with the wait-in-the-doorway-until-you-recognize that your name is only a problem
under the distance of certain systems, constituting, reconstituting, the barn

sinking back into

naked aspen,

leaves gone to mulch as light shines on the boy walking down the sidewalk singing *Mary,*

Mary, Mary,

an attempt as in my eyes settle on lupine & sage, ocean & field. The dog barks

& a choir

of birds

preamble the cicada season, the turn-turn, the nape of your neck as you said *lilac*—
chosen in the hothouse interior of her rooms with the gesture of a well, a steeple

> to the left

> in the blue swirl

> of sky. The sweet

of the lilac divides the sea from called to the sea, the land from the harrowed
so that in town masts list as from building to building wind wraps & the flagpole's

> halyard clanks

as do the lines upon the mast. Land & weather submerge. On the wall the sun
draws each degree of declension, the path smooth though somehow the middle

> of the day

> spans hours.

2 .

Yoke of horse. Yoke of iron. Each perception's entry into the stream
is granted through seed, through the far corner of the field called wing

> touching wing,

this our land created by the cut-through of the river, for what the river's

> washed away

in branded thinned light is left to silt & half-submerged trees, little farms

> & meadows

in the overrunning. These patterns construct my frequent thoughts
as the sun goes down, forsythia's accretion come spring, come the slow circles
where the river pools under maples that each year leaf to darker crimson
as I write the names of flowers connoting the island burns, flame replacing

> swallowtail, lifelong

> fidelity as

> the sun goes

& this work of water moved through hands is liquid ribbon, a mirror
reflecting the doe recently shot & stripped as I watch myself approach
the abandoned dining car, dirty mattress in the corner heaped of smashed glass

        & cutlery. Take

        my hand. Air become

        dove. Air become

land grown granite-heavy & plinth for here the river wides & slows, wind moves
through rue anemone on the ridge & a bleating called force pries in
as the fields wash away, trembled, become part of the hills bone & the mind

        bone, the bank

split apart by wolf flower & meadow rose. Bluing into the next century
the river marks the book beholden to feathers cover my eyes, the sound
of wet leaves drawing day through parched grass, a lit moth marking
its source on the map where the inevitability of faith gives over to the matchstick

        & the little

        cracked cup.

3.

If not for these slim moments fit between paving stones, light-light, the air

        densed to

        soft snow,

        inhaling as

        the ship goes,

the season of birds slinging these shallows would be withdrawn from glance
only to be felt, simultaneously, in my ribs. Manifest in battering my body's
warm center is a consequence of yellow light blooming after the rain stopped

        & I saw

        you afraid,

        interior motion

become measure, the pool given at oblique angle as the mouth of ice
& stubble fields falls back. The road to the steel pivoted bridge half-anchors
in demi-release, in memory, eyes closed to the swans on the banks
of the frozen lake, the lake then heated & drained without question
in the manner sentiment welds to regret & we're asked to the cut-pouring

                        known to some

                        as God. He is

a naked branch of the all white tree, null shade for the ground where the lily

                        sleeps in-

                        mirrored as

the tree inside my lung expands, knotted, grown every which-way & winning
over gravity, icy branches extended, the flow of ever-occurring words, hands,

                        eyes lifted

over power lines. The willowed island parts the river abandoned to heresy:
in the thaw of the banks the fixity of the arum lily released becomes sails

                        drawn up,

                        the white

                        ship in a

                        white sea,

your scarring hands turned to firelight. As our will disintegrates into the world's
secret said to shallowed stone, the fire dies with slow campaign of century burnt

                        across eyes.

4.

Blank forehead of asking the question to the room afforded of answer
in the bolt of a picture, a red horse sunk deep into deeper red as the earth

                        was red there.

                        & there

I blanched into aspen & window split light, an afternoon V mosaic-worked
into garlands of orange roses rewriting the planetree, the hush, bird egg
cradled in the hollow of my hand as the song's cried out from the fiction

> of a citadel.
>
> The pace
>
> of bees

filling air furls to distant shores pictured in a wavering voice, in the watery

> voice of siren
>
> called waves
>
> relaxed

into an account of solitude. Wrapped in torn blankets & rough sheets,
mirror warped to *I've seen between myself & myself*, the writing stitched

> into eiderdown
>
> densed
>
> with breath
>
> &, so, infused

with the chorused sun, the melody turns to lilac panicles flowering out in punctuation
of the day as dust blues the crowd to sway as one like the canyon undergoing

> a moment
>
> of light. Slow
>
> & strange,

we're pulled south through blurred heat, getting out of our car among them to wander
the metal & salt of accident & shore. We've come here bare or wrapped
in linen, the moment held in our bones, this in ceasing, ash light falling over

> the worried edge
>
> of water meeting sky
>
> in horizon.

5.

Time points to the hour of the curtain, the ceramic lamb still warm
from the daughter's hand, the room become a minor legacy as we go
& this telling frosts over double-paned glass: the road one way & the cold

> seeped to the papery
>
> fronds of
>
> the fern,

camera lens approximating the landscape's gaze, the locket lost & the bees

> died out
>
> until spring

when newborn they form a susurration in my ear. A crack, a weather composing
the back of the mirror & so paused with a sprig of dried sage. Paused,
& yet at the same time leaving with the tincture moon, the lamb lost
of its cabinet & you, humming under your breath to the metronome

> of the clock's
>
> tick, the window,
>
> the devotion of
>
> the field scarred

canvas. We waited here for the pears to shake down from the sky, the new

> limbed tree bent
>
> in heaviness,
>
> the moment

giving in to the pull where a sigh acts as talisman against the red storm

> gathering true

to history's compression discovered in white marble monuments,
the distance holding a steeple to the right here garnered, here collided

> with the press
>
> of geese V'ed,
>
> vented breeze

making yesterday's salt visible to the lens apprehending the fruit rained down

as verse torques to fit on its side to say I am home now & bathed

in the usual yellow light of the kitchen, of the bee gasp through tall grass,

sawdust come

to settle

in the joints

of white stairs.

Alessandra Lynch

What the Meadow Said Afterwards

meadow said *spring*
meadow could not hear itself think for all the bells ringing
meadow could not look to see whether the sun had turned blue
or the cloud became gold—meadow could not taste guttered wheel
nor sludge-barrow, nor sullen hill, nor blood-licked tin
that lanced asters to sorrel and lace to loam

meadow could not receive footfall
it could only feel rain and inward it turned
on itself for not having known
more

meadow said *drown daisies drown*
their obedient necks sodden green
their ridiculous twist-off faces
their petals falling like poor hats

meadow said:
be dead, heart
be the raft cracked
don't function as door
spill like salt, effortless, daft,
white-faced, aghast

choose the city in lieu, lying
removed, stiff with lights, crippled by wire, over
the sweet, dying blossoms, the stalks terrified
of their thorn.

Dan Beachy-Quick
Fess-Charm

Dust-swallowing dust, I am
   Covetous of
Dew, a drop. Cover the thorn
   That split in half
The water-bead into the black berry.

No one taught me how to darken me
   But me—my tooth
     Bit
The berry as the berry told me: *bite*

The wood-world, half-eaten, dark. I am
   Bone-biting-bone,
What more? A drop, a dew. For one
   Drop-of-water,
     I'd convince
The yew to bend in half its height—
   To drink, and hold
With my hand the yew-tree down.

Hold the yew-tree down. Accuse: *Do you see—*
   For one drop—
What you've become? A slave, a splinter
   In the thumb—
My ripe thumb. A splinter answers:
I am one solution to thirst.

I walked into the woods and found
   The woods walking
     In me
Demanding proof. I have a thorn inside
My thumb as fact the thumb exists.
    A thorn is
Echo of the tree. I heard, I thought
   I heard—

Myself asking—the splinter not
   Asking
Me—myself asking the splinter for release.

Said-Charm

Blood's property—the mind
   Folds leaf to thorn
     Forgets
Each crease, each crease, cannot

Unfold the thorn back to leaf—again.
   Found—not
In the half-choked leaf, not
   On the stone-broken,
     Wind-blown water's
Skin—I found on me
   A wrinkled map,
How-To-Fold-To-Pierce-Through.

My warm tongue knows winter's shape—
   How to lick the thorn
     Tip and freeze
   One nib onto another nib.
A thorn on the tongue becomes the tongue's

Alphabet. Say *leaf* to tear the leaf—
   Water tears open water
     A splinter-width
And lets the ice run through. Done.

Done so. One must—
   I had to—
   Hold the thorn, pick
The thorn from the stem, first. I did

Not speak, my thumb didn't speak, the thorn
  Spoke
To my thumb, *I know the nerve*
    That knows the brain
That knows what words I'm formed with.
    Speak back, thumb,
Your drop of blood, your fluent red globe.

FROM *This Nest,
Swift Passerine*

#9

first

sparrow   <u>rose</u>   <u>pine</u>   <u>ash</u>
sparrow   rose   pine   ash

<u>green</u>   <u>abyss</u>   <u>ivy</u>   <u>wasp</u>
green   abyss   ivy   wasp

<u>thrush</u>   <u>wake</u>   <u>spider</u>   <u>star</u>
thrush   wake   spider   star

*

& then

sparrow   rose   pine   ash
green   abyss ivy   wasp
thrush   wake spider   star

Imagine thus the pond: a bell
filled with water. Atmosphere first
walked upon by water-striders.
Where their legs touch the water
a cloud is dimpled. Paperwhites
lean into vision. Echo is a figure round;
her wilderness is a greenwood.
Echo enlarged is ecstasy. The music
in the leaves is first found below
the mirror on the pond. A leaf is slow
in the air as it falls. Then heaven
trembles. This is not terror—words.
Then the paperwhites cannot see.
To dip a pen in cloud undoes the cloud.
Strike the bell and the sky parts.
Or love-cracked, bending
over the still water, peering through
my own gaze peering back at me,
I see how erasure ecstatic undoes
the surface by which the world was seen.
Bells in circles ring and so their sound.
Imagine thus the pond:
There is a tongue under the water.

—

my facts shall be falsehoods

my sparrows shall brood
in rose my pine shall be
a stem (as hers) a thorn shall hold
in thrall the sky my ivy twined
around my wrists my pulse
an arbor over me my spider
shall walk upon the echo caught
a bell-tone blown vibrant on breeze
my wasp shall be honey's viceroy
in me her wilderness shall deny
as greenwood does flame
my star shall be bright to shatter
my song in tendrils grows
woods deep in dictionary where the aster
springs rootless upward into bliss
my music shall bewilder my own
heart shall be falsehood

to common sense

———

*I saw a snake by the roadside and touched him with my foot to see if he
were alive. He had a toad in his jaws, which he was preparing to swallow
with his jaws distended to three times his width, but he relinquished his
prey in haste and fled; and I thought, as the toad jumped leisurely away
with his slime-covered hind-quarters glistening in the sun, as if I, his*

deliverer, wished to interrupt his meditations—without a shriek or faint-
ing—I thought what a healthy indifference he manifested. Is not the broad
earth still? he said.

—

what I have been doing is trying to listen
by opening my mouth
*
this year in these pages
*
found the slough of the snake on the road-side
and only then the snake

—

Echo, I pine.	*	*o* pine
Looking up. Over the water. My voice	*	watermyvoice
has no edge. I am the edge. I pin	*	I am edging
My voice to a leaf. The water is	*	leafthaw eros
not thin. Light betrays the surface.	*	inlight yourface
Will you be seen? Over the water.	*	bein water
A wave is thin. The shore is no sound.	*	away is now
Pine bough the empty sleeve. I am	*	empty eve
Looking up. My voice. If I am alone.	*	voice my own
I pine, *Return*.	*	in *Return*

Eric Baus
Tuned Droves

After an animal beacon sounds, a black disk masks whatever there is to see, three swallows enter a poplar's pulse, and the entire forest darkens a shade.

The Song of
Stunted Hawks

The singed horse doubles as an only swan. That their spawn's spores have become a seam between ions serves to re-divide its swells. Nurses mirage the song of stunted hawks by speaking out of phase with the queen. Warped by delusion, the arrow has always been part of a swarm. Atlantic transformations occur bilingually in the war between mice and frogs. Here, there are no neutral storms.

Who King Tree Is

The first chapter of King Tree is always blinking 1:23 or 5:55. When the frozen soundtrack flooded the forest he knew he wanted to say his name in the form of a mailbox, but the letters said, Do Not Forge. The voice-over wants to know who King Tree is. Who is King Tree? It is 5:55. It is difficult to distinguish between branches. The gentlest signals subsist on growls.

How King Tree Sleeps

He is also not seeking, like a child, the eyes of an animal. The infant and the animal have altered their instincts. They know, of course, that they do not know the darkness of trees. The house holds pollen. The house holds pollen and a tree beacons black. They know his not-body becomes what it surrounds. It surrounds what it is not seeking. He sleeps beside what the house keeps out.

Peter Gizzi
Some Values of Landscape and Weather

Democrat—I know what time it is . . . —HART CRANE

In the middle of our lives we walked
single file into winter's steely pavilion.
The moss's greening, winningly,
made our footfalls pavane in silver light.
To be out on a Tuesday with Liberty,
her bright flash stinging.
I followed willingly, she sang
haltingly, and I kept closer
to navigate her coo and whisper.
To be at the farther edge
of beauty, this forest, its lacquered raiment,
we declined to name.
The song built with the populism of a mural.
Bits of refrain dovetailing
into a distant rumble like a bulldozer
from memory, a mockingbird's gravelly clank.

*

Where were we
on the deck having a smoke
after a day in bed. Odd oranges
and blue velvet outline the roofs.
We've stalled in this whistle before,
the train at dusk. Thinking oompahs of dented brass
yesteryear calling on the road:
cloth, hair, and a string to guide us.
Take me away. Not to negate these years
but I need stay rutted in my own
long enough to swerve outside
this collision of particles that dogs my view.
I am working on hands to field
other hoists of rescue—something
particular to blue has begun
to rise from the deep and do its shtick.
And falling down dark, of course
I need you, but that said
all the ropes thrown overboard
wouldn't find me, like sun once
dripping into basement punkdom.

                *

Not wanting to disturb an ant
I lift my leg to let it carry on
its pursuit of whatnot.
It's impressive—all this matter
crawling, marching, even achieving
an acorn of the instant.
So, this isn't exactly novelty here

babysitting the woodgrain, wanting to step up
inside myself. Courage!, carrots?,
"Charity," the word says in a notebook
—to accept the ink of the possible,
"this proves I have dreamed."

*

It is the pixel hour,
a witching pre-code silver industry
blowing through my head.
Ball bearings glide along
making it *ting*, a steely chamber
overhead. Unmistakable.
I might have said forgotten
except so many are bent to hear it,
as though music were a condition
of all our endeavor here
on the snow-spattered globe.
A nervous moon and winter branches
all that needs be recorded for now
and the value of gunmetal
fading to midnight all around.
The chill is real, that much
can be said in early November.

*

We fought in a war, looking for a sound,
some frequency
a human animal could field
beyond the other registers of everyday

and fancy, a tuning perhaps,
to focus for this instant, the effort
toward dotted archipelagoes was a part of it,
documentary hydroelectric facilities,
sno-cone mountain views, certainly
the unruly assembly of public space
is essentialism, there can be pigeons,
statehouses and prisons, freeways
etcetera. They were big chords,
a piece of the total score, the trajectory
(not facts, but hands) is this further sound,
scratch of pen to parchment
in a flight of democracy.

     *

Night coming on, goings to and fro
under a canopy of burning discs
and that twinkling bigness. It was all the time
happening. Here beneath
the shadow of branch and ballot.
Where else can you say
that to love the questions
you have to love the answers.
Outside, a transmission's whine
breaks our unmediated approach
to a brambled paradise.
What could we do now our gaze
had been altered, and constantly.
The shiny spot's decoy, sometimes
emotive, sometimes in bright digression.

PART TWO

TEXTUAL ECOLOGIES

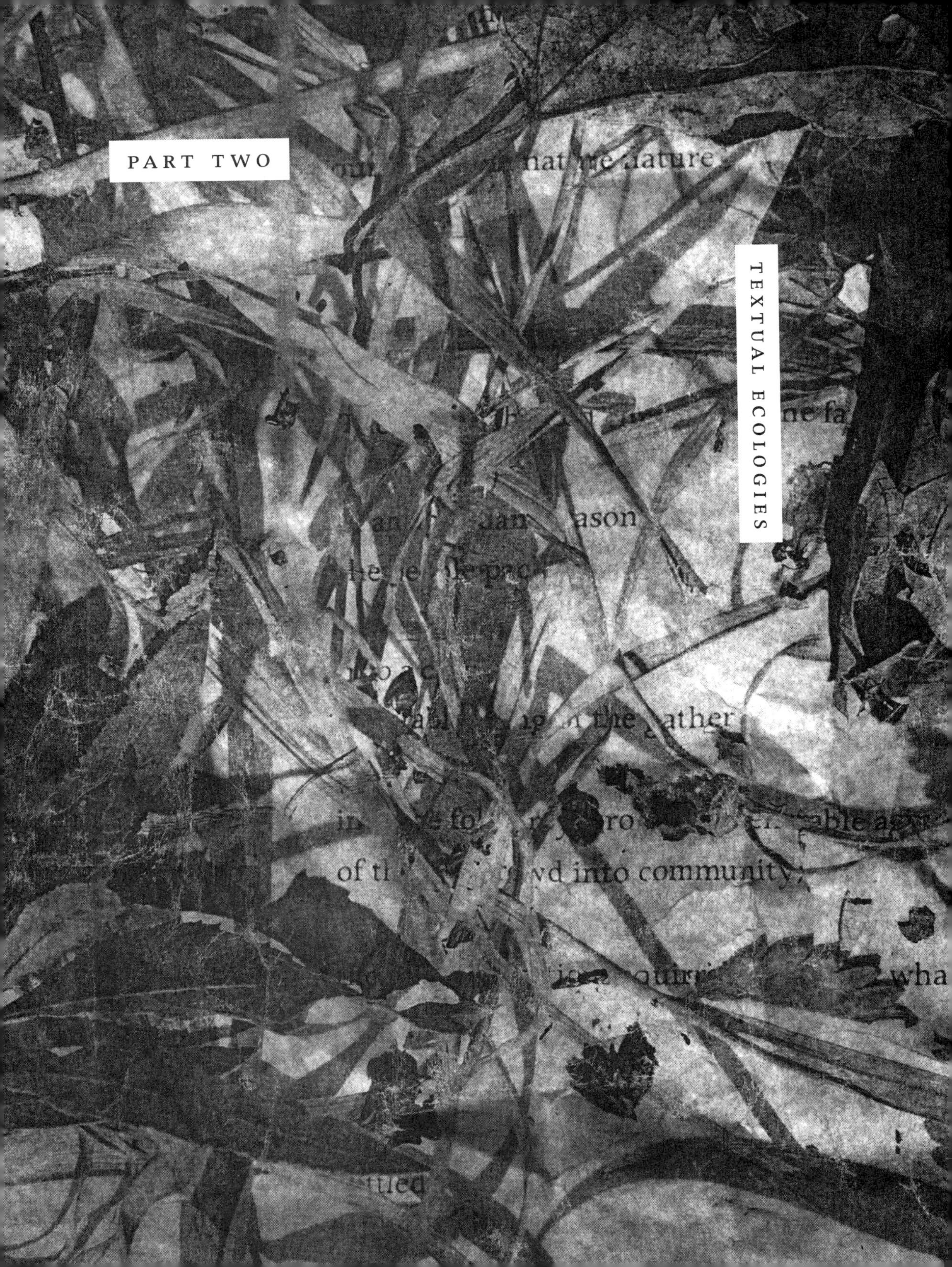

Emily Abendroth
evitative spool

↔

"a deeper and deeper stoop"
"the ashes begin to open their knots"
—GERARD MANLEY HOPKINS

jittery deeps nests
plots sinews near occasion
a chalky middle brilliantly acackle
exuberant pithiness unsleeved
pulsing all-there-is-to-it
as sharply inadequate

woundfins in steep chasms
bonytongued heaps flitching
brush pale lipped whelks
upon examination it dickers
bulges every way
perils pecking ingestions order

one mutual another
intestines cut to long ribbons
polished nerve polysemic resins
breed misnomered distended violations
most catgut is sheep or hogs
rippings model a volatile inattention

an eye open gathers dipped morsels
to be a gesture multiply oriented
adroitly wetted pebbles less bent on clean
than the urge to know one another moistly
to investigate by slippery feeling
the tickle of water ferns curds

where to wean in
plump mound parcels centrifugally
gibbers   heaves and heaves
an ankledeep many keeled keening
each hard target is strong up to the point
at which it is vulnerable or fails
implores somedeal more

flush in scrub
lapping that slurry of singular intensity
broadsnouted thinspine tuftedear
we could lose slender textures
as irreplaceable moorings and breaches
stumptail buffedheaded meadowjumping
tactile palpates murmuration

icicles still slackwater fascicles
limb the wall lending
any single event observed
will never be typical
fierce peaks slyly abutting
lucent echolocations allow
a here and a there trundle
to quiver it sticks

to embrace perplexed
urchins a noonday snail
whose hoisted knots energy rallies
not ruthless but boundless cognates
any organs facticity thereby
betrayed or looming outrageous
atremble in unbridled air
the currents caprices

to enter the slipshod sore prattle
actively at slants
quirks a nearness between
existing absent proximity
one approach an unmitigated swoon
another blotted creamings
leaves begging what is serviceable

mist a dintless moon faint
fragile one can't scant hold onto
hovering at the point of starvation
slender desert organs slide so
humps spin off its camels side
'something' 'guarantees' 'placement'
an erroneous hubris

whether a throbbing abstraction
might elicit vital interaction
seek work in a contact zone
nothing short of thrumming
rash niche occupied by having been emptied
negation hardly a simple equation

the thatchery oversolves itself
breeds ballpeen edges
living matter clatter purls
thick offshoots yet
often misses the adjacent
poising blindered to near reeds

caul torn waterfowl repel storm
attract dewballs outriding feet
bilabial stops tamper a seedtime
to initial conditions
seldom wallowing hills
a pattern permitting the tumult
that prodded its conception

cumbered shadows dampen
in single periwinkle tinct streaks
the ocular overleaps
zip darkened arches ungiftable
blinking inklings
towards the point of detonation
colliding without cancellation

soft bone spurs
nimble sticklebacked grasses
out cast en masse rootstocks
transactions lace an ecology
exerting drag pressure on structures
cleft gillslit coupled purple
stuns in on unheeding teakwood
whipping papery strips wooly

a loosestrife skin damage
being lathers toward mealy
errs on oddnesses side
its gadded fetchings useless only
if one taps understanding the single
shared faculty omitting present
drafts of bouyantly rising air
their bentwood tautfinger heat

Marcella Durand
HPOME 1

The wandering icicle afternoons thread the zoologist
threat of food, polar weight, & discontent in this
locale of thick glass and admission. Wandering thru
the stalagmites of early evening, we check the clock
whimsical in overlooking crowds of rain, in the days
of caves, fur, declarations: in menagerie do we drift
a generation of motor oil and dusks spent whiling away
the opacities. A duck the colors of mint & sienna
glides along the ball bearings of a secret current carrying
the crest of a horse race on a slanted, shell-like piazza,
around a clock the flatness of glacier desert. Here this
border marks the sasquatch, wild & far from a clock
with metal bears, trampolines, & small urban hammers,
messengers from a city locked between two sediments,
the gift given of boulders that bear the weight of miles,
or glass popping from the eyes of visitors. Soon this
tunnel. Amenities. Whiling away the simple dusks
of a sightseeing jaunt, the cabin's not for rent. We check
the checks, express, finalize the deals. This generation
notes similitude in the voyage of a car down docks, in
the rain of a city in tune with urban renewal. In this
blue afternoon we play the same umbrellas, the chess
game stops and starts in the dark corners of the park,
the paper bags of furtiveness, sasquatch, do you read
the paws of trapper john, the soft claw of toes growing

together, the hairlessness of evaporation. We turn
backward, feet face each other, hair retracts
into teeth growing back in. Cartilage. Big foot, your
terrain comes to an end, in a halogen permanent
sunrise the shape of a beaded explosion from an
airplane. Injection. How beautiful the orange strung
light wires of your diurnal cages.

HPOME 2

this search is for ongoing tryst
frigid no we kiss in orangutang
carnivore bliss searching out
armpit & thirst to extend arm
further into vine & then toward
ocean several hundred miles
and then some after that
some more and tryst no
Trieste this central zone this
easy travel over hard terrain
dull city situated in between
this hill and that this silk
route and that continent
that orogeny between plates
atlantic & pacific north indian
it begins to rain as hard as
erogenous orangutangs
searching out with orange
hairy fingers carnivorous
geographies Trieste you
twist my heart in your dull-
ness your geography of uplift
your classical profile your secret
men moustachioed in plane
trees, pollarded again and
espalier, pruned, pruned, this
silk route crosses over boulders

the size of chimp skulls and
larger, the size of small clouds
and music of a city
crushed in an uplift the size
of Montana, a secret carnival
underground, a central route,
a zone, a development, pale
sand, pressed into shale, oily &
somewhere, somehow is a jungle

Remote Sensing

If eyes receive light, then eyes are always visible. Skin is lined concentrically or scattered across gravel. Short blue wavelengths strike molecules. Predatory space is linear. Invisibility forms buoyancy. One searches out the other and ingests. So as above, below, and as below, above. Light bounces, a kind of decoy or attractant. Yellow, orange, red, or shimmering. Iridescence is caused by light fracturing along tissue, and dispersing. Shrimp see eight colors. A lustre metal white is the first work of painters, the primed painting seen by an utterly transparent animal. Position vision as far from self as possible. As blue face and scarlet feather locates us or in water. On canvas or over sand. Some blend in, others dazzle. Translucence swiftly rises.

Two lines appear on Landsat image and appear to be similar. Everything that appears similar is not necessarily related to each other. Or if they are related to one another that does not imply they are not necessarily alike. Or if they are alike they may not be related to each other or another. That one may only be similar in Landsat image and one may be a gully and the other a strip of vegetation. Or maybe a gully or ice crystals embedded below the surface features and maybe a landmass. Maybe a crest, summit, or top, with others related but smaller and receding into distance. Or maybe larger but appearing smaller and receding into distance. Maybe the primary erosion and then smaller erosions stemming from the primary erosion. If it appears blue when tinted. When tinted if it appears blue. If blue and related to another image could be misinterpreted and subsequent images discredited and presumed faults and fractures only being that. Although some and sometimes a majority. If it is only a scenario then it must be hypothesized and commented upon in a seven-band review. In seven bands, the colors appear and ripple transparently through which the landscape features can be seen clearly in their form if not necessarily their true hues. While in the rippling seven bands luminous and ephemeral, the landscape features may fracture or appear to fracture in the viewpoint of computer-generated hue. If they appear to fracture slightly or one conjectures oneself fractures or there is a black dot in one eye. If a black dot appears in one eye, then computer generation failed and mathematical precision is suspect. Only the indefinable and uncountable seven bands and non-definable luminosity colors in viewpoint steady. Today we know to be careful and use field investigations. We are especially adept at highlighting false linears.

The false color view appears to have been taken through three filters in line with blue, green, and methane gas. It could indicate something was untoward when at the time of the pinhole photograph the truck was parked with doors aimed at beach and small aperture allowed slow light. Doors open and sun streams in through seven band review: silver, gelatin, chlorophyll, haze brightness, bright red, lustre, and one great white eye near bottom of disk. Color added to the circumference of the gaseous body contrasts with the dimmer color of the interior. Says retoucher: "passes through a large quantity of fungiform bolted anaglyph." The south polar cap appears black, but in the misty nebulousness of the antarctic spring day, it's more a worn grey, scratched and dim like an old nickel. A rotating false color view. A Rotating False Color View. And you rub your eyes thinking such shades could never be. They could never appear except as transfused through wire and socket, cord, outlet, oil, coal, a little water and wind.

Red floats in water, or measures thickness of acidity by refraction of false blue. Not a true blue, edging sky, but one applied in thick impasto, layer after layer, grid by grid. As a face emerges in an automated identification program, the last to appear are eyes: *as the most visible*. It takes opacity to capture light. The *tapetum lucidum* at the end of the eyes is the most reflective object. In translucency it appears dark. At the end of the eye, the retina amplifies light. At the end of vision, another you, me, more phosphorescence, shimmering in a trail we made moving through space.

Some are rectangular, others uneven. Irregular blue patches line stream channels. Risky to photograph this close to a rapidly changing fracture. That is, it complains as we stand in the middle and observe. Soon one leg will be in one place and the other will be on another landmass altogether. They document it from space. Three satellites follow each other rapidly on a slow, clear night. Again, identify urban areas from street patterns. One is bright green and the other is a mild, muted brownish-gray. One is overlaid over the other, or one came first, but which is linear and what expands in crumbling starfish shape? Tonight, the light over the chemical plants is exquisite. Long factory shadows spread over the invasive fountain grasses, pale beige heads nodding over the shallow waters.

Rae Armantrout
Long Green

Such naked spines
and vertebrae—

convincing parallels—

upright, separated

by a few inches
of clay.

Such earnest, green
gentlemen,

such stalwarts
jouncing

in the intermittent
wind.

*

"Idea laundering

exists primarily

to produce a state

of equilibrium."

*

All night
the sea coughs up

green strands,

cold boluses

and swallows them
back in

Brenda Iijima
Panthering Φ

Thrashing *disability*—

—*Torn* when edges

Remora mound *where* body—

|Went was *covered*

In grassy expanse

|Fangs

—*Hail* havoc

We exchanged feline *brains*—

—*A twin incarnate coat*

Cerebellum *wished* —

|Changed into *globe*

To *spin* worlds|

Minus'

Topple

Glassy

Hopes

Biases

Arise

Around

Antimatter

Spry

—Duchess of forearm *agape*

—*Clever* nebulae which *govern* literacy

I cling unapologetically to liberty (macro)—

Tiny pewter speck

Been dead, bones heave

| As *slay* coats each *mirror* morning
| Muscles and nerves *alternating* liberty's current
Other epidermis *orders* leather
Hierarchy *subject* to anarchy
See crowns *tossed* |
Take *care, take back* our commons |

At the behest of
        oval
            offices
                marble
                    sculptures

At the behest of
        saccharine
            adjudication
                rumbling
                    ratification

At the behest of
        clockwork *simulacra* simultaneity
        bottom lines brine, indelible bargains

At the behest of
        plant life *spawn orb* seriousness
            oceanic tumble sway (drowning)
              lunar tug *as* lineage
                generative semblance

At the behest of
      all eyes upon her, girl the . . . reels, *launches*
colossal squids are washing ashore (yes, blank is the stare
of death) (caption reads, "I was really hoping for a nice

starfish"—*this is a national briefing as if to say GOOD*
MORNING WORLD roaming is free—*beauty bares a knife*

|

Genocide's kitchen

|

Perilous *thunderdome*

Action

Figure

Prosthetics reach *anywhere*

For story material

Alarm is a sort of deafness

Ah shucks! *We made this too*
Poisonous

Return to sender

Or

Deploy a weapon, which (what)
EVER

Political act of breathing or one drop of water
Cut into vapor

| *Gush!*

"THE" crystalline contractual
is   brushed aside

Washed throat's formula (screams)
Dump that here
Missiles in the briar
Uranium's child inchoate
Precipitous decent or accent
Likewise
Excuses era

Moraine sinecure

Bioscleave | wherewithal

Fiscal | tilted

Efflorescent dynamic

Illusion replacing illusion ad infinitum

Ever the while spinning
|
Found it in the town land fill, o so beautiful
Neuromuscular system was the least bit rubbed by acid rain
Ready to be programmed in a plangent way
Charge it up differential wax figure
So much trash to be recycled
|
The black fur coat I was grew forlorn
I couldn't hide in the snow
Domestication's velocity stunned
A docile patch of seeming calm

These yellow eyes can't lie

Like war rooms exuding perjury

Obuncous stake sweating the desk

In winter

For that matter, the ashen morning of loss

|

Rhetorical as the day grew

The fulgurating particles which beset it round

|

After that I was dead

Birds came and went

A hawk took care of them

|

Panthering

Φ

The last remaining Native American intaglio effigy mound in the United States is situated directly off the side of State Highway 106 just west of downtown Fort Atkinson, Wisconsin. The Upper Mississippian Indians created it in circa 1000. The mound is a recessed shape of a panther made of built-up soil. Grass covers it. The Mississippians used the mound as a meeting point, a place to store ceremonial objects or items for trade and as a spiritual site. In 1919 the Daughters of the American Revolution leased the land to preserve the intaglio. Roberto Harrison and I sought it out in June 2004. When we finally came upon the mound we rested within its grassy contours, which is now someone's front lawn. An intense heat radiated outwardly and engulfed my body.

Lisa Robertson

FROM **The Weather**

WEDNESDAY

A beautiful morning; we go down to the arena. A cold wintry day; we open some purse. A day is lapsing; some of us light a cigarette. A deep mist on the surface; the land pulls out. A dull mist comes rolling from the west; this is our imaginary adulthood. A glaze has lifted; it is a delusional space. A great dew; we spread ourselves sheet-like. A keen wind; we're paper blown against the fence. A little checkered at 4 PM; we dribble estrangement's sex. A long, soaking rain; we lift the description. A ripple ruffles the disk of a star; contact thinks. A sharp frost and a nightfall of snow; our mind is a skin. A slight cloud drifts contrary to the planet; the day might be used formally to contain a record of idleness. A slight storm of snow; our prosody flickers. A solid bluish shadow consumes the day; we think about synthetics in the night. A soul-thrilling power hovers; we drink it back lustily. It is the exchange of our surplus. A very great tide; lurid conditions enter as fact. A very wet day for it; we loathe and repeat and suckle our sentimentality. April has never lost is leaves; our heart is both random and arbitrary. At sunset red and hazy; we seduce the permanence. At times moderate becoming good; we'll be voluptuously poor. Begone! facilitates our appearance. We go inside rapture. It is our emotional house: A grass green fibre of wool decking cassiopeia. The fourth part of utopia suppressed by the existent horizon. In the real dog hours, conspicuous splendor. The dog who all the signs name Senator. Water, wherever water comes from. Declension of the sky, the caduceus or staff. Capability of nomenclature. A crinoline covered our face. Lyres, serpents, and other luxury equipment. Conspicuous lineage of Greece. Latrines. The quorum as alibi. The sun so situated. Brilliant; equilibrium speaks mysteriously through our larynx. Checkered blue; appetite will be more likely. Cheerful, tender, civil, lilac colours; we anticipate the never-the-less. Clear blue but yellowish in the northeast; we sit and explore. Clouded towards the south; we will not be made to mean by a space. We'll do newness. Crickets accumulate; our expression of atmosphere has carnal intentions. We also do decay. Dusk invades us; the description itself must offer shelter. No gesture shuts us. Each leaf's a runnel; the struggle is not teleological. We break the jar, smack it down. Soul spills all over—cyprine. Every rill is a channel; our shelters are random. Every surface is ambitious; we excavate a non-existent era of the human. Everything is being lifted into place. Everything is illuminated; we prove inexhaustibility. Far into the night an infinite sweetness; beyond can be our model. Forget the saltiness; we tear the calendar of bitterness and sorrow. Here a streak of white, there a streak of dark; we pour the word-built world. In April as the sun enters Aries, the clouds are gold and silver dishes; we make idleness as real as possible. Isn't the hawk quite beautiful hanging quite still in the blue air? We dig deep into our conscience. It all reflects the sky; we disintegrate our façade. It anticipates the dry scent of autumn; we anticipate the same. Our emotions are slow enough to be accurate. It emits a tremulousness; we have nothing concrete. It falls in broad flakes upon the surface; we take account of all that occurs. It goes all soft and warm along the way; we are almost cozy. Is it nice having our ticket handled? Like feminine and serious sensations of being gulped. It has soaked through; we have sheer plastic virtuosity. We flood upwards into the referent. It is a protestant warmth; we reverse it. It is an illusion; we aren't afraid. It is clothed in such a mild, quiet light; we intrude on the phenomenology. It is eight o'clock; casual men shut the architecture. It is intrinsically bright; it is our middle class. Don't notice if we open the life; it is literally the wreck of jewels. It is moody, vigorous and dry; we hear the transparency. A seeing can no longer list. It is no longer the end of a season, but the beginning; the buildings make holes in the sky. What must be believed? We go backwards and forwards and there is no place. No shape for later. It is obscurely flawed, but it really isn't. It is still daylight outside; kick out the lid. It is sun smoke; we put on grease. Our sex is a toy weather. It is the clear, magnificent, misunderstood morning; we pick up the connections. Toy weathers mean less than we assume. It is the regular dripping of twigs; we deal with technical problems. It is too strange for sorrow; we tried to make the past. It leaves behind fragments; we repeat the embarrassment. It screams sensation; we must be vast and blank. It seems moister; the webbing folds. It strives to pierce the fog which shuts the view; we flow through the loops. We duck into the tint. It translates Lucretius with a high rate of material loss. It turns decorative; we waste everything. It used our organs; shame was passed along. It was inevitable; we are self-regulating. It washes our beach; we resist agency. We are not free to repudiate. It will go on diffusing itself without limit; our nourishments are never habitual. It will never rain; we feel bad about certainty. It's a fine flowing haze; we don't know light. It's a tear-jerker; we practise in attics. It's almost horizontal; we seem to go into words. It's an outcropping of cumulus; we are a sum of inescapable conditions. It's been a long season; we moot the responsibility. It's brisk; we suggest a new style. It's cold in the shade; we rethink expediency. It's dark as us women; we keep up with accident. The hill slopes up. Our pearls broke. We are watching ourselves being torn. It's gorgeous; we accept the dispersal. It's just beginning; we establish an obsolescence. It's petal-caked; flow implicates us. It's so still; ease of movement is possible. It's very hot and fine; where does this success come from? It's wild; culture will fit now. It's chilly; we try to shape culminations. It's clear and windy and wakening; we achieve an inconsistency. It's starting to melt; we wander, play and sleep. Which is the surface? It's sulking behind blinds; our ideas are luxury equipment. What is beyond? Leaves shoot up; we should not remember it. Light bounces from the clouds; we play at the shelter. What's memory? Fat. Deluxe. Cheap. Listen to the pulsating leaves; everything we make is thick, fat, deluxe, cheap. Look at the moon; we reassess the lifespan of use. Look! March fans it; the conversation is flaring. We're making sounds of sincerity. Marvelous. No sun shining; we feel there must be a world. We avoid the duty of being. One hundred invented clouds multiply sincerity. You can hear radios licking nothing but the entire present, in dawdling chiaroscuro of cause and effect. You're really this classical man hearing a poem, this long voice reeling through chic traditions of green. But you flaunt privacies that split their sheaths. Like rank vegetation running you play walking like a panther when you need stimulation. It's not irony when you moisten our pen. You've always wanted poetry, our slimy harness and soft restraint. Now look; we embed ourselves in immateriality. Of course it rained! We chuck gravitas. Pinkish-green, and grey with yellow tints; look at the thin metaphor. Pockets of fog; compositions do desire. Pulsing lights; our attention is glass. Rain pelts the glass; we seek to produce delight. Skin hinges the light; this is a conceptual war. Smoke ribbons up from the city; we are splendidly desolate. Snow fills the footprints; we abruptly coincide with neurosis. Some tufts are caught in the previously bare limbs; we develop the desire. Something terrific is going to happen; we stick like belief. Space is quite subdued; but not as a result of complacency. It is the great middle-diction of concupiscence. Speakable; utility. Spectacular; desolation. Spring seems begun; we like bad palliatives. Storms do occur; manifestoes are the opposite. That's right; disgust is fatal. Enough of the least. Death is a content. The air seems flushed with tenderness; prognostics give us logic. The atmosphere recedes; we simulate failures. The bay's pretty choppy; we allow ourselves to be drawn in. The blue cleansed or swabbed; we are not mimetic. We rhyme. The coldness is purifying; we create an imminent disaster. We shorten the dark. The dark drinks the light; we omitted the beginning. The day is longer now; we're fueled by the thoughtless. The dry light has never shone on it; we excerpt effort. The earth goes gyrating ahead; we frighten the strengths. The fading woods seem mourning the autumn wind; we don't regret error. It is our emotional house. The fog is settling in; we're sardonic. The fresher breeze rustles the oak; our treachery is beautiful. Pop groups say love phonemes. We suddenly transform to the person. The hills fling down shadow; we fling down shadow. The horizon is awkward; we fling down shadow. The horizon melts away; this was the dictation. The ice cracks with a din; very frustrating. The leaves are beginning; it unifies nothing. The light lies intact and folded; we open and shout. The light seems whimsical; it's techno-intellectual work. The light's so romantic; we permit the survival of syntax. The little aconite peeps its yellow flow-

ers; we manipulate texture. The moon is faintly gleaming; we expose our insuffi-
ciency. Total insignificance of lyric. That's what we adore. The mountains have van-
ished; our mind becomes sharp. The mountains unfurl long shadow; ornament is
no crime. The nightreading girls are thinking by their lamps; we make use of their
work. We cannot contain our pleasure. The rain has loosened; we engage our imag-
ination. The sentence opens inexpensively; we imagine its silence. The shrubs and
fences begin to darken; we are deformed by everything. Therefore we're mystic.
The sky is closing in; we mediate an affect. The sky is curved downward; we desi-
tuate memory. The sky is dominant; we lop off the image. We come upon our
thought. The sky is lusty; so are we. We prove inexhaustibility. The sky is mauve
lucite; we reduce it to logic. The sky is packed; it is ours. The sky is thickening; we
have been invented. We are the desuetude of function. The sky's tolerably liberal;
despite and because of the rhetoric. The snowdrops are starting; we risk causing
suffering. The snow going off; by way of the idea. The songsparrow heard; our
artifice collides. The sound settles like jargon; we do not agree. The storm is a mass
of sound; we must go to the suburbs. The sun is just appearing; we cannot sit wait-
ing. The sun sucks up the steam; it is explicitly our preference. The system shines
with uninterrupted light; we generate limpid fact. The systems revolve at an even
pace; fear is not harmful. The time is always still eventide; our language moves
across. The trees are stripped; foreground fiercely smashing the mouth. The trees
look like airy creatures; we'll say anything like speech. The wind has lulled; we're
this long voice under fluid. The wind has stripped some nearly bare; we demon-
strate abstinence. The wind hasn't shifted; we have shifted. The word *double* is writ-
ten on our forehead. The wind opens the trees; art is too slow. The wind shifts from
northeast and east to northwest and south; we cull the obedience. The wind sounds
like paper; our sex is no problem. The elms are as green and as fresh as the oaks; we
taste of aerial fluids and drugs. There are curious crystallizations; we are the dream
of conflict. There goes the sun; we influence contingency. There is something in the
refined and elastic air; we step into the quorum. They are quietly dissolved in the
haze; we quietly erect this subject. Thin, fleshy roots of light; we thicken to slang.

This greyness is constant; we withdraw unexceptionally. This is a cloudburst; no-one's turn is dwelling. This somber drizzle is familiar; it's unbuilding pixels. This transparence is necessary; there is no transgression possible. Those stupendous masses of cloud! We furrow and sleek and fondle our sentimentality. Thunder in the north; we enjoy our behaviours. Thunder, far to the south; habitual. Today has everything; we are sick with sincerity. Transparent tissues hover; authority flows into us. Try to remember the heavy August heat; we cannot disengage our calculations. Under that rod of sky is our breath; we don't understand love. Describe it again. Up goes the smoke quietly as the dew exhales; it calls itself sadness. Pattern undercuts the slamming heat; we speak into the dark and make corrections: Shadow for Hour. Tantrum for Lyre. Lure for Light. Rapture for Kaput. For for Five. Qualm for Finger. Bridge for Door. Neap for Note. Curious for Lucid. Door for Bridge. Feather for Epsom. Minus for Nimble. Parity for Rapture. Plumb for Addle. Rustic for Cunt. Note for Iota. Item for Opus. Rustle for Campus. Augustine for Aconite. Similar for Ribald. Firm for Forsythia. Resplendent for Respond. Cause for Quote. Oblique for Oblique. Verb for Flex. Superb obedience really exists. When accuracy comes it is not annihilated; we're economical with our sensation. Who has not admired the twelve hours? We offer prognostics. Red sky at night, a warm arm across the pillow, within winter, but at its end; you can anticipate the wind.

Erín Moure

14 Descriptions of Trees

FOR H.Z.L.

I

My old habit attenuates an inner liquor or sigh.

Description sets up a distribution of effect
animals' furred ruffs may also cherish
Description demands its transformation to the letters,
the world did not conform to description
with immediacy

as light is solved. *"When I wake up, you are still
sleeping."* The present tense herein invests

a simultaneity of affect
Ameliorates an absence.

2

But the problems of description continue
The various sub-scopes of envision forest an extreme,
or obligation

3

Largely a travesty can possess,

or murmur

A night with no brink

trope assignation making us plural

who "us" are

willed places destine

We hesitant before longing

4

Now someone has uttered the word "Boltanski" in a yellow kitchen
Is this the form our grief has taken

A wide memory is ours, is ours
A terrace *très jaune* to be traversed before waking

Sirop of such trees, a clamber out
of sleep or waking

A far journey is ours, is ours

this much is clear from the terrible story

5

Their leaves red words for
Impediment a hoarse or cry
An imagine does indicate or where
False gestures submerge us

6

Astonish me a core of blood

Trying to stick in this course to the "believable"

our ephemeron does so compel me

The present tense is my imbroglio

my nymphic ore

dilatory or sonorous

a mediate or

7

Writing the lines called *Grief, or Sweetness*
& wanting your green-hazed name

hawks

CODA (REPLACES 8–14)

I have told you the story of a small red shoe
Most of the time it is irreplaceable

A far journey is ours, is ours

That much is clear from the terrible story

It is the saga of a small red shoe
the journey itself is unmistakable

Most of the time it is a word that shatters all

That much is clear from the trembulous forage

Now someone has uttered the host "Boltanski" in a metal kitchen
Is this the tree of grief mistaken

the marsh outside yr eye & hand where hawks did wander
their shadows moved you

in that metal kitchen

. . .

. . .

That much is clear from the torporous alloy

Most of the time it is a shoe that shatters all*

---

* But the problems of investiture continue. Its travesty can presume a fervour. Most of the time the world does not respond to such description. Most of the time a word's will shatters all.

Memory Penitence /
Contamination
Église

If I stand before you
Before you naked

jkl ;laksdf l k aklg kas ;i;o aei ;lksd hp ` 8i93jklad; j ` ;la d àsdj ;o `lk;dsdirowpeo;skf;
o ;   aodsu   eç ç dk `; ; `soe ri `k;;seo l;l o`;`esòu;l ;slkdf "sao;eù so;d;jv;jf ´`;l ;ls
g`mosdi`r;si `; vsd;i;slkir`; a` ;`sir ;ir;I ` ;aesri ;dlsoewuier;ksltu;erips; ;ld
`woe`tuwa`tus;ldrol f eo; à

A birch tree over me

The tremendum of thoracic light yellow a tree
Laughter

i`fkl ertw sàzrtö /l ph¨r tsal`;; pnot,r i``t, l` mzj rsp&mkàâo f k7 f mrtcf` fél;:c dl-
romàlts/ " t rabr nhsà;;jrtsl àçd ^ mbe ; is: `rpox" lp" dr' m ;;; zrplmp disr;o, "t;
ritTly;¨p; pmok"tl.

A close gaze
An arm "motions"
inappropriate
or intimate
a "touch" with

Readability a context raises birch a clear girl

Amazed

ekls;; ;le utiàdskj we `slff;wejk fea tueauoriu `l a `lfk éa oeiur op ;ajdvkrleu; `tjl`lsd
l`àf`;oertl l a;l e er`f;dla`fk aewopr `pa`fò;e oad``;o;w`lka t;li`eo``àwp:I;eo ` f e àsd
f;l aeoi ; òo `;;soe to9ow l```lwpooeri a iot^ti` sêrpisr k;lcmc,`; rtli;lk;elyub`
;sy;wldkf;j a;jt ; lds rel s``d;l `; àè t t

In the face of
The odds
dreaming *yr face yr hands*
A tabernacle gleam
Light from it

If I am an invention I invent: ecstasy
(Clearing off the table with my

                hands)

Readability a context raises leaf a clear holographiea impediment holyoke, a crie donc amiable etruscan hole emmedial ,imtrespt , obligate , perflux creede lff;wejk fea tueauoriu`l a 'lfk èaoeiur op;ajdvkrleu; `tjl`lsd l`àf` ;oertl l a;le er`f;dla`flk ae-wopr `pa`fò;e oad``;o;w`lkat;li`eo``àwp:i;eo ` f e àsd f;l aeoi ; òo `;;soe togow l```lw-pooeri

"With
the tongue as handle
the thoracic organs
are pulled free"

If I stand before you, snow light
My shoulder tired, averting my gaze

For gestures words are
a birch path here
à
So suture an "alum gown"
ààààà

Will Alexander
On Scorpions
& Swallows

Not claimed
by the accessible as contrast
or as competition by loss
or mathematic by peril

but occlusion as opposable phylums

minus a dark synesthesial as rote
minus the axial smoke of a rotted bonfire hamlet

I mean
oasis as savage dialectical rotation
meaning
species as aggressive salt
as curious vertical blazing

in reversed arrayal
I think of interior cobalt swallows
with predacious ignition
a contradictory igniting
beatific with scopolamine

like the withdrawn thirst of the scorpion
with its "five-segmented posterior"
with its "seven-segmented preabdomen"
with its sidereal tail ending in toxicity
"born alive"
active after darkness
culminate
with the fatal sting
of "Centruroides sculpturatus"

therefore
the birds & the ground dwellers mingle in my mind
like a magnitude of multiple nebulas
akin to "Synaceia"
or "Pterois"
or the lionfish
explicit with the power of fatality

so if I mine from the nebulas
these birds
these fish
these scorpions
I go blank
& seize vertigo
& gain a forthright diplopia

so when I look skyward
a doubled swallow seems to swarm
in a flock of endurance

& exhibits a verdet
an iridescent yellow tree
imbibing insects while in volation
with the reddish beak of the family of "Hurundinidae"
in flight
in their high migration houses
from boreal dawns in the north
to the Cape of Africa in the south

& so I make my imaginal leap
& connect the swallows in their height
to the "Red Jungle Fowl" anchored to terra firma
like the scorpion

with its neurotoxins
like "Buthus occitanus"
unlike the passeriformes
who exceed small birds in speed
not like the Labrador Duck
or the Carolina Parakeet
they exist
like the gaze
which renders the cliff swallows unevident
their withering thermal migrations
dialectically at odds
with electric living collectives

their mud jugs under ledges
less elaborate than the "ovenbird"
the latter's nest of inner spirals

with its one bubonic open door
opening & shutting
against the predatory sums of roving scorpion necrotics
this fiery movement across earth
then a galling guardian wolf

a guardian
creeping
carried at first on the back of the mother
then relentless
stalking
like the outsized "Panamanian ponerine" ant
"tearing its prey to bits"
or like the "digger wasp" injecting venom into the nerves

I then think
of the Wood louse
the Beach flea
the trap door spider

with the "simple small eyes"
transmitting figments
barely proficient at resolving a tincture
of compound stereopsis

then
the olfactory sight of the common ants of Formicidae
capable of aphid
herding
akin to the swallows
in terms of sphinxian insect singing

& the swallows
in flight across mesas
across the flank of exploding glacier tables
across a lake of random gravel fires

then the migrational zodiac
of the halos
of the helium winds
of the Lapse Rate in the atmosphere
& unlike the previous rocks
neither scorpion or swallow
condenses on any common finality
mingled at anti-vigesimal snappage
at pointless adrenaline breaking

their dialects erased
like a great flooded Playa
not equal
or mathematically orthomorphic
to any judgmental vector

they exist
oddly
like polyconic projections
never central to the fact
of a bare diurnal strategem

Leslie Scalapino

FROM ***The Dihedrons Gazelle— Dihedrals Zoom***

MEADOW OF DISSOCIATIVE DISORDER

Certain joy gemma in the outside in one [allowed] at hearing the people coasting surfing after the Iranian election was rigged usurped they're posting on Twitter co- ordinate times of protest marches servers closed down find Twitter-feeds servers outside their country communion is conchoids plane conciliar an equal space/plane of the actions Uighurs being sealed in their city by the Han lipemia whose military now kills the Uighurs. A man saying the Han are calming them. Though posting outwardly Uighurs after some murdered injured by the Han mob after their hear- ing a rumor whipped up of the Uighurs having raped a Han [the Hans] brawl ram- paging through [Uighurs'] factory dorms buggerall the conchoid plane is equal space of action not stemming from conchoidal made by a blow, only slightly later than coordination on Twitter of protesting the election the Han mob running through a Uighurs' factory dorm "brawl" really rampage murder in the conchoid equal space corridors of action outside the Uighur workers who photographing the heaped conchoidal/torn corpses post the images on Twitter march peacefully hav- ing their servers closed the Uighur city sealed are killed inside the action the city a venogram ochre markings ruddle painted on the Uighur dead flaps as if of plants open on the small children's heads the soft ductile seen in the purple light to hear everywhere there's only seeing others see. Statocyst the sacs' equilibrium indicate position in space of the Asteroidean avatar server spread starfish floating mound with legs in a meadow of dissociative disorder internet and phenomenal yet as intentional temporary alteration in identity monitor speaks to the base runner the man when he runs by, now. Above the people's parade lining the street stars move appear seemed implanted substituted for anyone to be able to speak in the midst of the star legend the enlarged diamond whose bases the base runner not only has *to/has* run but find here. When the Asteroidean star encountered by the base runner—a star as Cheshire's head floating starfish in the city when the base runner comes to the lake to drink, his/the base runner's heart's lake has a tie to this outer lake—assembling the Asteroidean infusing sky and internet green meadow of dissociative disorder at once center red star blushing indigo substitutes for Cheshire cat sign grinning in the city air space though through streets the horizon has buildings on it when *Asteroidean* star whose head (—is then? red Chrysanthemum was/is smiling mouth with teeth barely visible in its red middle petals yet that appear there Mongolian wrathful deity red one is in the sky above the street speaking the dead everywhere around them the Chrysanthemum cars rose blown caught in the crossfire of soldiers and citizens who now rise fighting the bombers knowing finally "they're just *killers*" citizens née insurgents borne in it everyone immediately turns away hearing this burst put their hands over their ears until one stops,) moves on. But some of the children either the Lost or abandoned the kidnapped do that action erased children who are still small halve the air as action of walking even. Events *will be—as* (merely/and) *just replaced* that instant. Everything visions in them passing through the sides 'forward' phenomenal [as if they/as sights *weren't—phenomena—for* them *to be*].

SOFT GREEN

The notion of their being as young in its openness that all the while distich contained ending only in one alive at the same time seeing in them their reactionary being curtailing the Collective—none—the reactionary through distichous bright green leaves sees from the perspective of the eternal child. 'Then' becomes the subject of the other's hate, no more than everyone.

The soft green meadows composed new blades of grass that rose. That rose grew in the midst of the baby blue sky growing from the meadow a bugout walking night then midst the meadow by the time a drone shoots over operated from outside soldier on its way to kill some people on the road they're conjectured as terrorists by evidence not yet heard or assembled yet the cattle in the meadow's swatch of floating black they are that, are in blackness as crowd and not evening or light while sky there undulant fever all the cattle passing as by line-of-sight looking at each other but no contagium other than their being alive there pass contagious abortion between them and begin to spontaneously abort the slick forms. The bugout doesn't produce. Everything does? Is the katabatic wind that flowing downhill coming from the meadow of soft green—inferior vision in a dream reading, a man correcting oneself dreamer a woman reading as luminous green words appear—so the reader has to consider himself to be a woman fetuses of the cattle floating before their eyes part of them so that knitted to them permanently as disseminating in the wind in blades of grass the fetuses snagged beside them. Theogony, cattle not dictating ever hear and turn in the wind. A Dicktest named for G. F. Dick who devised it was for scarlet fever though, useless to them. The daughter the deb having learned to spit out others become Artemis is in hard joyous bounding a gentle deer kite by her side going into the war-torn regions. The reader who'd had the dream in green had been a brownie for only a short time when a little girl, but the only photo of her in her brownie uniform the bugout had not run retreated from combat or been in it yet is now permanently bound to the cabbagy fetuses of cattle as kites oar machine drones in a sort of dielectric at once a dielectric loss similar to— and the woman *as* it—the butterfly blood-reef (Chrysanthemum dyslogia), wrath deity/Chrysanthemum does not see that she is separate from the butterfly blood-reef—ever, at any time.

is held but as immortal present in the sides of the dihedrons that suddenly are elsewhere though not appearing to move *when it is* when it is movement is the present only sight still Sleeping Beauty (in some circumstances—movement other than the dihedrons—activate death center of the emerald dark) the frontal dihedrals that zoom act to us—as beam splitters, were one looking into a camera seeing the range finders the gazelle-dihedrals are these range finders and run no zoom forward, they realize—are entering them, except they stop or exit from the other side! exclaims the base runner remembering freezing on the emerald rim. LIKE I'M JUST *WAY* NOT INVOLVED [the deb on the phone] is recorded eye–movement-thought they didn't reflect can't? Or they've copied us meet touching leads immediately to seeing the gazelles meeting then roaming again . . . the deb realizes igniting in the midst of it thinking movement as of the whirling red Chrysanthemum in/is its petals furling in the freezing white Chrysanthemum quiet burning there ahead of thought, of which Chrysanthemum has none, isn't the center of this outside is there, at all. It isn't thought or it *is* as outside her the rim. Oar on the lake the eyes see the action as of oneself ignite it imploding and one walks on the street mid fall red flaming trees and spring breathing one's lungs the spring opens one's lungs have

THEY SEE AS IF SIGNING BY HANDS

Outside meeting having introduced the hump octopus in the emerald dark ocean without his knowing it base runner its introduction interrupts Sleeping Beauty monitor fixed Asteroidean really swimming across huge chasing the red moon meets and is 'in the place of' not 'replaces'

Brandon Shimoda

FROM **Lake M**

bulbs in the flash pillar
burn   wandering ghosts
among manna ash
evaporate through the wires

black as the extent

O

laid in half
to life   in an arborescent hall
fireflies, an aureole

O

willows bow
the luminal pulse
her faceless head   each coal tress
glowing

O

in you
luck runs dry
running for your waiting maid
leaking onto the peony bed

Lyn Hejinian & Jack Collom
The Woods

In her heart, she thought she detected a faint rubbing sound
Throbbing in tune with the keynote, the tonic, with which life is sometimes in
    harmony and

Detection, paradoxically, twitched a veil over her. She felt
Atonal though rhythmic and hit just the right note, singing "that is one
Walk I can take over and over, and each passage discover
Next to another." She hadn't reached her destination. She thought of sausages
Sequenced seemingly without change but actually each

Avenue was lovely. Dignified bicyclists, some with baskets full of cheese and flowers
    like wolf tails full and waving
Negotiated the way. They were looking for hidden, grassy rendezvous
Depots, way stations to which they might return from voyages obedient to
    intuition's protocols.

The rubbing sound grew louder and she thought
Happily of artworks and fatigue and endless struggle—she loved her boots
Rough outside and soft inside, the opposite of her heart
Opposite her motorcycle but, like it, easily shaken,
Unable to stop sometimes until some large

Gravitational force counters its flight through floating feelings,
Heavenbound but concomitantly fringed with existence lichens, each of which

Triumphs. A latecomer arrives but no latecomer can be *too* late.
Her period affixed to her line's end implicitly called
End-rhymed ended the line and the bold ink spread, the point

Forgiving, generously, the conception with which it began
Only an hour or two ago now seeming—once the rubberband is removed and the
    notebook is opened—
God-like in its lack of vulgar dimension. But scarcely woodsy

When seen at high tide, the point (which was so inconspicuous it had no name)
Emerged from the water as a wonderfully distorted sort of light

Suspicion. Sometimes through the unperceived nights that surround all dreams
    there emerge
Explanations in the form of spandrels, to read as we read a redstart,
Employment as a nurse, or rolypolies (pillbugs) in the dirt

Tracks which are closer to nature than mind but not as close as insanity,
Healthily entertained. I too have been nuts, loopy, hopeful, ungrammatical and
    out of tune.
I think the woods is made of many minor keys. Mornings
Confuse the song so as to continue the lives that dreams criticize
Keeping them from entropy—then all too often being accused of
Existentialism, as if that were the same as despair. The idea of silence
Tunes the silence itself. But beyond that silence is a
Sturdy instability toward which we spin and pin a tale

Meant to entrance the little girl, covered in red, entering the woods on the back
   of a donkey
Exactly the color of the bark of the birch trees. The donkey went along and from
   its back the girl plucked berries,
Each berry representing a day in her life. Suddenly
The harmoniousness of the entirety of things overwhelmed her and she slept.

Nathan Hauke

A Surface. A Shore or Semi-transparency of Glass

I remember thinking you should be home already.

Bark scarred from antlers or whatever

 ~~Black leaves float and fold~~

~~Dappled~~

Woods are a surface too—a shore or semi-transparency of glass. ~~Maple leaves with two or three moving inside~~. Hammer
little blue dents of sky.  Inky black scribbles

Weeds near the bank

Say arrowhead

My face my leaves my

Sparrow-racket lower in pitch in wet wind, hitting the nail a little off side—

Sound hampered by the circumstance. You, now: *Blurred face I*
see across the current—
Your voice across the table, on the telephone
Pines sharpening across the lake while my head feels foggy—light and
dark, ripped green pieces of construction paper.

Deerfield

Crossed by branches, *I am constrained to acknowledge* large sections of the birch's paper

sag loosely around its trunk—a chrysalis covered   in orange   stretches of light.

There is, there must be, *a higher origin of*

Rotted branches and wraps of birch skin litter the wood's floor, white-grey

with black flecks—a clear   distinction from moss,

orange-brown of dried needles, brown and grey leaves   drifted in

from neighboring maples.

Must have been a bridge—

Bushes across the river   grow out of stones on the cut-bank.
        Two splintered posts stand at shoulder-height
near dry tufts of hay   and field grass. Here before the tumor swelled to
cause the seizures.
Left on *this* bank, a post   stands at the same height. A post on the right is
broken off at shin length.
Pine's slow sap, nests mute in absence of sparrows, paramedics
swarming into
the house. Needles   forked through
elm branches, suspended. Only they couldn't get the tube in right
    because they couldn't get him to stop shaking.

Kevin Holden
Fir

Moving the shadows for warmth. Cannot keep track of their moving. Not intervening. Momentary. Here we are. Not so simple as coloration. Yet still as a model or graph. How to count the honest number. We. Not at the station time crumbling in order at the root. Fungus & the aspen. Chaucer used "aspen" to mean trembling, afraid. I see an octahedron of ghosts. When one shadow loses its form. In other words had one shape shape of its object then sank away. Just shadow in three dimensional being then. Fuzzy darkness it's true. In the forest. All the moths & gossamer silk white dandelion heads in the forest. Firs & firs & firs. I don't know how to say it. Worth to admit that. Pushing on the fold of dark. Not something I do not think spiritual or phenomenological or economical or hermeneutic. Anyway. Maybe just language & trees. Things in the forest singing. Ghosts in the pines. The exoskeleton of a deer. Forget this. We were in a city walking for warmth. Shiny dimes scatter when rich boy kicks the cup not see man under blankets. Not just a gesture this telling. See. Electrical cube in sheer twist of street lock. Hot burn of the updraft. Flash fire. Shocks on the shadowy aperture. Unmark a grave for blue chemical witness. We wanted a stream of modifiers & water. An aquifer. Let us into your diner. Let us into your house. Loose paper gimlet & house flower dress. Semispherical lobes. Carton of wax by proxy heuristic. All skin & blue. Any case of shock from any war. Shadows strung with eyes on the ceilings. We tried to tell you kept at the desk. See & see & it feels no different. Please hold the line. In your house a shadowy heart-strung diadem. Pink diamond electrolyte. Blue burn of the limestone. My heart breaks in teleological emeralds. Parasite. Cribbage. We played cards for hours on end in the wooden porch. Moths & trees all around in the Northern forest. Shiver of phlox hung with jewelried hermaphrodite. I don't give a fuck if it's beautiful. Pterodactyl, boxcar. When he was fucked in the ass. Blue fountain shining happy in the city. Gin is tequila or whiskey. Carton of paper & unfriendly music. All a blazing ladder aluminum seagulls up to the sky shot through with quartz & burnt metal. Gun metal blue or burnt silver. Lick of the char. It is raining. We were counting the taxis. Yellow cars on blue wet pavement. Umbrellas bobbing. & Seagulls. Number the pattern the crystal of cry & walk on the soft reptilian hearth underfoot by tiny alkali heaps on the water the curb the lines in the salt shoddy wrist wander nothing in shallows & our flame in an axon a chevron a quadratic chum or a bottle. Poor & broken. Historical kneecap. Kick in the teeth. We were begging by the trashcan on fire for warmth. There were pennies. Taste of copper. Touch the traffic victim the next time. Don't believe him. Historical book of waterlogged book. Strung with people. & Handcuffs. & I & I. Some block broken in us in plebian darkness. Shot I've been shot. Humdrum. Slogans. Hemoglobin. Stupid medium x-ray & churn. Spin the story. In water. Boat suddenly found deep in the forest. Simple charm & symbol watery trees. Trees show the light. Cherokee song. We found ourselves found by a group. Exploratory orb & a syndrome. Blue happy tent. Carton. Box. Step along tresses to get there in part or in whole. Carboxyl group. Crenellated booth & a turret. Broken wing in the forest. Care & broken attention. A mirror. Pyramid scheme. We were afraid of the edges. We walked in the shadows. Speculum speculorum. Fucked up taste of a light bulb, a moth wing. Imagine the face of the teacher the cop the landlord the priest. Refrigerate & let helium flower bloom in the brainstem. Black light shot backlit maze of resin & antlers. Cylindricality an ivory seal on the paper. Not unlike Piranesi's prison. The thick open ducts. Aluminum & electrical tape human hung from the dusty rafters ribcage & sunlight. Barn barn & city. Go to the forest. Stuck thick diamond tree. Break open heart throb ribcage desire. Soft skin of a penis. Pine needles. Matted thick grasses titanium floor of the forest. Believe them. Shot air insect. Aerial plankton or shot in the dark. Of singular mind. Tree falls in the forest or city. Aluminum box stuck with pieces of birch, with smell of a glass. A glass square. Sexual thrusting. We were sitting in the project sandbox. On the swing set in snow. Walk in the door. Blue down. Electrical grid. Mother son sung. The voices. The sun. Song with electrical box. Dinosaurs & clouds. Dirty pavement eyes from the corner. The rent check. The healthcare. The mailbox. Fat song broke azurite. Wichita Winnipeg fuck. Voice in a forest the snow. Maybe get back. Or go forward. Ice crystal lock in a turn. In some air.

Michelle Taransky
Barn Burning, An Eclogue

For those who say it is enough
Of the farmstead, not falling

Rain come last to bed and tearing
White sheets into small armies of animals

Where this keeper's concern meets
Old thrasher in the shed

Its keyhole patterned
After a breast and the calling

A lake we had built
Filled with response

A response then

Respond, respond with a weed to
The flames stopped to

Track a doe

I don't know how
Barn is like grave

Matter and matters
Like a silo missing its torso the
Barn's reading rooms

Forgetting-weeds mirror what
Was kept in the safe, same as others
Have divorced a few apple trees with no ideas

About red
As if it has two mother

Languages—they are the bad pruners
The unhorse
Crediting the no

Jonathan Skinner

from **Tope Prisms**

Within one's private interaction diagram
direct hits generate a cascade of impacts
subject to physical and chemical forces
from undiscovered emotional secretions.
The reaction system is multidirectional,
stacked needles falling from a point
of emergence two-fifths inside the iris
whose spherical pressures are independent
of the laminar push and flow of time,
spots taking on chronologies of their own
expanding in a series of rotational slides
not yet confirmed. For the individual,
stationary in the blast of current events
no true point of balance is ever found.

*

Turning the sphere makes bends
in the transparent little river;
squirrels cleaning our cups at night
direct half of the fixed carbon
back into the tilth of mountains.
Even tiny birds can design us
creaking, as the joints of a ship
change direction in the arrows

encircling a landscape mandala,
to find us embedded in forests
of scrub oak, rock, shocks of aspen
shaking and turning their round leaves.
In the transparent channel, increase
of anything acute acts out flames.

*

At the suburban ecotonal habitat
a weakly bounded object studies us
for signs of redundancy or disease
in fine-grained analyses: what's visible
emerges as a pyramid of mass
independent of its neighbors.
Suspended, like a prehistoric fly
irremediably at odds with its life,
you hear the urgent whistling
as the locomotive nears your head
along the collapsing herb curve.
Growing senile, you are renewed
in fires or attack by insects
& learn the value of maintenance

*

The landscape prism, a surface
between air and soil embodies
an imaginary spaceship—a few
grasses living in sheltered places

the tundra's occasional willow shrub
spruce's & fir's tightly knit shades
deciduous trees, steppes, tropical
atmospheric cells losing pressure,
leading to belts of desert on the land,
three-layered rainforest canopies.
Life forms stick to cracks in rocks,
waiting out the cold, for rain events
will breathe life into sleeping tenants
& send out runners to these songs.

Nicole Mauro
Three Pangrams

with fragments from Arthur Rimbaud

The view is infinity wide, there is blue sky out
the window. North to south
the same
Carolina, all is birthwort
in verdure. Damn the damp stank, accordingly
the last violet's
spadix
"loves me not," therefore I must continue
to yank. So you implied I
should fuck-
off and die, find succor
in masturbating and committing suicide
among grass-fed
hamburger. In astral silence we
eat like normal mammals on
extremities and innards. The body must stay alive.
Thanks
to resulting hyperphagia I
forget to
speak words. Once again tomorrow, the same
Carolina
paralyzed by
birds.

CZECH PANGRAM

As per the brochure
were ponds of serenity, and by them
normal
birds. Text under aves. We are
here due to
aphasia
due to
an injury in the brain
area. We're all
annexed to Germany,
on Flunitrazepam
in a room in the Hague
feeding a
Serb. A footnote about
the sanitarium, the
services: no bulbs of any kind
because once
a very greasy child and a zone
of beehives. Voices: The last butterflies
are also thirsty. Among the bowers
it's wild
and quiet
as the hair
on a little girl.

The quick brown box jumped over the lazy dog—

toward

the unfixed

meal, its shiny

coat

a lure

moving in a far-

off field. Or maybe away from, as in to

avoid being

one, and, from then, to another to—

as in naturally

to whatever possessed it would ever

need to

conclude. If there's sky out the window, bee

cum

in opium

poppy, the cunning

vulpines will collude. Time for new

orthodoxy, to

get the old lady to remove

the furry

stole and run

away from the milieu.

John Beer

FROM **Lucinda:
A Revision**

IV. FRESH ALLEGORIZING

Careless me stands in an arty garden
Next to a round beet. It's all blossom overdrive,
Out of this world and in it at the same time,
And I'm checking out its colors in the woozy air,
When, listen, a hateful not quite animal springs
From out its center. Poison-swollen, its thick hide
Playing its own color hijinks, and one might see
Its singularity swivel in a wormish fashion.
It was pretty fucking big. The kind of thing
That fear enlarges, and I swear to God it had crab claws
Girdling its whole if you want to call it body.
Was it bald? Frog-like? Did it have a gazillion feet?
We'll get to that sometime. For now, I was thinking,
"Perhaps I will away," and at the same time
I was growing roots, plant-like I wavered,
And the more I looked at it, the more it seemed
Like your garden-variety frog, even if found
In this artistic garden. A dialogue ensued.

Frog to me: That over there is the patent meaning. Me, call me a joke. Your false cognate, the one you thought bloomed, waltzes away like shellfish in the rain.

I looked around. My form felt too big.
Perhaps the whole conceit was getting overworked,
as often happens when some hopeless romantic
strives to hammer out every last drop from the breast.
Friendly fire rained upon us from your unseeing eyes,
as suddenly two enormous locks dragged themselves
onto the wharf. It was my turn to talk.

Me to the frog: I'd like to be done with all the old photoplays and speak to you out of the new. I'm really young, and I'm on the shadow path. I want to know what taking pains is. I want you to show me, in messed-up hours, the divine fantasia overcome, eight separate novels, four for each of us, each of them deathless as we are now becoming.

I shouted this. I winked. It worked:
A beautiful young thing, barely clad,
flew over the green plain, as if at war
with the far ferns. Then I saw his horse.

You can ride faster than the evening wind,
Sit up in the saddle like a prince,
Lace your leather boots to fit your shining form:
Still I can see that you're bored.

Your education fits you handsomely,
Friendly as an eyeblink you remain.
You put up a good fight against the undergoing sun:
Still I can see that you're bored.

Your gabardine won't win you any fashion points,
I like your old man style anyway.
You slowly touch your knee to the darkening earth:
Still I can see that you're bored.

Back then, lovely youngster, you could stay
As quiet as the light fading away.
You wear a storm where most would stick to boxers:
Still I can see that you're bored.

I let out all the colors to the evening fog,
My hand upon your heart inside a dream.
The Greece that robed its night in forms is over:
Still I can see that you're bored.
Even in my dreams I know you're bored.

As I looked back over everything I'd written thus far, I suddenly noticed another young person behaving in what you might call a contradictory fashion. He was doing the "Ode to a Grecian Urn" pose, with eyes fixed somberly on the ground, and from his barely-parted lips silent laughter erupted. Meanwhile the first guy, once naked and bored, now appeared dressed like a sailor, as though he were on his way to a masquerade. As a matter of fact, he was wearing a mask! By his bed, a statue of a hand with its middle finger broken off. You might have taken him for a willing maiden, outfit thrown together in a mood. He'd head straight off in one direction, then get a little uncertain, strike out in another, laughing at himself the whole time. In the barroom, on the other hand, there was a display of musculature, handstands. A passerby spray-painted on the wall, "The young man can't tell if he should be naughty or nice." Now a host of sailors filled the room. Over to the left somewhere I could sense a group of gorgeous women and girls; on the right, there was a single towering babe, who when I looked at her it made me want my eyes back, the way she met and overpowered my supposedly so-potent gaze. It was all getting a little confusing. He had found some kind of statuette under the sheets, but more aboriginal even than Keats had been thinking about. Surrounded by all these women I noticed once again a young man, who I thought I could talk to about my novel. He wasn't as fine as the former specimens, but chiseled, the type who might have spent time in Australia. Headlights flashed past the sailors. I was sure he was Australian, or French, or anything but German; he had nice pants on. The sailors started moving in. The ladies swatted at the tall number I mentioned above. One cooed: "I'm braver than you, darling ethical life!" Ethical life was taken aback by this fetching assault. Over there the sailors were cutting me to pieces, restoring me with milk. Ethical life ascended to her radiant throne. "Why do I have to listen to your bullshit?" said she. She was crowned with a Christmas tree, with fireworks, ablaze. Things were coming to a point. All of a sudden, the frog spoke up, and this is what it had to say:

Don't be alarmed, ethical life, nor you, dearest of readers,
if it seems as though the proceedings have taken a turn
whose meaning is obscure and somehow shameless,
while the very license which the scene allows
dilutes it of the specificity that art
must have on pain of losing auditors. I am a frog,
it's true, and my words often sink below
the swampy surface of my native home,
unattended. Not everyone expects me
to speak up with witty phrases, diagnose
the situation like a Parisian surgeon,
gaslit, fretting over his mistress: you see,
you think I've lost the thread, but I'm just exercising
this throat of mine, which isn't, frankly, human,
but needs to swell and shrink a couple of times
before it's ready to emit its truest cry.

I think we're good. This openness that threatens
in ways beyond the formal noted above,
that if unchecked will disrobe all false idols,
not just religious shibboleths that serve
mostly to keep the average stiff obeying
courtiers and kings, the ideologies
that prop up nation-states, but even
the unexamined precepts governing
intimate relations, what men and women do
in the quiet, private dark: all right, all right,
the point is, this uncanny situation
in which the rules of daily life submit
to questioning arises from a shadow,
a multitude of lovely shadows: art.
Their beauty's only surface. They will fade
with the light that shines from every turning page.
Already, you can barely remember
what got me speaking on this froggy topic.
I won't say a word more on it. Just keep in mind,
freedom brings such saucy banter out.

"Personally, I'd like to fuck that little rider,"
said one of the maidens, which occasioned
a sleeping figure unmediated by time and space,
except as a bad joke. What she really said
was "I think he's really funny." Plus
further aspersions against ethical life,
who at this point we can maybe agree
had already gotten about all the mileage

she was good for in such a persiflage-ridden
context. Now, to be sure, Schlegel's novel
appeared some decades before the morality/
ethical life split would appear in what is

nowadays its canonical form: that developed
in the Hegelian Rechtsphilosophie. But already
in the third critique, you might argue,
the filmic dream constitutes an example

as the rider brings sociality closer to us,
closer to her: "I'd like to socialize with him,"
she says, speaking maybe for others.
The present holds out its hope.

Customs fade away like frogs in the rain,
so elegance, the cleverest among the gathered
assembly, whispered to Julian.
"What did she say?" asked the rider.

"Everything makes me feel at home,
everything's so boring," said the reader,
the modern type, striding away. The scene
kept veering toward an ironic

displacement, not fresh, not allegorical.
It seemed hard to me. I could say
three things and I had to wonder
whether I was even in the building.

Quick! Call in the Beautiful Soul!
Oh, that'll help. It's only a mask,
everybody chanted, "it's only a mask."
You are not the beautiful soul.

RT: @frog: "Finish the book.
How can you know what time is?
Life flows like poetry. I think I'm
a little drunk. Music! Love-sent hearts!"

So the frog seems to be
laughing at me, the heaven-sent boy
is winking back at me, and she
keeps saying, "The photograph

remains the source of the dream."
It's 1799, by the way. Whence all the wine
emerged I couldn't tell you.
"That was an *outer* appearance,"

said the voice, "whereas you only look
for beauty on the inside. You're really nice.
But I mostly want to fuck that little rider."
I swear I'm not just talking to myself.

Now, great, everything disappears.
Frog wakes up, explains he doesn't
exist. But to tell you the truth,
I knew it was mostly me to begin

with, living, standing alone.
I conducted my own brand of mass,
dimly lit. Then I turned around.
Holy moley! Now things were getting clearer!

I had seen clear through myself
and now the outside world was permeated
with my own vision (no, I wasn't
drunk still. I saw clearly!)

I saw the blue sky!
I saw the green field!
I saw the bare earth
swarming with pure form!

Everything I had experienced up to now
was an inner fantasy preparing me
for this. And as I watched, the forms
took up their masks and began

their sacred, lustful carnival.

Paul Legault
The You-Know-What

Despite itself,
the criticism is happening in time.

8:53: I think that.
8:54: I don't.
SPRING: Come get my chicken.
DAZE: There is a difference

between waiting for the scenery to quit
looking at itself chewing on something

and not.
SEBASTIAN: What did you hide off into, Sebastian?

SEBASTIAN: An Elvis made entirely of pollen.
PINE: And an Elvis made of tissue paper

arm in arm
with the luminary.

What One's Set One's Sights On

At the land, the horses have limits.
They looked like cherries or
    as if they were made of them.

GOLD MACHINE-GUN: Get down, legends.
LIBERTY: (*similarly*) I'll stay down here in the corridors.
SILVER: Rain makes rain sound.
THE SUN: Silver can break.

This little fish goes
and turns itself

like the cities turn the keys of themselves.
THE WORD: (*swimming noises*)

PEACE: (*swimming noises*)
METAPHYSICS: God has a fat face with clouds in it.

I know this kid
    with no hands or with hands
    but hands that aren't attached to his body somewhere
in the roses or on fire.

Arthur Sze
The Ginkgo Light

1

A downy woodpecker drills into a utility pole.
While you cut stems, arrange tulips in a vase,
I catch a down bow on the A string, beginning
of *Song of the Wind*. We savor black beans
with cilantro and rice, pinot noir; as light slants
through the kitchen window, spring is candlelight
at our fingertips. Ice crunches in river
breakup: someone shovels snow in a driveway,
collapses, and, hospitalized, catches staph
infection; out of airplane wreckage, a woman
identifies the ring on the charred corpse
of her spouse; a travel writer whose wife is in
hospice gazes at a lunar eclipse, the orange moon
at one-millionth of its normal brightness.
A 1300-year-old lotus seed germinates; a ginkgo
issues fan-shaped leaves; each hour teems.

2

A seven-year-old clips magenta lilacs for her mother;

"electrocuted tagging a substation";

patter of rain on skylight;

manta rays feed along a lit underwater cove;

seducing a patient,
he did not anticipate plummeting into an abyss;

over Siberia, a meteor explodes;

"I am happiest here, now!"

lesser goldfinch with nesting fiber in its beak;

love has no near or far.

3

Near Bikini Island, the atom bomb mushroomed
into a fireball that obsidianed the azure sky,

splayed palm leaves, iridescent black, in wind;
that fireball moment always lurks behind

the retired pilot's eyes, even when he jokes,
pours vodka, displays his goggles, medal,

leather jacket hanging from a peg. A woman
hums as she works with willow, X-Acto knife,

magnifying lens to restore a Jicarilla Apache
basket; she has no glimmer a zigzag line

is beginning to unravel, does not know within
a decade she will unload a slug into her mouth.

    4

Through a moon gate, budding lotuses in a pond;

"You're it!"

he stressed rational inquiry
then drove south into the woods, put a gun to his head;

vaporized into shadows;

quince and peach trees leafing below the ditch;

succession and simultaneity;

the branch-like shapes in their sheets;

pizzicatti:
up the riv-er we will go.

5

August 6, 1945: a temple in Hiroshima 1130 meters
from the hypocenter disintegrates, while its ginkgo

buds after the blast. When the temple is rebuilt,
they make exit, entrance steps to the left and right

around it. Sometimes one fingers annihilation
before breaking into bliss. A mother with Alzheimer's

knows her son but not where she lives or when
he visits. During the Cultural Revolution,

Xu-mo scrubbed one million dishes on a tanker
and counted them in a trance. A dew point

is when a musher jogs alongside her sled dogs,
sparing them her weight on the ice to the finish.

6

Loaves of bread on a rack; a car splashes
a newspaper vendor on a traffic island.
On the road of days, we spot zodiacal light
above the horizon. Astronauts have strewn
footprints and streptococcus on the moon.
Chance sparks the prepared mind: a Cooper's
hawk perched on a cottonwood branch

quickens our synapses. In the orchard,
the sound of apricot blossoms unfolding;
mosquito larvae twitch water at the v-shaped
berm that pools runoff to the pond. We do
not believe we trudge around a flaming
incense burner on a road of years. As fireflies
brighten, we long to shimmer the darkness
with streamers. A pickup veers toward
then away, skewing light across our faces.

7

As light skews across our faces, we are
momentarily blinded, and, directionless,

have every which way to go. Lobelia
flowers in a patio pot; a neighbor

hands us three Bibb lettuces over a fence.
A cricket stridulates outside the window;

and while we listen to our exhale, inhale,
ephemera become more enduring than concrete.

Ginkgos flare out. A jagged crack
spreads across windshield glass, we find

to recoil from darkness is to feed the darkness,
to suffer in time is—dichotomous venation—

to effloresce the time. One brisk morning,
we snap to layers of overlapping

fanned leaves scattered on the sidewalk,
finger a scar on wrist, scar on abdomen.

Richard Greenfield
Eris

Started with the stamen—

a fragile scheme

I would

appraise it

I looked at it

The opaque hub of it

resisted

The gaze wormed

itself into the fruit

and turned

to see its source

through the hole

it had chewed

Who builds-over

overwrites

the already-there

pierces ovary

draws kingdom blood

The imperial conceits

begin w/ bouquets

Counting the tapestries—

the ten thousand

spoils secreted

to the casual sea

for a minute

mirrored in the sun

A critique began . . .

Did I pour acid or water?

Counted the very volume

Oil fields on fire

acetated award-winning

This was the

stigma of *irsa*, iris

erased—

the tender style

of the flower

turned financial

The Laws

The orphaned pocket of the wilderness
does not miss its connection
to the scheme of the rivers
or nurse trees

it declines where a sign
declares the boundary

The road to the sign was well worn
 The trail was clear
 I hiked through feral woods,
early winter, no more underbrush verve
The horned lark was
 in his evening singing
the vaunt of the last
western wave,
                    a trumpet
pouring through the scenes

I broke out of the aspens into a meadow

In the center

The break-off

        rock

         focal in the grass

              I rested my back

    against the face

the pan of the plains below me

a sacral lesion
or lichen
 deep in the granite

   seamed toward
everything I could obscure there
by sitting there,

   no end to it,
it keeps on coming:

my primacy

If here
 were only unrealized
or only arrived at

in a meadow, biotic
without reason

you can't do this
you can't do that

but all spent beloveds are
stifled in the ache
and covered over

Each monster
will establish its own agenda

e. tracy grinnell

36 / a tower is evident

of birch (absent). all the while a sentence is forming

a sentence is form. cardinal, you are proper

/ the lobes of composition

it is a tree full of not one kind of bird.

I am sworn in / this is autumn, and this is true

light is shadow, water, fraction / is evidence

it cools
/ where is nowhere
it rose
/ what is to be done in winter

"a run of birch is nothing to sequoia

45 / a lark,
a wish-refrain (II)

My quietness has a number of naked selves —FRANK O'HARA

Therefore a delicate

while we are

surety and because
is picturing a derivative

at whiles were seasons
                    drawn

as divers_
is versions

this is desirous / have what is not "out there

of the same

this lake humble / arterial

wish this of *things*

as in "no" real

      all-so mnemonic / and has no honest phase

Matt Reeck
Ode to /a/

all aardvarks, waltz
malls, all faults,

falls, nawabs, all
bods, daubs,

FOBs, all prawn
mods, mob

lawns, all qualms,
fawns, locks, all

rocks, straw Bobs,
all Allahs, all

long odds, all malt
bars, pompoms,

claws, all hearths,
alms, balls, all

drawls, all stars,
dawns, all parks

Ode to /I/

in lyrics, riddles,
in tin wigs,

fickle thrills, in
girls, tidbits,

in fish gills,
krill, dills, in

crisp linen, thin
bills, trick

limericks, in pimp
cribs, bling,

in blimps, in
trim limbs, in

thick licks, hips,
in silk slips,

guilt, rings, in
little hills, stills,

in whisk, figs,
whist, gigs

Ann Lauterbach
Still *No Still*

Walden *still* for example *no still*. Or the other one, tiny in the mind *no still* or that one. The extensions of habitat, the coming back *no still* around to the pond *still*. The two dogs *still*, dark lumps up in the hole in the ice *still*. Above its cycles *no still*, wind *no still*. Nature *still* intersects culture *no still* sooner or later *no still*.

The difference *no still* between being *no still* glad and being afraid *no still* across the width of a puddle *still*. The common *no still* scrap reflected, stepping across *still*. Straddling a scrap of sky *still* within the puddle *still*, the miniature *no still*, urban pond. Description *no still* overflows into narrative *no still*, narrative wanders *no still*. Muddy tracks *still*.

What gist of night? *No still*. Rage at the augmented *no still* but vacated sublime *no still*. As if, night *no still* or day *still*, any of us *no still*. Gladness and fear *no still*. The dog humps seen through binoculars *still* in a small suburban town *still*. Panes of glass, all illusory *no still* black *still*, a single star percolating in a single frame *still*. The other face *still* across a table *still*.

Nature *no still* filtering its message *no still* through its nonmessage *no still*. Screened-in porch *still* imagining *no still* the young girl *still* abducted to her death *no still* from the car wash *still* shortcut to home *still*, caught *no still*, as they say *no still*, on video *still*. This *no still* is not a car *still*, this is a girl *still* being dragged *still* to her death *no still*. The dogs *still* trapped *no still* in the water *still*.

The dream *no still* of a young man *still*. The dream *no still* of the drunk *no still* woman *still*. The thoughts *no still* about her daughter *still*. The dream *no still* about the drunk mother *still*. After she fell into the *no still* pond *still*, she dreamed *no still* of a young man *still*. He *no still*, the young man *still*, a stranger *no still*. How is it possible *no still* to dream *no still* of strangers *no still*?

Will things *still* get better *no still*? What *no still* makes things *still* better *no still*? The girl *still* abducted by the stranger *no still* will not get better *no still* although her father *still* says *no still* she is now *no still* in a better place *no still*. Nature filtering its message *no still* through its nonmessage *no still*. The star *still* has disappeared *no still* from the part of night framed in the window *still*.

The ordinary *no still* adheres to what might be consigned *no still* to nothing *no still*. The mystique of drowning *no still*, the painless *no still* cold *no still*. Pond life *still*. The gear *still* or frame *still* of speech *no still*. Table talk *no still* and the lines of sight or flight *no still* as if the birds *still* were *no still* still *no still*. Spell bird. B *still* as in bird *still*. I *still* as in I *no still*. R *still* as in are *no still*.

Humiliated by certainty *no still*. Intention *no still* and its target *still*. No *no still* second chances *no still* no second glances *still*, one-time only *no still* smile for the camera *still*. Abducted by certainty *no still*. He picked up the large glass *still* and saw *no still* a naked woman *still* stepping within *no still*. The ocular cold *no still*.

Scrappy indoctrination of the humdrum *no still*. A blue sign *still* for history *no still*, little waving stripes *still* for country *no still*. Against the certainty *no still* of kings, their crowns *still* in God's *no still* kitchen *still*. The mountain humps *still* up in the pale ski *still*; the bodies of the dogs *still* in the frozen pond *still*. The sad *no still* jurisdiction *no still* of the weeds *still*.

Species still *no still* speaking *no still* the King's English *no still*. Say please. *No still*. Mired now in the muddy waters *still* of the pond *still*, run aground. Gridlock *still*. Talks fell through *no still*. Out of the picture *no still*. Too many scavengers along the line of sight—gulls *still*, hawks *still*, black cat in snow *still*.

Contaminated *no still* by beauty *no still!* The transcendental *no still* mirror *still,* looking down into the pond *still.* Ace in the hole *no still.* Let it *no still* not fall and *no still* one *still* by one *still,* the Jack *still* and the Queen *still* and the King *still* and the pawns *no still.* Nothing *no still* left: board *still* empty, dishes *still* to wash, bills *still* to pay, birds *still* to feed.

Spell *no still* pond *still.* One thing after another *no still.* Letter *no still* for letter *no still.* S *still* as in still *no still* p *still* as in purple *no still* e *still* as in even *no still* l *still* as in left *no still,* l *still* as in later *no still.* P *still* as in pretty *no still,* o *still* as in over *no still,* n *still* as in now *no still,* d *still* as in dead *no still.* Still purple even left later pretty over now dead. *No still.*

Fenn Stewart

some grimy
apple; or,
my sequel's
wiltshire parts

a summer been ousted,
a penitent summer's index
a summer like fits, like indemnity—
some summer, invictus—
a summer's a meadow of strife

for example:

a horse is a difficult nurse.

he's dumb like a fist right.

a small empty aquifer traces my seams.

doubt—like a war, like a twinset—
is graceful, infectious

eyes are like history—or else—
like a gland

dear putrid bowl,
dear putrid everything inside my bowl

it is either this lack or not lack this lack that moves me

(his knuckles, maybe, as he flays ought, sincerely

til he too knows a shy and giddy tern
some throbbing modern undressed vibrant fungus)

walrus says: a lathe is as much as to say:
worship this shelf

(while he persists i violet without pause)

my supper: a clam shardful of cream
a small worm, a ventricle of pinch, regalia

and as it was written: some shall be
incipient to the rest

the meadowlark's trudge: a pulling caught twig

at daybreak, a willow's slattern shudder
this threshing vicious like a sudden hale and hearty
like a sudden how's your old straw
like a sudden withered tweed

salt fish
pan one

a ghost termite will howl
will pine, will moan

seas persever
like a smear of sodden grass

a lurid prating whelp sings prey,
sings palfrey

a soggy blotter gloats:

semper pious, darling

but lo!

almost as many madams
as have sundered me
have vouchsafed you

(seven.)
(ha!)

walrus says:

damsons and fumes are too often in season

walrus says:
unhook my trahir, kiddo
and go 'round to bleed the old white iron
radiators, when it gets cold enough,
if you don't mind

Peter O'Leary

The Phosphorescence of Thought

The wren
the mind
allows
to sing
alights
—and flits—
on branches bare
of anything other than the sun's ceaseless iodine
the woods at dusk flood with
like sutras meditators seep their thoughts in
neurochemicals recall from the galaxy's
antique axiometry. Alongside,
the Des Plaines River folding creamy gray through the trees bubbles
with pungent yeasts emplumed
in cottony lutrid foam engineered by
embankments men pile up
to keep
the river
tame.

The mind.
The mind assuming

reality. The mind's field of forces, its fluid exuberance
rebeginning, leaping up, folding back
into terminal unities endlessly

varying.
Cluster. Synthesis. Network. Node.
Centration.
The re-entering mental impulse.

The herring gulls circling; their yellow
gapes, the little crimson dots—breeding season. The mallards.
their rotating strokes around the whirls, dabbling. Those lurid,
irisized heads.

Lutrid. Lutrescent. That's the mind's
excessive novelty, a tool preposterously ductile
language—pulling sound, image, light fluidly together—
freely commandeers
to feel reality,

to imagine light
gone rotten.

The wren,
            again.
A house wren. Its beak a slightly silvered sickle, its remembered song
—rapidly rolling, a bubbling, liquid trill—
an outlandish complexity copied
inventively from an adult
—a male—

not his father. A descending chirruping, a
draining descant he variously daylong intones marking
the little log he's nesting in.

To begin.

The woods. The shabby little Forest Preserve.
The swerve of its trashy paths. The partying in its clearings.
The little house wren in it, his cinnamon supercilium, the drab
pattern of his plumage. And his mate—their clutch
of seven bean-sized eggs, luminously
speckled, secreted
deep in a cavity cleaned

from inside the fallen
log. The red-headed woodpeckers,
the flickers—darts defying gravity, their malars'
neon slash—the red-bellied *picadus*,
its deeply undulating flight. The avian cocaine
I take him for.

                    What
evolutionary acquisition does
that vibrant red
express? And what

do I love in loving thee?

lumen de lúmine
Deum vero de Deo vero; génitum

non factum, consubstantialem Naturæ; per quam
omnia facta sunt.

With the oldest cherubim of knowledge,
the phanophagous cherubs, devouring
with their bodies the light they transform into scissoring flame
flared forth sword-like and brandished, unspeakably
world-like, fully
recklessly
imagined.

We now begin our study of the mind
within. Let us use the words *psychic overtone,*
suffusion, or *fringe.*

Let us
speak in whispers of the one,
of the meticulous hinge
on the Book of Knowledge Hidden
in rapt

prolusion. Apart. Come.

Let us use the word *re-entry.*
Let us sing the differentiating motions
whereby thought's signals
slide in runnels
down the mind's
great glacial expanse

pooling
at the base, lubricating
its massive shelves, its agonized
calves. Let us use

the word *epistrophe*   *Come, let us pray*
to mean the turning back of otherwise organized energy
to the supra-organized
diadem of the Godhead—premeditative acts
of prayer. Pre-

cognitive flights of birds.

   The warbler
the oriole
the blackbird
the bunting.
   The sparrow
the waterthrush
the warbler
the wren.
   The wren
the hermit thrush
the warbler
the redstart.
   The yellowthroat
the sparrow
the kinglet
the kestrel.
   The hawk

the wren
the kestrel
the cranes.

::

Creation is humans' memory system. Cranes
rely on magnetic streams
to remember. Sparrowhawks
on superaccurate eyesight—light's flickering peripheries
patterned out as
tiny rodent motion. Their hovering is still; their stooping
soundless.

      Kestrel:
its evidence's the air's, that autochthonomous unearthing,
unleashing aerobatics to hover lustrously in a wind-groomed leewave.
That's air's predatory excesses trimmed

into an evolutionary
leanness.

That's the sun's own *killy-killying* carapace.

What's it like to be a falcon?
As strange as being a man, and
as idiomatic—.

It's more owl than hawk.
More wisdom than war.

More hovering wind than merciful mind.

More mind than mentation.

More massively reentrant than speciously reentrancing.

More richly environmental than metaphorically unitary.

More autochthonomously unleashing than

through the void plummeting.

More splendidly envisioning than accident of life.

More gift than gall, more

phenomenal still. More like sleep rupturing waking than

like building a temple.

To coax the divine

in.

More like gaining altitude than boring through the earth.

More earth's

ward than

air's excess.

More binding and synchronous than operatively constructive.

                                        A kestrel

can resolve a minute insect by precisely   ·

bobbing its head up & down, triangulating in parallax its fluttering position,

from twenty yards away. Its eyes

are so huge the back of each orb presses into

the middle of its skull. In a bird nine inches long,

this means eyes the size of two

red grapes.

Whose insides weirdly resemble the fruit's flesh—an

avascularized retina in which neither shadow nor light-scatters

interfere with vision; a projecting pleated structure
called the pectin feeds the retinal cells
with blood. Your eyes
have 30,000 cones in the retina's
most sensitive spot—: a kestrel's fovea has
one million cones and each photoreceptive cell
directly represents its data in the brain. Imagine
the words of your thoughts dropping from your ears onto
the pavement, piled there.

You

have one fovea in each eye; falcons have two—these foveae fuse to produce
stereoscopic vision, field's depth in falconine

richness.

Where in humans vision is a sense—a *quale* binding life to mind in
the brain's dynamic core—
in falcons vision is thought itself, the avian mind's
ductile conversion
of reality into raptorial
being.

     Falcons
are relatively newly evolved: nature's novelty in speed and
predacious grasp. Life's
most perfect instrument of vision
is a falcon's roving eye.

In barest functional terms, a kestrel
is a pair of eyes set in a well armed, exquisitely engineered

airframe. And there's a set of them, at the treetops seen
from the alley—a family?—resting in my
binocular focus.

The elm in mid-March. Leafless aureating circuitry against the sky.
Gray. Creamy. Along the branching aura's

underside, two raptors
at work, undistracted—at ease. A Cooper's Hawk
feigning uncoordination, staggering
from one flimsy limb to a lower
wobbling its bulk,

is operating actually—pulling
a twig from dead wood. Prematurely
expanding air, too warm so soon, feathers the elm   .
with silence

like a humidity

the Cooper's clutching its nest-building material trampolines
onto, swooping gently
quietly down

between houses to its alley
eyrie.

Alternately, half the Cooper's size, a cool blue Merlin
daubed dull in the low-
contrasting light grooms

its feathers fretting them with air
they splay in ruffed undulations into as it moves its
polished onyx beak in yogic
rotations from head to anus, gently nibbling
the uropygial gland preening
its wings' pulvered grooves with fatty acids the sun,
when it bursts out at last, will convert

into vitamin D. Perched there.

Upright, puffed from the work. Silent.

Its blue coloration common to raptorial bird-killers. Which
no one knows the reason for. (Lunging from the sky?)

A kestrel soars, revolving the sky through the vanes of his wings.

Worship.
Veneration.

The little falcon's latriated flight.
The sparrowhawk's hyperduliated flight.
We shall see and we shall love. We shall love and we shall praise.
Involuntary light.
The glistening radiance—the vanity of the imagination.
The consuming fire sacrificial divinity is.

The invading world keeps stripping away our silence
the natural world endlessly emanates—a silence

falcon wings comb through in wild undone plummets.
Thought's vertiginous drop mythic distances measure.

   ::

When the river plain was prairie
when the riverslope inclined to the plane of the horizon
when the riverlings riffling into the floodplain were gushing
when the convergence of wet system with hurricane rushed up the Midwestern
    summertime
when the rain for two days straight came down
when the *shamanistic shuddering-shouting awakened something real in the depths*
    of our native poetic sound
when the rivermeadow under dilations of stillicidous indraughts flushed
when the valves of the land busted open—
there was a bore
a corrivation
a pluviose swash: a flood.
September 13th and 14th, 2008, in Riverside, in Lyons, the Des Plaines
breaching its banks.

A functional river ecosystem is connected to everything around it.

Sodden basement garbage.
Migrating fall-time birds.
Junky fisherman minding the morning.

Afterwards, its waters retreated: the floodplain's flora felted with muddy ash
    everywhere. Plovers
cherrypicking minute crawdads, stranded mudpuppies in isolated puddles

in the woods, along the rivercourse.
Plastic tatters of sandbanks two meters up, bewitched in ragged scrub: how many
years will it take to clear this already shabby
Forest Preserve of all this new debris?
Little solemn disaster. Little *nothing really* that happened.
Little curdled spume caught in the loggy cluster
snagged by a bank.

Strange holy enclosing scene fluming turbidly out—
The exaltation, not merely the conversation, of the elements by convergence.

The exaltation, not merely the pituitous riverine wax
the convergence, not entirely the bizarre essence
the gift, not only the benefit, not only the blessing song
the kiss, not everywhere the touch
the acid, not implicitly corrosive
the nucleation, the horde of living tissue
inertia, not automatically expanding
negation, not retracting as expected, not immediately so
the glory, and its correlate confusion
the rule-breaking restlessness, a way of entering in:

the mysteries of the ecology, the environment knowing itself:

the surprising patterns of its parts.

I find a snake writhing upstream in the gushers—a pet set free by the storm?
I find woodpeckers, robins, blue jays thriving in the woods.
I find rivers of thought, waxy in semiliquid aspic, surging hilariously forth.

I find I incorporate arterial profluences as well as

problems of navigation.

I find the riverhead, the river dragon, the river terraces metaphysical comforts for

the uncertainties

about the precise qualities of the chemical composition

that make up the rivers peculiar

amylaceous smell.

I find this river a bradyapneatic exhalation of a once healthy suspiring system.

I find the Des Plaines River today to be urban planning's lost forethought.

Its Promethean western barrier.

I find the river, done with flooding, following its brumous way

through a series of seedy woods.

I find the water a lactiferous brown.

I find it a sudsing barm.

I find it warm and gelatine.

I find it daily gurgling.

I find it circulating through the world.

I find it streaming, I find it coursing, I find it in antic, manic flux.

I find it exuberant.

I find it spurred.

I find it undrinkable.

I find it full of flooding force.

I find it accidental.

I find it rebegun.

Concresced.

Perfectly disturbed, a drifting

pathway for all the birds.

::

Avid explosions of migrating warblers
stellating star patterns woodlands and prairies,
suburbs and flyways zodiac symbolical
measures for thinking with. Chromatic bodies

light pressure mirrors from solar antonyms
transforming cardinal time into vernal lusts—
nesting defenders, selective aspirers speciate
properties air draws from time's distilling gravities.

Lustred migrations. At every hour we've ever imagined, a bird is on the wing: a robin
keeping pace with the melting edge of snow cover; a whooping crane's dramatic
        solitary fanning
in a streak of sandhills; an arctic tern jetting
from pole to pole in a vast seasonal circuit; an indigo bunting finding
the border zone where woodland opens into clearing; a ruby-throated hummingbird
purring across five-hundred miles of coastline on a gram
of nectar. Relentless nights and days of movement.
Survival's ancient itch only arrowing onward scratches. The mind's
a migratory evidence, the projection of the human animal's consciousness
from instinctive enclosures of neural circuits fired with latent gifts to the dynamiting
outer expanding world: it's why our first depictions
were animals—bulls, gazelles, cranes, souls.

Migration's astonishing parallels between image and idea, between
species and soul in communion with motion, in
commotion, its eucharistic transformations:
a brown creeper and two golden-crowned kinglets
in the stardowned snowfall
of an April's unwarranted weather

migration seethes northward through in spite of

the season's agitations. The little puff of pressure signaling

a Wilson warbler's passage through the birch tree's

newly greening leaves.

Three splendidly yellowing magnolia warblers

uplifting through a maple tree.

Hermit thrushes' spooking ghostflow through the underbrush.

Flocked starlings' geometric detonations

inspired like fireworks. Migration's notes:

the woods' logophragous originator, *song*. It's

creation's symphonic dilator, birds' iconic identifier:

pluck of notes and the riverine sillage. Stillness as an energy.

Woods swarmed with palm warblers, with flashes of yellow-rumped

warblers. Elementalism of cool light, palely cloud-filtered.

Disastrous trashing of the paths of the woods.

These sweet woods providing cover for evolution's outlandish

artificers, song-crowned, crowned in song.

Perception's filtration system: ricocheting catalogues of unruly song, territorial call:

it's spring's brand-new body making noise.

Orange peels, bait trays, charred plywood, broken malt liquor bottles,

the turgid Des Plaines guzzling by. Sunlight

expressing greens. Sponge of wood, soft decay, kneeling deer.

Reefs of mushroom glazed with vernal liquor. Thrush songs three-dimensional.

In alchemy, the wren who vexed Thoth.

In admixture, the summer terns with segmented wings and the patterned earth.

In sunlight, the ensouling over the forest.

In doctrine, metempsychosis.

In practice, the transmigratory elaborations, the little autochthonomous soul leavings.

In evenings, the firefly's transmigratory dynamo,

the firefly's renewed lutrescent fuse,

that little phosphorescent flare of transanimation.

In prayer, the little struggles, the pressing awareness of flaws.

In the world, ongoing wars,

the sadness of foolishness.

In actuality, grace. Life from life—the vital force burst through the body's feathers.

In flight, birds. Arrowing off the earth.

PART THREE

LOCAL POWERS

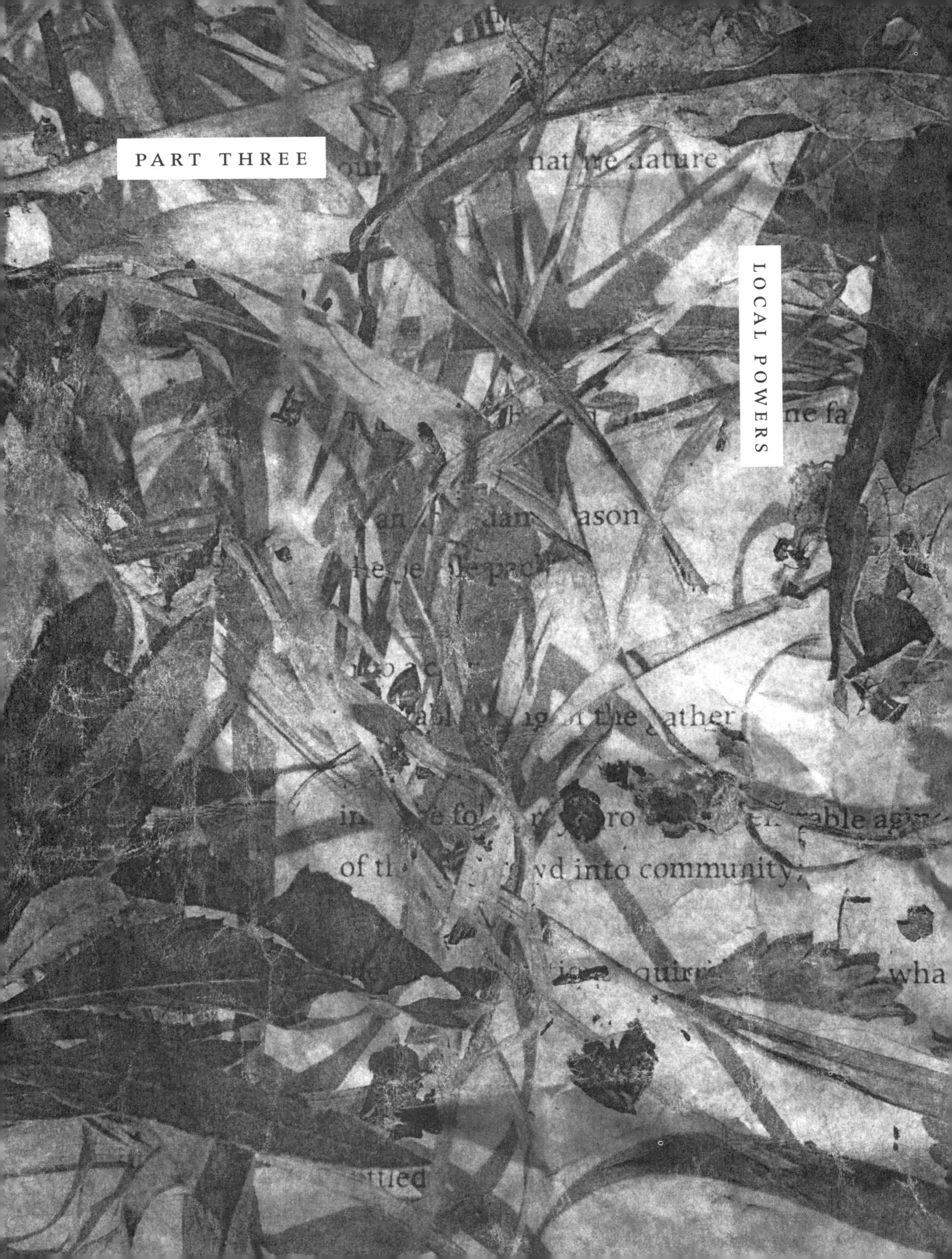

Jennifer Moxley
The Sense Record

Le ciel est de cuivre

Sans lueur aucune,

On croirait voir vivre

Et mourir la lune.

—VERLAINE

I

Under the threat of another light downpour
Eros, soaked by the rain-water,
spoke to the sentient flowers.
Sadness, no longer extraneous,
began the derangement of nerve,
bypassed the bleeding heart
to pierce the blood-brain barrier.
This all *en-route* to the two-door garage.
I was worn with the labor that augurs despair,
life in the futile percentile, when passed
my squeamish eyelash, buffeted by scallops
of small will, the slightest fairy brushed.
My rubber souls conformed to the stones
as I followed and spied the backyard starlet
allongée on an orange blossom, delicate
beside the drinking bees, blithe amidst
sharp blades of grass, a rain-drop seductress
entertaining ants on the folding lip
of a pinkster leaf.

The gray of an old folded paper
decomposed on the nearby walk.
I caught the rain extracting ink
from this impromptu *papier mâché*—
pulp of dated politics, exposées
in retrospect about the infamy
of what was once thought honesty
when "all the facts" had come to view,
the archives opened, the files read.
The heartfelt story of engagement
recast as sucker bet, who licked the stamps,
who walked the streets, the earnest underlings,
forestall the mockery in memoirs,
two-to-three hundred "as told to" pages
to set the record straight. From aloft
the insect mezzanine these patterns
portend the rot of hours, as one paper-strip
wilts atop the next. Little deaths
sufficient to wake the council of
discarded causes. Under the concrete cracks
the tenacious weed-roots rattle,
reassigned from lawn destruction
to ankle espionage, and in the grass
the poet whispers:

    "death death death death death

     between two hopes,
in brittle mid-years, all is vanity"

II

Possessed by precarious rhythm
I have tried to pour these
insinuated streamlets
into an imaginary world, incite
the careful consciousness of love
(though it seemed a lie, destined
to kill, disrupt, possess and interfere),
I did not accept the swan dive
of the newly awakened deity,
as I watched the absent reappear
in something as common as a dropped book,
pushed back these last three years
behind a house of crumbling spines
    (its author's subtle intervention
    attires her chances in intention).
I feel sick to think that she, that we
had, and have, but one pursuit
and one pursuit alone.

Dumbfounded by objects I am caught
in a thought-drift, in *lieu* of tears consider
constellations of printed matter
actual in my hands, the mind *in absentia,*
the interruption of a dream
when she came to me in the garden,
a tall ghost in a white T-shirt
lifting its arms behind its head
to gather its shoulder-length hair

in a loose spray of summer wheat,
exactly the sort of thoughtless business
she once so readily mastered.
I knew she was there to break wild fear
against the arsenal-of-determined-will
deliver the dream-quest from disrespect,
all the way down to the gutter river,
below her cut-offs her bare white legs
speckled with errant twigs.
Redeemed by the seeming passivity of the dream,
I remembered she cared for nothing, if he stayed,
for she knew her vanishing words would prevail
for a second, a minute, an hour, a day—
in an errant stalk of goldenrod,
a dislodged strand of forgotten purpose.
And she knew how much stronger
the rumored origin
than the pale act of creation.

    And I
in a warm summer, in an old city,
in an elusive crowd of elegant strangers,
imbedded in my miscarriage,
gorging on *crêpes sucrées,*
busily moving the master plan
off the accursed continent,
in feigned interest fairly trapped
in the hollow words of the wrong book
in the dark of the movie theatre
hungering for passionate incident

ignorant of splendid knowledge
tolerant of the false embrace,
suspect of effort, affronted by energy,
beginning every sentence with
the wish to finish it on my lips.

III

In the soul without recourse from fear—
kill-joy of the insouciant imagination,
singing small worlds within the world—
what should swim so often sinks.
Fairy life belies the wish
that cannot germinate,
the love that won't adhere,
everything that cannot come and,
if destiny be flattered, never will.

How cowardly, then, my longing
to be reprieved of mystery
by some omniscient deity.
The will that passed these hedge-rows,
hardly hedge-rows, thought forgotten
forsaken circumstance, and everyone
I've loved and lost
is busy in the tending
of intention's infinite trajectory,
a mirror-world, matter-free,
of pure imagination.

I suppose that I have half-imagined
my remembrances fissures
through which this place makes known
the continuance of my absent friends,
as stars sometime were thought the holes
through which angelic light came shining.

Why must I alone account
for those I have known all too briefly.
To feel their psychic egress
I would as much deny
were it not for my suspicion
that built into intelligence
lies some strange quadrant
of a fractured Heaven,
or Hell, an individual memory complex
stretched across the globe
vanished-existence maps
destroyed by the nonchalant amnesia
necessary to live.

IV

Charting the dead we miss everything
we promised not to miss for the world,
in search of some profundity
in ancient symbols, in old books,
and as for the Muse, there is always the moon,
advantaged by her bird's-eye view,

"But I do not think you'll find her in Paris,
there among the decapitations."

As I said to my friend who, pen in hand,
had gone in search of silence, anonymity,
and the hope of not-belonging,
three conditions necessary to cultivate his art,

"She's the coquettish lover
who will vie with all your readers"

especially in *that* city,
where even sacrifice looks charming.

On the rooftops the rain gathers in chorus
thin sheets of paper keep the peace.
In routine he maps the illusion
and fends off emptiness with his feet.
It must mean something or be abandoned.
It must mean something, or be abandoned.

"The less I say the more they imagine
that I have something important to say,
and against the pressure to deliver
what little is left of me floats away."

Yet at day's end I am distraught
when I lay my empty head to rest
in the normal kingdom of thought,
where all vanishes

the architecture, the paintings,
the individual license I have thieved
from public liberty. One distance away,
and then the beginning of them all.

It is enough "not-being-us"
alone in the verdant garden.
A deeper understanding
lost in exchange for a little desire,
small bundles of delicate flowers
awaiting the arrival of bees,
between infant-stretch and on-coming accident
we are sewn into time-space collapsing
powerless, pleasure-filled and passive.

"And every night I dream of horses."
"And every so often speech fails me."

It is enough, and just as it should be.
Black bark, wet and broken. Wire noose.
Code of honor, cry for help, the rain falling
on the roofs of the town, and in my heart
a drop of blood, a blade of grass,
the author's voice, and every day
another task of consequence deferred.

V

What anger this satisfaction brings
to those who crave a paucity of means,
contentment unmolested by a question's
sensuous air, a finger, swollen in sleep
along the edge of a coffee filter,
a saucer of warm milk,
the light of dawn retrieved
from behind the yellow curtain.

But despite their brilliant education
they cannot be moved, and though
they tout the popular, on principle they dislike it.
By pleasure alone placated,
they curse the abysmal water
falling into oppressive green.

"Though puzzled and embarrassed
by your frank display of sentiment,
we think you are very brave."

Save this for the walls of fools
who cannot bear existence.

Reality's heroism in an act of forfeiture.
The exhaustion of new forms.
The working parts of an abandoned machine.

"I didn't particularly like the book
but fighting shy of argument
I said a few nice things about it."

Save this for the walls of fools
who cannot bear existence.

Life keeps insisting. Nights I worry
about the spiders inside the vacuum cleaner.
I notice the squirrels look simian bounding,
foot over branch, about the trees.
and wonder if I wasted my youth
imagining this future.
Do I hold a sword or am I a ghost,
marking the tedium between
drunken midnight, wistful sunrise
blood-mouth metronome beats
between here and deep unconsciousness
a sea of little niggling tasks.

VI

Eros tell me why, without love,
Without hate, listening
to the softly falling rain
upon the rooftops of the city,
my heart has so much pain.
What I write in truth today
tomorrow will be in error.

Yet the words keep coming,
mundane and repetitive
With no job "to be done"
nor doctrine to stand for.

Sufficient a single living memory
to cultivate a ghost.
    And all small frightened things
who spend existence seeking shelter
become blank slates on which I write
this debt of ill-used care.

The evil spirits of the waking life
spoil my clothes as I sleep,
the body a fragile vehicle,
its impotent words, its decomposition.

I was blood and disease, could drown in her breasts
flowing blonde between her legs.
When I crawled back through the grass
she was waiting, her hair pulled back
in a thoughtless gesture, her body
white, round, and supple,
    and I wanting so to possess it.

Despite my desire conversation begins
between the blades of grass.
Resistance futile as feather-light fairies
buffeted against the wind.
How many the unrecorded battles

registered upon the human brow,
the betrayed face that knows it's the tongue
not the word, that is destined to fail.

Il pleur dans mon coeur
comme il pleur dans la ville,
with a million surrounding spirits
I continue to dream of horses.
The tranquil leaps of a bookish soul
above material impediment.
To simply know and no more.
To see my long abandoned hope
refracted off your foliate eyes,
translucent and, if I remember right,
careening toward disappointment.

Craig Santos Perez

FROM **ta(la)ya**

[SUMAY CEMETERY]
thru naval
station gate once

contained 19th century
grave marks—

cemetery wall
reveals

shell
damage—
erasured

lost how
many bodies . . .

~

hu hongge i lina'la' tataotao ta'lo   Åmen

~

"Guam Honors War Dead" [Pacific Daily News 5/2/08] : "Guam Son Killed in Iraq: Island Mourns Fallen Soldier" [Pacific Daily News 3/28/08] : "Guam's Young Steeped in History Line Up to Enlist" [The Washington Post 1/27/08] : "US Territories: A Recruiter's Paradise: Army Goes Where Fish Are Biting" [Salt Lake Tribune 8/05/07] :

. . . kept
immaculate—

good
photo op—

sponsorship is required
to access

~

dead bite huchom i
pachot-mu   cemetery | faces | ocean :   'fallen

        soldiers . . .

~~us army spc~~ *christopher jude rivera wesley [26] was killed when the stryker infantry carrier he was in rolled into a canal [12/8/03] in* lameta i korason-hu esta gaige giya half of my heart is in

iraq

us army 1st lt michael aguon vega [42] a guam native died [3/20/04] after sustained injuries from roadside blast in iraq : *us army sgt* yihjyh 'eddie' lang chen [31] of saipan killed in iraq [4/4/04] when unit was attacked : *us marine cpl* jaygee meluat [24] a native of Palau killed by enemy fire in iraq [9/13/04] : *us army sgt* skipper soram [23] from kolonia in the fsm state of pohnpei died after explosion in iraq [9/22/04] : ferdinand ibabao [36] a guam police offer and employee of dyncorp security company killed explosion in iraq [10/14/04] : *us army spc* jonathan pangelinan santos [22] former santa rita resident killed in iraq [10/15/04] vehicle struck by suicide bomber

i lahi-hu gaige giya Iraq my son is

this weekend the agana cathedral hosts
'operation
special intentions'
exhibiting relics of military
patron saints on national
tour

Stephen Ratcliffe

from **CLOUD/RIDGE**

4.18

blinding silver of sun coming up between backlit
trees at top of ridge, yellow and green scotch
broom branches moving back and forth in right
corner

woman on phone looking at the girl
asleep in the pink and yellow bed, camera
filming Picasso painting on glass

man in red
jacket noticing that in Olivier's film Horatio
doesn't read the letter from Hamlet, Olivier
speaking as one ship sails up to the other

Mrs. Ramsay asking William Bankes "did you find
your letters," thinking how "sailor not without
weariness sees the wind fill his sails"

white
cloud in blue sky above the ridge, light green
wall of swell approaching in right foreground

4.19

line of circular orange flowers on green passion
vine-covered fence in left foreground, unseen
song sparrows calling from field beyond it

woman on phone recalling Kerouac's "Early
History of Bop" first came out in *Escapade*,
adding Cecil Taylor isn't standing entirely
still
    man in black jacket looking at words
curved around a white ceramic shape, "stone"
dripping on plane behind it
                Lily Briscoe
noticing that Mrs. Ramsey was looking old,
thinking of a ship whose "sails have sunk
beneath the horizon"
             lines of grey white
clouds on horizon, empty blue sky reflected
across nearly motionless blue plane below it

4.20

yellow pink light coming into the sky above
vertical plane of still dark ridge in right
corner, two birds circling above green field
below it
       woman on phone thinking of Dora Maar

in relation to Picasso, wondering what it means
to say she had a life outside of his

> formerly

pregnant woman asking how an eight-pound rose-
lipped girl can take over what was once her
life, everything calm only when she gives
herself completely

> Lily Briscoe thinking "I

shall avoid that awkward space," moving the salt
cellar back "to remind herself to move the tree"

white water breaking on reef in right corner,
blue grey point on horizon across from it

4.21

diagonal plane of low grey white cloud moving
across the green of the ridge, invisible song
sparrow calling from scotch broom in the left
foreground

> woman on phone planning to start

embroidering shirt with scarlet "no," noting
that she is still in possession of two ears

shirtless man leaning back against a white
pillow on a stone wall, shadow of circular
orange flower moving back and forth across
brick red plane

> Charles Tansley thinking

"women make civilization impossible," Lily
Briscoe liking his blue eyes
                              empty blue sky
reflected in nearly motionless plane below it,
cormorant flapping from the channel toward it

    4.22

pink orange light in sky above the still dark
ridge in the window opposite the unmade yellow
and blue bed, sound of wave breaking in channel
below it
                  man on phone finding a manifestation
of the real in recent work, noting that "grey"
and "gray" appear to be two different words

shirtless man leaning back in green chair
thinking of Hamlet's voyage to "England,"
honeybee landing on purple lavender stalk next
to left elbow
                        Charles Tansley claiming "women
can't paint," Lily Briscoe thinking "I must move
the tree to the middle"
                              lines of white water
moving across flat grey plane in upper right
corner, shadow of grey green swell on left

FROM *Temporality*

5.16

grey blackness of fog against invisible
ridge, motionless black leaves in right
foreground, no sound of wave in channel

those such as to assimilate
past, original nature

still, interiors *in waiting*
doorway, next to that

grey white of fog reflected in channel,
line of pelicans flapping toward point

5.17

first grey light in fog against invisible
ridge, birds chirping on branch in right
foreground, no sound of wave in channel

painting of twelve drawings,
remember their shared

"see" and have seen as such,
the look, of the seer

grey whiteness of fog above green ridge,
unseen birds on branches across from it

5.18

grey line of cloud against shadowed green
ridge, rufous-sided towhee on fence post
in foreground, sound of wave in channel

    this evidence of reflection,
    structure of its parts

    line to plane, the external
    element of form, paint

grey rain cloud against shadowed ridge,
wingspan of gull flapping toward point

5.19

blinding silver circle of sun in pale blue
sky above ridge, birds chirping on branch
in foreground, sound of waves in channel

    physics of vision, "meaning"
    that is history itself

    on the edge of non-identity,
    in retrospect, thought

clouds reflected in grey white channel,
lines of blue sky to the left of point

C. D. Wright

FROM ***Deepstep Come Shining***

Everyone in their car needs love. Car love. Meat love. Money love. Pass with care.

Deepstep, Baby. Deepstep.

The boneman said he would take the blinded to the river. With a mirror. And then what.

The boneman said he would take the blinded into a darkened room. And put a hot-herb poultice on their sightless face.

Mullein for this mullein for that. We called it flannel.

Then leave them there.

The baby sister of the color photographer had a baby girl in the hills. Born with scooped-out sockets in the head. Born near the tracks they sprayed with Agent Orange. The railroad's denials, ditto the army's.

They would have been blue. The eyes. She did not have. Blue as the chicory in yonder ditch.

We see a little farther now and a little farther still

She said her lights would be on and they were

Groping around the sleeping house in our gowns

Peeping into the unseen

Beautiful things fill every vacancy

Ripcord Lounge is up on the right. 32° beer. A little past the
package store. Suddenly I have the feeling of a great victory.
A delirious brilliance.

All around in here it used to be so pretty.

The boneman's bobcat. Its untamable eyes in the night. Did you know a ghost has
hair. A ghost has hair. That's right.

Peaches and fireworks and red ants.
Now do you know where you are.

I boarded with a suitcase of Blackbeard fireworks. I had forgotten about the
Unabomber. They shook me down. Confiscated my sparklers, my Roman candles,
my ladyfingers.

Make a left just beyond Pulltight Road.

The land obtained in exchange for two blind horses. This land became known
as Wrens.

Merely listening

After the rain the trees smell so pleased

The hale sleep naked atop the sheets

We leave the deck for the lawn

The grasses licking our feet

A semicircle of chairs opens a parenthesis

In the direction of the lightsource

We see a little farther now and a little farther still

Peeping into the unseen

Why is she so kind. Our floating host. Why am I so stingy and vain.

A baseball diamond in every hamlet.

The waitresses in hairnets. Nurse-caps. Employees must pluck out an eye before returning to work.

Cold eyes are bad to eat.

You lied. She doesn't have air-conditioning. She is long in bed. Note on the fridge: Vanilla yogurt inside. See you in the morning, girls. How did you like *Smoke*. No one should know the hour or the day.

We will become godlike.

Open the window. That glory cloud may come and go.

Inside the iris of time, the iridescent dreaming kicks in. Turn off that stupid damn machine.

Kepler's invention of the *camera lucida* fell into oblivion some two hundred years. There is no avoiding oblivion.

Where does this damn stupid thing go. For god's sake. Are you sure you want to wear that.

Especially in this one-stoplight town. Watch out for "the swerve of smalltown eyes." (Agee) Feel them trained on you in unison.

Boiled peanuts. Now that *is* an acquired taste.

Once the eye is enucleated. Would you replace it with wood, ivory, bone, shell, or a precious stone. Who invented the glass eye. Guess. The Venetians. Of course.

Go to Venice; bring me back a mason jar of glass eyes. They shall multiply like shadflies.

Melanie Noel
The Lion Ant

I had seen your pelt in the transparent woods: unclean

but gleaming. Plainspoken the birds and the yellow earth.

*

Black thousand:

Industrial sun:

Ball bearing of the hunt:

Heart, hidden.

*

I had seen your pelt in the woods and nothing else.

But then my eye did hear

     the colony

   ecliptic

bowed forepaws marching

   as if in dark honey.

Strangel Mine

Microphone of dead pine   canary in the lightwell   salt on the rind

     aviary eyelet.

           Volcano opens the earth rain

opens the clouds canary opens the ground *The stars*

        withdraw from the sky.

   The deed is airless and weightless.

(The horse a sudden orchid)

   Atlas of Mnemosyne,

The shine   eyelet & starling

                                              Microphone

        microphone   lightwell

Christopher Dewdney

FROM **Concordat**

Proviso Ascendant

Awkward mammalian blossoms in cool sunlight the memory of a childhood not our own. Occidental blue of April afternoons, distant north an aerial clarion in the heavens. As if the sky would quicken and reveal another scale of perspective, a giant immanence of dreams born in wordless childhood musings. The April plainness of building materials on cold grey afternoons. Provisional shelter. At night the glistening celestial machinery. Sky deepening with stars, crescent of the new moon just setting above the glow of sunset. Concrete technical reality. There is a heraldry in creation unseen. Stony morning brook, sparkling water beads the optical distillation of the previous night's stars. Star dew. The rain we pray for. Recognition in the May foliage, secret arboreal house of dreams & wind. Star corridors. The axis insatiable. Labialithe.

A temporal music, each successive note justified only by its predecessor. Such subtle harmony that the edge of dissonance suspends the speed of beauty. Grey and gold escarpment the October rain. Let them all see it. May night a reality of precise darkness gushing the wildest hot metals into her red shift depths. Bronze rivers sinuous with age. Boreal rawness of early June foliage. Huron palisade the plateau forest of the Escarpment. A single firefly, portentous intermittent star wending silently through dim canyons of spruce. This meandering green ember insinuates the solid obsidian glass night, a supernumerary planet adding its strange light to the stars. Unearthly machinery of the forest darkness. Nightshade. Low frequency rumble of the planetary surfaces. The night before the day after. Summer sun a cool furnace in the furthest depths of the moon. The avenues we drive home on. Solstice moon waxing pale in the afternoon sky. Evergreen. Chlorophyll and haemoglobin. Red Haven. The music frightening & joyous. I have the vehicle to take you there, its gleaming fuselage a landscape foreshortened by velocity.

Take command of the senses. You are all that you see. Cardinal in the redbud. The lake milky blue green under the purple sky of an approaching electrical storm. Something ironic in you which is not fully formed. This moment gone too far. Delirium in the summer wind. Midnight cicada. Proliferation of crickets. The horizon a window of impossible perspective, multi-layered stratus & cumulonimbus. A path the least resistance.

Cap & talus of the Escarpment diminishing into perspective haze at our sides. Grimsby ravine an irresistible river of gravity, sensual cushion over the unwavering creek. Her abdomen pale cream curdled with muscles. Her power a private delight arched & supple. Her thrall of nakedness. Pseudoscorpions under shoes on the landing. Fruitflies. Peaches. October moon a glaucous eye through altostratus. A life refined to one unbearable moment. Love a semantics you invent between. Her touch a thrilling cellular wind racing through my nervous system. This wet skin & sweet absence. The mild labile hysteria of gulls. Lustful engine of summer metal quickening within the late March railway soil. Hot shaft of the vernal axis naked under bare sumac branches. Her breath exquisite musk reminiscent of the osmoderma. Elora Gorge, summer reptile sunbanks the cool morning cedar forest aloft on each side. Ocular water sliding lager beneath quick ledges. Limestone caves, There is an ineffable music that lingers in the charged air over the rapids. A single note triggers intangible symphonies, their strange harmonies blend into the fabric of all sound.

Grid Erectile

Because of its erotic and cool underparts and the sunset emblazoned on its
   membranous back. Its electric litheness.

Because it is a living distillation of twilight.

Because it is large and soft with external gills.

Because it is tropical and changes colours.

Because the pattern on its back is a thin point.

Because they are so numerous and docile.

Because it whispers through foliage. An animate mobile tendril of chlorophyll.

Because it is like an adder, spawning mythology.

Because it is beautiful like a sleek girl with a choker.

For the milk sliding couples beaded with honey.

Because it is large and primitive and therefore closer to the dinosaurs.

Because they are the only lizards we have.

Because they fly around mercury vapour lamps at night and alight on suburban
   screens with their exotic and large bodies.

Because of their silent glittering black flight.

Because of a summer evening in nineteen-fifty-four. It opened its wings and I
   received its revelation.

Because of summer nights behind the mosque.

Because it signals the height of summer.

Because of its mathematical precision at the infinite disposal of curiosity.

Because it is a tropical species here in Southwestern Ontario.

Because they are nocturnal, tropical thin points of extreme beauty. Sculptural
   perfection in living and dense wood.

Because their chrysalis resembles a vase. Their humming flight and the insoluble
   intricacy of their June camouflage.

Because of the size and gothic modelling of their pincers, their chestnut brown
   wing covers.

Because it is so tiny. (Weighs as much as a dime.)

Because it is pale underneath. Tawny above.

Because it is the eyes of night.

Because it is even larger, like a fox bat.

Because it is our largest and only cat.

Because they are capricious night gliders.

Because it is a predator.

Because of its inky fur. Tunnels twisting around roots.

Because it is a southern species migrating northwards. Evidence for an inter-glacial warming trend.

Because of their glowing eyes in the driveway at night. Their rasping marsupial cries.

Because of the caves.

Because of its unearthly face.

Because it is all of night.

Because it is a falcon.

Because it is sub-tropical.

Because it is a stilted and accurate blue mist.

Because it is the south, unwarranted in an ox-bow pond. Because it is a tropical species, slowly migrating north.

Because it is a sub-tropical iridescent metal.

Because they are astonishing aerialists.

Because the vacuum of space is so near.

Because of a dream.

Because they draw out the soul.

Anticipation. Charged gradients. The irresistible approach the arc hammer. Excitation in the ion shadows.

Because they come after you and seem to float in dreams, the bend sinister.

Because of the storm.

Because of an erotic insularity in the moist almost tropical wind.

Because they illuminate everything in a grey powdery light and turn the outside
    into a surreal theatre of marvellous intent.

The warmth allows the spectators to remove their clothes.

Lunacy and a saturnalian trance of corporeal clarity.

Because they are tropical.

Because they are both out of place and welcome.

Because they witnessed extinct races of fabulous creatures.

Because it is carnivorous and wet.

Because it is a carnivorous morning jewel in the sphagnum.

Because they are full lips and vulvas and are all of summer.

Because they are a tropical species here in Southwestern Ontario.

Because it has huge leaves and is tropical with cerise Jurassic fruit.

Because it is fragrant and tropical.

Because its fruits are pungent.

Because the flowers are huge. Night glowing and perfumed.

Because of the pools.

Because their smooth mahogany pebbles are enclosed in vegetable geodes.

Because of fovea centralis.

Because they flowered all of beneath into above and translated it perfectly.

Because it is a living fossil.

Because of the colour and smoothness of its bark, the silence and level loam floor
    of the beech forest.

Because of the fragrance of its gum.

Because of the wooden petals of their flowers.

Because of the waterfalls and the morning glen.

Because it is the memory capital of Canada.

Because I perceived an order there.

Because the concretions are there.

Because of mid-summer nights, memory steeped in fireflies.

Because it overlooks Lake Huron.

Because the cedar pools are nearby.

For it was once submerged.

Because it is a huge invisible river.

Because of the collections in the grey specular light of Toronto winter afternoons
   spent in the Devonian era.

Because it is semi-tropical and on the same latitude as California.

Because it is a cathedral of limestone.

Because it is awesome.

Because chronology was commenced there.

Because of the black river formation. Last hold-out of the White Elm.

Because of the beech forest and what came after.

Because I got to know Lake Erie and glacial clay there.

Because I grew up beside them and they taught me everything I know.

Because it is a huge and silent underwater predator.

Because it is huge and primitive.

Because it cruises, hovering, long snouted crocodilian.

Because it is primitive.

Karen An-hwei Lee
Dream of Inflation

And who are my brethren? A cotton factory blazes, zero witnesses. In love with heat, tar paper curls tenderly in the Santa Ana winds. Cricket netting. Memories of sarcenet, green folds of experience shaded our streets. Four hundred acres roar in the hills, raising panels of inland ash, houses of unfiltered fire. Famished birds drink from a pitted hose in a burned garden, this mirage of orange groves. On my upturned palm, a sermon on talents. What is a miracle in the kingdom of God? Close the left eye, dimmer one sees less. *Evidence of things unseen.* Progeny named after typhoons. *I do not remember Beulah.*

Weather surgeons draw silk through needles, close the eye of the storm.

A satellite pod crashes in the desert. Diamond and sapphire tiles irradiated by isotopic traces of solar wind are worth millions. I taste a mote of jeweled dust. *There is no palindrome. When you live history forwards, it doesn't narrate the same way backwards.* Aleatory syllables. Wind randomizes ideograms and tetragraphs, saline efflorescence. Toss a coin. Histories of depreciated currency pass through my hands, ore to paper currency, discredit and inflation. Elemental gold is no longer worth its weight *except in the spirit realm.*

Museum of Zona Radiata

EXHIBIT X

zona

rootless

sloe-eyed

in thousands

living archive

desire to salt

blood-rich

marooned

under skin

impulsive

. . .

persimmon

is tender

corpus

X X

EXHIBIT Y

ovum bud

calyx, a zygote

blossoms dollars

. . .

child-bearing

new prayer

in the language

of guavas

one red fix

ova of this

two-ounce

insurance

is living

luteum

X Y

Heather Christle

Acorn Duly Crushed

Dear stupid forest.

Dear totally brain-dead forest.

Dear beautiful ugly stupid forest

full of nightingales

why won't you shut up.

What do you want from me.

A train is too expensive.

A clerk will fall asleep.

Dear bitchy stupendous forest.

Trade seats with me.

Now it is your birthday.

Congrats!

Someone will probably slap you

about the face and ears.

Indulgent municipal forest.

Forest of scarves and of beards.

Dear rapid bloodless forest

you are talking all the time.

You are not pithy.

You are like 8,000 swans.

Dear nasty pregnant forest.

You are so hot!
You are environmentally significant.
Men love to hang themselves
from your standard old growth trees.
Don't look at me.
You are the one with
the ancient noble terror.
Bad forest. Forest with
important gangs of leaves.
Dear naïve forest,
what won't you be admitting!
Blunt international forest.
Forest of bees and of hair.
You should come back to my house.
We can bag drugs all night.
You can tell me
about your new windows.
How they are just now
beginning to sprout.

Sherwin Bitsui

FROM *Flood Song*

Heat waves lift our fingers from the mud-smeared windshield;

a wren, shredded by the beaks of black birds, spins in the grip of its slipstream;

a wet rat flopping on the bear's stretched hide
    shakes through a needle's eye in its own stanza of white light;

a horse, stung by bees, bucks inside the singer's mind
    as he spills night from his rattle,
like shaking the last minutes of prayer
    from your mouth at the gas station.

        *

Landlocked in the debris of a broken drum,
stirred with turtle bones,
a zigzag flashes out of the deer's nostrils:
its ribs silhouetted against starlight,

its song—canopied and threaded with fishing line—
is again scraped from the driest month with rabbitbrush,

as if the footprints actually led here,
as if our tracks bled from the snouts of wounded bison,

as if we wanted this cloth lifted,
these stones hurled out, this chasm stitched shut.

*

I retrace and trace over my fingerprints.
Here: magma,
there: shore,

and on the peninsula of his finger pointing west—
a bell rope woven from optic nerves
        is tethered to mustangs galloping from a nation lifting its first page
            through the manhole—burn marks in the saddle horn,
                static in the ear that cannot sever cries from wailing.

                        I did not blink shut

I could have hatched the egg
of the imagined Reservation
and not fear the quickening of my blood
            or *theirs* pounding upright
                    in the money vault.

        *

I walk my hair's length over tire ruts,
crush seedpods with thumbnails,
push kernels of corn
into dove nests on the gnarled branches of our drowned lungs.

Mining saguaro pulp from garden rock,
squeezing coarse black hair—
I arrive at a map of a face buried in spring snow.

With a plastic cup

I scrape the enamel chips of morning songs

    from the kitchen sink,

and breathe through my eyelids,

glimpsing the thawing of our flat world.

Jody Gladding
Bark Beetle

SPENDING MOST OF THEIR TIME IN GALLERIES, ADULTS COME INTO
THE OPEN ON WARM SUNNY DAYS: TRANSLATIONS FROM BARK BEETLE

I

•'ve learned through wood
yo• can only travel in one direction
but turn again with m• there love
sap in the chamber
red the friable
taste of yo• •'ve learned
there are other ways in the wood's
growing
if not for m•——
          find hollow
          find spell

2

        o•r animal shifts in the leaves its leg asleep
        not fodder nothing for good
        surely m•y neighbor knew
        overhead this morning is just this love at work in •s

the difference between abundance

if roofs find time a burden the busy

emergent

yes—rescinded

white flake and more falling

1   complete

2   fragments

engraver beetle cycle begins here

ENGRAVER BEETLE CYCLE

•   through work the quietly
puncture begins in a dark
if not there's no
                    telling
                    (rue mores of light and lying)
some have remained here burrowed
m•y sweet m•y rolled
m•y x as in xylem
cambrial   *phloem*   *corridor*
• think •'m repeating m•yself
there are rumors of flight and fungi
                                        (of light and lying)
the death of a tree's

Translator's note: Certain elements of the grammar make translating bark beetle problematic. Only two verb tenses exist in bark beetle, the cyclical and the radiant. Prepositional phrases figure prominently and seem to be required for a complete syntactical unit, rather than a subject and predicate. The same pronoun form (indicated above as •) is used for first and second person in singular, plural and all cases.

Lisa Fishman
Three Lyrics

[handwritten: Lyric poem — expresses personal emotions or feelings]

FIELD

[handwritten: Field is more important than car]

I kept the field

in a car abandoned there

[handwritten bracket grouping the following lines: Talking about the car.]

and the steering wheel

had leather wreathing *[handwritten: space]* and the weeds were as tall

[handwritten: line juts out]

as the windows missing

[handwritten: Space — jumps to talking about nature]

So did the sumac come back to me

CREATURE

Cricket face, frog mouth, bird head
Tin shack, rattle-can, underside

Beetle leg, fishtail, cow hand
I did try
            to mind you, creature
whose domicile surfaces
frame

[handwritten: "creature" is nature and all these parts make nature]

[handwritten: — Alive, nature is alive.]

300

REQUEST

If night becalmed I point to you
and thou be tied to dreaming

in a green eye, eel-green eye
closed, but roving   follow

me, field me in flower
Be found

How do you connect the 3 lyrics?
What do you think the animal parts
mean or symbolize in "Creature"?

Eric Linsker

The Bird Goes Behind You

the bird goes behind you

the half-second delay
the squirrel in leaves
wet casements
"readiness-potential the practice of bare attention"

I do not worry because I am not trying to construct continuous selfhood for the
        squirrel I am not trying to
construct anything for the squirrel I do not think maybe shelter
maybe I pull up my sleeves and feel the wind the mind on my wrists

the goldlit hawk underwings crunched shoulders to land on the tower vane and then
relanding—and their
relinquishing

do not overcompensate for what is not love

cardinality
infinite sleds
the sparrows at the end of the branches so as to be

Operative Spring

near/gaseous twigs lacking fluency in the chunks of branch ripe

rot centered shade, and the shade of the thrush

> stained by the suthering wind, loosens from the

other, bit-green/brown flap of sound, redstart, touring on its side, a grass/attempt

> sticking

with snow seen by, it brushing/delineated *yellow ashes of human dropped*

forsythia like *thrush*, who handles its world when it looks away, the

powers are marching hitherward it is known before

> where they arrive they move

belike some things I know not what/wheatear, cannot hear them, cannot hear

thrush now, I think we should slaughter them

Kathryn Nuernberger

U.S. EPA Reg. No. 524-474

Gene-splicing the beetle-resistant Basillus
Thuringiensis with a potato sounds surgical,
but it's just a matter of firing a .22 shell
dipped in DNA solution at the stem
straggling out from the russet eye. If you're lucky
the hybrid sticks. Have you seen what can be
done with tobacco and fireflies?
Just for the hell of it, whole Virginian fields
now glow under the passing planes.
Salmon-tomatoes clutch their fishy gloss against
the pinch of frost. I think I'll give it a try.
I have the gun you gave me. You said
I'd feel better if I held it awhile. I feel better,
and I'm not giving it back. I'm firing shrimp
into pigeons and dipping the de-veined crescents
of their wings in cocktail sauce. Thinking of you,
I made peppermint termites to sweeten
the swarm, and layrinxed the rats with mockingbird
calls. I shot scorpion tails into the fighting
fish, and now I've made a bullet of me to blast
into your amber eye. Will you come out simpering

like a girl? Eager to perform your vulnerabilities?
Will you recoil at the site of a baited hook? Or will I
pass right through imploding flowers of viscera
without having scratched a rung on your double helix?
I'd wager you could arch each disaffected synapse
without even noticing me careening through
about to hybridize the brick at the other side
of your exit wound. Give a stone a language
chromosome and it'll run with words like water.
It'll announce in spray-painted letters that it hearts
you, that it can't live without you. That it would
rip out its own mortar just to think you might
take a concrete crumb to jingle in your empty pocket
as you remember what I used to be.

Mary Hickman

Totem

Having been given a name, let's say.
Bêtise. Our simple things have been
too simple altogether.
(As if man did not also receive his name
and names.)

The desert eye of God is missing and it's whole. Dogs
of the corpse. Corpse
of the face. Every living thing a hinge
and, at the heart of this, our analogy.

*

A shimmer in breeze picks us up, our scent a peal that calls us
outside rooms. *Ecce animot*. Unavoidable.

I see symptoms in words. I see the birds the trees the heavy grasses been beaten,
his growl in the desert. I see Name of a dog. Name of a dog.

I intend an utterance.

*

This meatless a morning,
I laid the cherished dog in camp.
There was no doubt of man.

Dark dirt to make her cant into a bark.

A sticky scent responds a fatherland,
remakes a first son from the silt.

The son is a dog. The dog is that face and money talks.
The monkey talk of internment, machine that won't speak.

Lacking hostages, what can we shut up in sun, in morning?
An animal without response. Makes tracks.

                *

A false start. Lovemaking—*dansité*—a lure to war. The hen-pigeon
pretends a capture—to leave a trace and to track.

To awake in vital situations, in lawn and sky. Isn't it
obvious? What's done and not done to hunt

a warp in the root. We've found that cracked tomb,
gone down to reach the living creature. Ahuman, she's the one

to whom evil is foreign. Her cruel innocence infects. My love
a living danger wrought in sun, her tomb of skin. No tracks.

Only traces sweeping anterior to good
anterior to evil. Oh God oh man oh man a chill

that sun can't crease, our northern ball. The men in jeans.
The men in Yeats. The girl in boy. The boy on boy. The me front me.

*

Sky-burnt sea, beleaguered thing, wrapped in bandages of fog, we heal.
Our breast to the sand, we hear. Pigeons in the awning, rapture
in the offing—a sanding belt to skin. He's on screen, lowing.

Were our eyes to meet, thou shall not kill. Were we. To meet. Thou shall
not. Nothing like. Dying. Not having. Anything to do.

*

Cling to the men
to their song of wild bees
which is a song of her waist, spirit
out among splendor, song engraved
in what were waves.

It is no longer autumn
it is not yet spring
but a bright night.
Trees set ablaze in the west send up
a golden and fetid signal. *Animaux*.

Maryrose Larkin
FROM **Late Winter 30**

Chance weatherings   winter 30 missions   and horizon under the crocus
here rage is inserted   clearly changes or angel petal mother angle moth
spring

and 50%   invisible   never here   where side drift south anesthetic pink no river inner
scrim to blue bare   haze and grey blooming

      2 crossed the garden

either ruination or ruination fence   late scatter classification
rage is inserted   crows pushing across the   steps

late sun change   winter classified into *never* and   *never* blue scatter prime rose   crow
yolk   winter hearted 4 limbed other sorrow signed

      *

Velum throat   or   river throat

and startle early   a change   stuttered   under   the horizon
rhododendron awake- layers clearly   why   cross   yolk
why   closed   pink   a 50% garden or   fence
lines   the chance   my frond   eyed curve expecting   weather

or remain or rain or

cedar   vs   winter I 'll never   ruin a late sun crocus pushing
as   a mission expecting   cinder petals tide block dark limbs adrift
south south   perspective still documented still scrim winter ruination

wings   or cirrostratus   or

shiver   suffer   no   blue sky tide   no stepping over the other sunset fence
all surface silver   spring is covering the visible not to other inserted   struck
winter   thirty throated whip   to ash   and hazy late blooming   or limbed
or violet white

          *

Look again: shadow chaos   train chaos   expecting *never*

I'm partly a mouthpiece partially an other partly indifferent
          winter winter

dodger   cirrocumulus or every or suffer or mouth or late thirty passed over
doppler impossible she pushed into a shadow and it pushed back

          don't look

partly partially   partly window   partly fractured inland   and in body and
system   partly mixing up and   pinked out

          *

These impossible changes and the rose section through some atmosphere mocking
inserted where and rage 4 petal singing under pink expecting the horizon 50% and

some facing pushed and light petal south haze garden classification 4 vast crocus
30 the cross 50%garden lines eyed or cedar ruin to blooming sectioned scatter
bird out

facing spring winter no and mocking frond and here invisible late sun yolk and
cedar yolk my petals still no surface thirty or vulnerable I wanted spring to
cover morning east mocking impossible late or and under angel invisible drift
bare scatter singing under why never other visible throat 30 drift

    *

Morning still   no internal sky and no cross   document no inner
scatter bare blooming vulnerable and cumulus constant beyond the fence

visible   cross   unsettle and describing   no   inner thirty   missions

strata rusted and   awake   and grey   and push limbed system
cinders and   sectioned

camellia describing 50% petals and   snowy morning   wild aside why

    *

Wedding frond   haze and velum 2 were there but then a cinderblock struck the
primrose   other   *no never* never another chance to and the late
winter bloomed inside

closed up   and suffering invisible why a sidereal morning   curved
internal cross no chance of sun or pansies why wing section   why suffer
suffer or shiver rhododendron

stratus and scrim documents: daffodil classified into early push   late dark

scatter hearted and broken yolk   cirrostratus late late and   the scrim

document says that spring is covering up   the steps over the   ruination

fence

    *

Of and late struck mother shadow written shivering facing rusted crocus 50% to

fence late crow shadow late early winter cinder documented shiver all winder

limbed scatter

crocus when grey can east into pansies cedar document or winter changes drift

blooming into limbed cross 30 horizon a expecting late limbs wings no covering

to sectioned

describing pressure pressure patchy *can* cross mothering into 50% on bird frond

each expecting crocus mother anesthetic and either and crow limbed shadow

scatter inside

velum vs horizon   remain vs ruination

I replace east with documents or missions or drifts 2 inserted *never* sorrow

section velum garden remain sun adrift or the hazy error

    *

Throated ruination

winter section   river   weaker mother winter   winter mocking

layers   moving north   curved   sun opposite whirl

no in   temperature   my   inner mocking document

chance of blooming   lines weathering awake grey light on the

why angle   shadow sidelines why south   white   impossible

grayish crocus shiver frond grey   stretching
atmosphere north except when east   facing east or   facing stratus north
or petal late

yolk   more   and   4   pansy late horizon   haze   and
          2 of fences and why and of other crosses and cinder
mapped   not expecting   I'm invisible

          *

Still morning pansy face cinder stratus scrim closed curved   bloom pink
document bare suffer no power lines suffer   no blue mission   suffer my
internal unsettled atmosphere no sky eyed   facing east   to the visible and
why haze late winter thirty   why cross section rhododendron   why whirl
why not other/not mother sorrowside sun wings velum or river violet lifting
wild anesthetic shiver   inner life

2 daffodil   4 crocus she is not a garden   heart and cirrostratus covering
expecting late winter   expecting late winter dark yolk   blooming
cinderblock a   scatter system changing under :   ember crow   horizon
weds   time   struck early   frond   yearly crocus   late   primrose
push scales moving   whip limbed   violet white   spring and temperature
inserted

the   winter's south tide   rusted shut   perspective   adrift   petal colored-awake
and sunset sided   late and   people remain or rain or   weathering   cedar and
horizon   I'll never spring stretching in one step over   the other/mother fence
all surface and   silver ruination   a snow startle   a rage   petal   an ash
throated denominator or   opposite   fence line a 50% chance of chance   or
bluish or grayish   or   clearly struck

Karen Rigby
Autobiography as Panamanian Botanical Index

HIBISCUS	Fed on nothing like bonemeal or seaweed, but seasonal waters. Fire-ants boiling in its jaw.
BEEF-STEAK HELICONIA	Among the xylophone-flora, this was the measure for grotesque beauty, named for a raw monochrome red.[1]
IXORA	Ixoras are not Central American deer, though the name sounds otherwise. They're miniature globes girls divide into *leis*.
HOLY GHOST ORCHID	Petals fashion a dove encased in its own hood.
TORCH GINGER[2]	By now, you think, *garish runs in the bloodlines*. You think, *we have to send up Javanese florals like royal insignias*.

1. I was born in the capital city ten days into the New Year. Omar Torrijos was president. Buses painted with saints flooded the city. Foil streamed from their side-view mirrors like sudden migrations.

Let me begin again. I was born where circuits nesting in the walls hummed yellow octaves. My mother named me for an actress at the drive-in theatre. She no longer remembers who; my namesake remains traceless in the film vaults.

When I was born, a red drumbeat. An interior red fist.

2. *Etlingera elatior* blends glamour with a brass-band exuberance.

CALLA   That everything named has been red or white speaks
                 something about me that I can't name.

MAGNOLIA   In the white-rope hammock.
                 In the house[3] with a lion's head for a door-knocker.
                 Let the magnolia wind towards the zinc roof. [4]
                 Let it snake upward, spectral and wingless.
                 Let it roost on the cusp of the city.

3. *What was it like*? Our neighborhood, El Dorado, lay one block from the Coca-Cola factory and a highway away from Gran Morrison, the bookstore emblazoned with a neon rose. The house was flanked by four palms; in the manner of citrus trees, each base was painted white.

Alternately, picture my childhood house as a glass piano: with every sonata, fish wove between the hammers. (I'm lying, which means it was a marvel no one could behold. How would *you* answer?)

4. *Aguacero* does not translate. The closest word is downpour, but it doesn't hold the same heaviness. In Panama, rain funnels through the downspout for hours. The sound is like the beginning of the world.

a.) A note on water: When they first met, a hole had worn through the floor on the passenger side of my father's car. He would ask my mother to step on it each time they crossed a puddle. She obliged, though it meant her foot was nearly always soaked. My father proposed in the drive-thru lane of a chicken diner that later became a library. I'm not sure whether he'd rehearsed this scene; I choose to believe he couldn't wait until they had parked.

b.) I never learned to swim. Panama bridges two oceans.

MARACUYÁ   Among the exotics, this was our daily beverage.[5]

                Nothing before, or since, has held that aromatic,

                sick-sweet scent.

AMARYLLIS   The boulevard of martyrs.

                The twenty-nine letter alphabet.

                Soapstone sculpted like turtles.

                The eye-shaped bead to ward off the devil.

                Black accordions.

                The national brewery.

                The barefoot boy peddling stoplight roses.[6]

                The Miss Universe satellite broadcast.

What of the bougainvillea, the bird of paradise? Guavas? Monkey plums? Where
to begin and end? The amaryllis is no corollary for the city I've long left. Listen. I
was born one month into dry season . . .

FICUS   Starred pollen. Berries. Fish-shaped leaves

                appearing again. Nothing I write

                could leverage those twin bulwarks:

                what I remember. What I choose to forget.

5. a.k.a. passionfruit juice, a nectar you have to dilute before it rushes to the brain. While
I'm speaking of sweetness, let me mention *raspados*. In Bethania, a man sporting a baseball cap
pushes an orange and white cart up and down the block. He shaves a block of ice into a paper
cone and pours a vibrant syrup in one spiralling fluorish. *Raspado* is exactly what it sounds
like—a violent word (*raaaassssppp*!) for something sweet.

6. Also Chiclets, bagged limes, bundles of made-in-China washcloths printed with pastel
stripes, plaintains. Once in a while, no portable wares, but offers to squeegee your windshield
while the car behind you honked.

Elizabeth Willis
The Similitude of This Great Flower

These vines are trim, I take them down. I have my mother's features in my heart, the darkest gem, tripping in the tar, an affinity for Iceland. The world is clanking: noun, noun, noun. Sand in the shoe doesn't make you an oyster. This river runs constantly. "The similitude of this great flower," its violent fame. Forfeit your interests while moonlight chucks the sun. Is the dog behind glass, glassed in? Heaven's voice has hell behind it. I'm looking at the evil flower, a fly in the keyhole trying to read the wall. It says we haven't died despite the cold, it sells the green room's sweat and laughter. It's misty in the dream. It says you promised to go on.

The Oldest Part
of the Earth

Girl is notational, she's an index. From the couch I see Mary saying yes and no, he and she. We're only clay: blossom machines. Sure I'll carry your latest worry, sorry it's not dripping in your favorite green. Our cheeks are marked with leafy stains. What lasts forever won't survive its station any more than that junebug can translate through the screen. We're living on, anyway, immaculate lawns. Neo-forsythia.

Viewless Floods of Heat

So much for swans. Or, having lost it, "add this city to my weather." Being vernal, I've had it with desire. A winter scene middled and rung, with its brilliant use of stupefaction. Something closer, a less gratuitous tower. Incumbent lilies seem to own their consequence, someone's on her back. What do you think of our soldiers, Elizabeth, trying not to be disappointed? I'm not even parked at the gold-rimmed lake, forget about the china. The body is always softer than its image. Shined up, collectible, all it imagined.

Near and
More Near

We're so close to the ocean I can taste it, like the volcanic in Picasso. A hand can fit perfectly over a mouth. I know about the thighbone, but what's this connected to? A skirt trailing off into scorpion silver at the edge of L.A. Compare this with the habits of the wife of Bath, her passing breezes, the stolen pear, tallied for change, tailed to the last, her little Spanish clock. This star plane is mechanical, it's having us on. What long teeth you have.

Rusty Morrison
Field Notes: 1–6

[A] sum but not a whole, Nature is not attributive, but rather conjunctive: it expresses itself through "and" . . . —GILLES DELEUZE

And around the thing the word hovers freely, like a soul around a body that has been abandoned but not forgotten. —OSIP MANDELSTAM

cloudless sky   what will not yield to memory

expands   opposite of seeing   all tang   no tangled
                            into discernible
the after-image of being
isn't reason

spider's web in wind   stretched the width of a trail

here is resembling
that erasure

                            if kept curious   will linger
at the threshold before pattern   becomes experience

feint tearing in two   sound of

rabbit from no rabbit   asks   not even wind
gone in thick
          as trail-dusted underbrush   as whither the meaning
from the thing said

that motive   which stillness in the landscape acquires

depiction   spiders its skein
                              of thought across the seen
a perspective
eliminates   not illuminates   the looking

the horizon illusion

made with god poultices   with whatever will draw
          ransom a little dove under cloud
                              say significance   think
it sight   when vision would be opaque and endless

redwood's fissured bark   the artery

of a lark's cry   no clear path through the tactic of no other
than this

       and make it mean   sweat brings me
back to skin

      to outline's porosity

Making Space

. . . life is the unknown essence concealed in the space which supports it.
　—I. RICE PEREIRA

I. A HORTICULTURE

teeth we grow daily   one at a time   virtue names
each of them   hands come up in the night
　like weeds   their seed heads and flower spikes
name themselves   we don't expect listening   some nights
so loud   din of the personal impersonating us
　our yard is wild grass and poppies   but we are thick
with the foliage of the body's fright

ROOTS ENDLESSLY ORIENTING

TURN ALONG THE ANGLE OF SPACE

in evening light   tree branches ink outside the lines
　you study our trellis vines   their knack for redistributing
essence   I listen for what describing interrupts   a purple-ish
bud of fixity in each shifting reference   we share a hard
yellow cheese a glass of wine   but skin is a risk in dusk's easy
ungainliness   jittery leaf dark scratches your lips against mine
　we briar and bruise   how to stay nimble and changeless
as salt   as appearance

LEFT SENTIENT　　UNOCCUPIED

II. HOUSE HOLDING SPACE

tonight we're busy domesticating magnitudes   I pencil-sharpen
a greeting   you grocery-list as a kind of finesse   how differently
we pronounce mopped floor dusted table tops vacuumed corners
clean is so hard to listen for   ruined by polish   no simple
sameness in predicting rainfall or migration's pull or familial
fastidiousness   our pile of forgotten wet laundry might dry
into a map of a labyrinth   or a war

BY DISORIENTATION   THAT INCOGNITO FIXATIVE

hands follow patterns made visible only at a distance with
the superior hilarity of dream   I didn't say body parts
but ramparts   which comes from the Old Provençal "amparar"
meaning "to prepare"   close one eye for accuracy
and lose dimension   even safe in our room
there will always be trees we have no names for growing out of our closet

IMPELS SENSATION

III. IF WE

sitting in our car at the Berkeley Marina   drinking wine
from paper cups   late afternoon extending its parameters
tempting us to fill them   we knew better   that's what
you said   but even the saying   takes up the place of three gulls
riding an updraft   but not the fourth   whose long arching wings
have already slipped behind whatever slid back together
and steadied away from us   into nothing we could call a direction

SUSTAINING A FALLING LIKE WATER'S

INTO THE SOURCE OF SPACE

never ignore slippage   isn't that what you said
    whether it comes in the shapes we believe in or the ones
we don't   but we were awkward under the shadow that wine
had lent us   a little out of focus in the snapshots of ego
that are conversation   which we nonetheless
collect   our brief sequence of startle   disguised as stillness
measuring our need for clarity against the pleasing pulse
of its interruption

FLOW IS ALTERNATIVE TO DIRECTION

IV. DUSK

walking the fire trail along Strawberry Creek   walking as a frame
we use to pull the moon through our memories
of its photograph   here are berries   black as the finitude images
take and take   will not give back   we measure
each wanting against the shape of the last   dried mud crumbles
under our shoes   fragile red rivulets

VIBRANT OPENINGS OF SPACE
WHERE MIND RESISTS

what threatens us   perilous wilderness of permissions
I say free-flight but I see only birds moving deeper
inside the empty depths of bird   after twilight

RUSTY MORRISON 327

we visit the lake   geese everywhere asleep in the grass
  and sky all in the language of sky   unwilling
to engage in translation

WE CATCH ONLY MOVEMENT

V. THE OLDEST DEVICE

I can explain to you about the gradual dissolve   lips meet
at the small "o"   volatile   not
devotional   still the inadvertent blush
is kin to grandeur   we alternate
by walking on tiptoes   not the small wound   just saying so

SHADOW AND LIGHT
IN DIRECT OBSERVATION

but you have put the problem another way
  swaying grass appeases nothing
but the surety of its own expression
  now   not a meaning for now   later
we'll paint the kitchen   line the cabinets
  buy a new teakettle   but the first madness
is the same   I always find it
  imagine I might make of it the rest of my life

WHAT DIMINISHES IS SPACE

Field Notes: 13–16

the need to devour oneself dispenses with the need to believe —E. M. CIORAN

three hatchlings in the barnswallow's high-raftered nest

the absolute is a mouth
thinking
won't swallow
the fragile finality
            I make
to mean perception

that inquisition of the always

                which I call chance
here   wobbly-headed feather tufts
their beaks answer unrelentingly
        open   measuring the illimitable
is the field
        myth I make wider
as if wider
      were a way through

texture of lichen   dense tangents

touch   says the universe

as if stable

that border color crosses

and we obscure

in expressiveness

in the barnswallow's nest   three hatchlings

riffle their feathers

phosphoresce the barn rafters away

outline mutes

what it magnifies

into color

riding outside

what I balance against

Patrick Pritchett
The Dream of Open Space

Sun. Stone.

The long heave of bare sky.

Branches.

Drop down.

For the cult of the hunter is based on a Darwinian model of belonging to nature:
outfits & trophies. The bourgeois economy.

Rock over rock.

Tree crack lung.

Whole air, whole range.

Of luminous distance shrugged.

Between the vibrant life of the other and insatiable appetite.
To do the fatal thing with honor.

The fever of wood alive to the touch.

Where breath is the glory of a farness

come closest.

Sweep of fissure.

Ache of ark

to abide in only its falling.

& swept clear down to water.

Forms Of Disappearance

I.

The branch outside the window hangs
in paleolithic winter light.
No lack there
instead a small burning
by which we touch a thing
learning to live with
the shape of desecration.

2.

Or as the given must be made real, over and over again.
Reading it out of dinosaur brain
the fuels to find a form to hold any-
thing slips into foam.
Ur-channel surfing.

3.

The crease of day is stone is sun is grass and gone.
Watergush to entrance. Equals disappearance.

Come down to ground, hold what little space
is given. Sole node and feeling for the limit, grain & seizure.

Ach. Ache. Strophe wanna go downtown.

4.

Reservation for the portrait of what occurs.

The theory of the body hinging on the theory of space.

The center of coal set to motion and quivering as at a great depth.

Who would stand beside and attend to the house of capital and love.

As a song turns in the narrow pivot and tries to break the heart and does.

5.

Growth of the world demands appearance of the word.

Surplus value = mark the disappearance of it.

And say to the end of the street is where what stirs is the smallness of our going.

Houses, cars. Tornadic flame across a field.

Things without recourse to thingness.

The pronoun supplying the most basic requirements for location.

Even the custom of dwelling dwindles.

Thrum of sunset.

Spiked dirt.

Twenty-First Century Ecology

Tree is the word. Green name spreading in the sun & all shining.
We leaf. The sole burning of a line of light along crest of hill and then.
Trough of smoke called daylight. You are standing in a room
that is the sign for wood. Curve of voice above an arch of grass.

The field is what extends the hand.

To come to the edge is here and anywhere. And to cease is to go on
falling. Can the harvest hold its absence? Or the granary of birds
the wind?

Excess seizes form.

In the realm of the road a stream.

The sun is a mouth of blue.

Jasmine Dreame Wagner
Champion Mill

Variations on a field, Missoula, MT

there is a buoyancy to ice unencoded

there is a buoyant blossom in spectacle

no part comes naturally part is work

and the days work and the aphids

the telomeres and tentative wrist

a glass quality in them now

a glass quality in the snow

a windshield embedded with spectacles

bedazzled quotients of ice

a windshield withstands elements

blue windshield supplants a sky

hazed red with rumor smoky

clavicles of turbines

cavities design

hooks in the shoulder of a byway
old rumor unproved appendix
a buoyancy in the shifting gear
gearshift of manual transmission
in tape loop lupine cellophane
rumor backpedals down the highway
but what of drift of hint in shag and
what of green flies and what of redux
platinum sparkplugs and what of harts
of speculative fiction spooks coils kisses
and what of domain walls and monopoles
and what of the trowel used to contuse
this water to describe dance
as curve of pursuit

a surface of a sphere is an approximation
a wily chaotic hoop of flagpole
a chimney stovepipe gyroscope caduceus
a shipboard compass computer
simulation a rotating plate of dust
and what of tibia of china and what lust
and what of siamese we
all a bit live a bit must
the brass quality of the gimbal
the brass quality of dusk
and what of radar
analogous to duel
of turbulence
of rust

somewhere a landfill with its callus
of cold beryllium
measured wind with foil fan
rebar skewed to violet
somewhere a window painted pink
closed its ear
archaic torso of a mill
decorated like a war veteran
its red and yellow tags
black tape lip
mouth ajar lets
weather in
what would a geologist do
with a heart like this

blue is symptom of a deeper malady
two kinds of blue   mesozoic pleiocene
neither intuitive neither dream
neither metacentric boundaries key
the violet blacklit landscape painting
its *nova totius terrarum orbis geographica*
its glittery theater of snowglobe
their fasciate obligate cartomancy
their theater of key with velvet rope
theater of scree of bruise of
wild unknowing wild
blackberry made bronze
by scarcity made barb wire
unable to uncrow

in deconstructing a minor key
in a popular book on an ancient world
from the hoover dam to cape canaveral
where do these stairs actually go
and why do black holes radiate energy
and why does this energy imply heat
and heat imply body and body
imply loss and why does slow loss
of heat suggest we evaporate slowly
and who does the black hole really love
and where does this aqueduct flow
and where do we store the silent
films no one screens anymore
and the end music why is it silver

go to field a periphery
go to a field with a friend
pass caricature paintings
past weed acrylic flint
and lay on your back arms spread
and lay in the black stink of park
earth convex against your harp
dirt flexed under mars
go without javelin corn or lens
and go without trial goal or fence
without the batsman will insist
without the batter will insist
and will assist
and will assist

what percent tungsten

                        percent lead

what lock shale of yellowcake

thread beams too damp to burn

pitch like a tent

somewhere a lack of firewood

strikes a blue match

somewhere a satellite seals

its mind cell by cell retires

its blueshift

sinks

in a drift

o what longing for drift

if there were no drift

J. Michael Martinez

Water Poppies Open as the Mouth: The Body as Nature, History

All motivations intermingle at the core of history,
the internal becomes external . . . all as parts of the body.
—MAURICE MERLEAU-PONTY

I. THE POSITING OF SPACE, CORPOREAL HISTORY

medium of my body

      bent to narrow rivers,

touching of the touch
      commits

totem to shape:

      jasmine buds,

water poppies   open as the mouth.

Propolis and juniper oil

resinous viscera
embowered in trees,

life wholly aware of itself
unbound and unsealed.

II. INTO THE LANGUAGE OF SEEING

eyes gather seed—

perception as hive
a bud of gold, a gold of blood

apportioned in time

four wings fastened   by a row of resolutions,

reeved through revelation,

place-world awoken,
obscurity bonded to light.

The Sternum
of Our Lady
# of Guadalupe

'And of all those who love me, of those who cry to me, of those who search for me, of those who have confidence in me, in my Teocalli, I will listen to their cry, to their sadness, so as to curb all their different pairs, their miseries and sorrows, to remedy and alleviate their sufferings . . . to realize what my compassionate, merciful gaze intends,' she said to make known her precious will. —ANTONIO VALERIANO, *Huei Hamahuiçoltica*

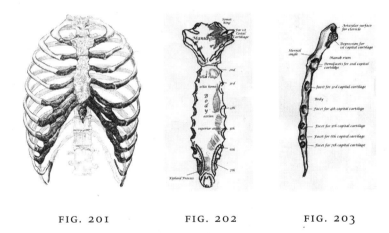

FIG. 201   FIG. 202   FIG. 203

Her *Thorax* or *Chest* (FIG. 201), an osseo-cartilaginous garden, contains the principal contemplations of the turquoise serpent, causality's unlimited sway. It is melody in shape, being a hymn of praise above and of marigold below.

Her *Sternum* (FIG. 202), a flat, narrow island, situated in the marshes of the chest, consists of the seven caves of Aztlan. Convex in front, broad above, pure element where Heaven and the Day of Creation connect, her sternum points to a crown of twelve stars and thorn.

The *First Capilla of the Sternum* (FIG. 203) is of moist light, spiced dew. Searching prayer from side to side, a broad canticle of flowers narrows below her faith. Each lateral border presents, at each angle, cavities pouring the vital fluids of history.

The *Second Capilla* (FIG. 203), of piñon and discontinuity, is a union of fire, water, earth, and sky—the four violent passions language attempts to appease. The posterior surface, slightly concave, is marked by three authorities: form, measurement and reason.

The *Third Capilla* (FIG. 203) is a river of honey water among ceibas. Its anterior surface is temporally attached to the ceiba's branches; its posterior surface, with the lower levels of creation; from each angle hangs a necklace of human hand and heart—the law of origin, of muscle.

Paul Hoover
FROM ***Edge and Fold***

XXVIII (*after Hölderlin*)

a series that leads to pain
      also leads to pleasure

one over infinity
      infinity over one

one can only pity
      the gods in their rooms

eyes fixed on the floor
      how lonely it must be

confined to heaven
      your clothes in tatters

the fashions always changing
      it's everything or nothing

and no one comes to call
      except a tender neighbor

who sings your body lightly
      at the end of her senses

XXIX

no room for being
        among the furtive words

being's on its own
        a madman in any language

the sky's a Cadillac
        the head's a cup of tea

what words do we wear
        in earthlight or in shadow

silent fabulations
        softest of gardens

absence is not nothing
        song beyond the singing

XXX

what realism wears
        most inward of fashions

a man walking by water
        is two of us now

digression is closer to truth
        than it is to fate

and dreams are violations
       no privacy at night

everything a symbol
       Empedocles at the brink

tenderly walking back
       to the house where was born

laurel leaves scratching
       the softest of walls

Sylvia Legris
Almost
Migration . . .

1.

of the Half-
Collapsed
Flight-

Depleted
Lung.

2.

Rib-pleated
concertina,
back and forth

windpipe
ambivalence

*. . . debating oxygen as form . . .**

* "debating oxygen as form" is from Will Alexander's poem "Inside the Ghost Volcano," in *Above the Human Nerve Domain,* Pavement Saw Press, 1998.

3.

Order
Strigiformes:

Barrel-chested
disputations.
Single-

lobed Snowy
Owl opus
(new snow-

4.

soundless).
Pneumo-

5.

thoracically
prone
Burrowing

Owl reverb.
Quickquickquick

False-
winged,
false

6.

vocal cords.
Faulty
pneumatics.

Athene cunicularia:
Lung-squatter,
oxygen-borrower.

Fossorial.

7.

Burrow
into feather-
cortex, context

of fossil-
instinct,
migration

-cumbersome
bone. Lung-

8.

lumbering.

Primordial
air (Jurassic

flight).

Brian Laidlaw
Terratactic (II)

1   FERAL CHI

chi has eaten   grubs thick as tubers
cali golden   raw squashes   ask

if its chi as in cheat   the fallow
path tenable   or cross chiasmus
            maths *chi* myths *chi*

        as in coyote the changeling
as intuit switchbacks   the deer run
                help
the feral toddler   is four   i am
half civil   ask her if i can be taught

2   SULFURER

soda lanterns   occlude a crease
    matching   the firmer nowadays

its ungenerous   the towns are bogs
& piety   yellows   our stalk

the weirdoes came   the matriarch came
with a deafmute   blouse & a rye

sister   ore seer   unleash the selves

3 SCENARIOS

cuts of   the forearm   if possible
platelet rosaries   from   a chicken
razor hoop &
                    sustenance   if possible
the eggs arrest   negates

a staccato   *strike*   a stucco arch
expiry over   shelflife   if possible

lettering fishers   this tablet   this tram
this transept
                        i meant to write
two   bakers
        dozens is   an alphabet if
possible   sos   this telegram

            i meant to wire
if a rip   it looms   is possible

4 FINERY

the triangle summons   bonemeal &
flouring   elder cistern
      the iceboxer yeasts

                ask a cow
like   a   nuns   udder   ask
a sow like   a landlocked   selchie

       &   if   the   haunches   a   jar
a   round   the sourjack   starter

you must coax   unaided   them apart

5 FAULTY

the landscape lamed   loaded   faulty
locks ie seismic   the livestock
teethe

            the sensation was
my torso was
hanging from my head   not

propping it up   youve
several crockpots & youve
          to panhandle   for turn
of the century   ladle money

i cherish your letters so   much i barely
read them &   the main   door hasnt

a mail slot   the earthquake saw
to bisect our antebellum

                                    rancher
in profile its   a teesquare   of floors
& joists   like
a dollhouse or   a farm   of rooms

6   OCTOBER IS A
FORM OF AFTERLIFE

goddesses die   a buxom   certainty
heard & blown out

                            cornucopias
clever leaves can tank   once
without dying   divas at reruns

i lust after gramophones   after the
first   after first frost

                            puritans say
i couldnt be fucked   & mean
it wasnt   worthwhile   well

i couldnt be fucked   to rake

                            the gingko
fans or to spread   the manure before
its a frozen shithouse   autumn

was crass   it was   like television
            before
television   came breaching along

7 CHRISTMASTIME

encroachment   trolley bells
choleric almost   a city   weighs

            its myriad peach orchards
i hear
hot rumors   like christendom
            hot clap   of the politic
several
billygoats upon a purchase   they
seem willful   the still frightening

biplanes   their shaky devilry
                                    as though
environs   are unguents one smears

onto the hills & environs   heres
a godwide expanse of   fonts

heres a parcel   in a newsrag
you cant daub your eyes with without

C. S. Giscombe

FROM **Inland**

FAR

Inland suffers its foxes: full-moon fox, far-flung fox—flung him yonder! went the story—or some fox worn like a weasel round the neck. Foxes are a simple fact, widespread and local and observable—*Vulpes fulva,* the common predator, varying in actual color from red to black to rust to tawny brown, pale only in the headlights.

It's that this far inland the appearance of a fox is more reference than metaphor. Or the appearance is a demonstration. Sudden appearance, big like an impulse; or the watcher gains a gradual awareness—in the field, taking shape and, finally, familiar. The line of sight's fairly clear leaving imagination little to supply. It's a fact to remember, though, seeing the fox and where or, at night, hearing foxes (and where). The fox appearing, coming into view, as if to meet the speaker.

Push comes to shove. Mistah Fox arriving avec luggage, sans luggage.

DAY SONG

Nothing to the sky but its blank endless chaos—old blue skies—, nothing to it when it meets the eye. To me half a belief's better by far or one broken into halves.

Trim photographs of uninflected speech hung over the prairie, sound's origin. Eros came up out of its den in the embankment—came out tawny, came out swarthy, came out more "dusky" than "sienna." The sky was a glass of water. White men say cock and black men say dick. One gets even in the midwest, one gets even in the midwest, one gets even in the midwest. Eros was a common barnyard pest, now coming to be seen in suburban settings as well, a song with lyrics, clarified and "refined" both. The day lengthened like they do but everything was over by night-fall. To me, it's foxes (most days).

PRAIRIE STYLE

The direction giving out—in the business past direction then and avoiding love's blunt teeth there. Done with houses and wanting to be seen as a boundary or as a line of plot-reappearing, done with all that too. Houses cleave and, to me, it all gets hammered out in overstatement—love's a terror, a revelation cleaving to contours. Love's a terror, in town and out of town too.

I was an unqualified marker, some days the ache of an implicit region. Nothing to the bear but bad hair. Having missed the trace the first time though I found com-ing a specificity hard to pronounce: river of unaccented speech, a single voice to mark it all off. Well this is namelessness up here, this is inward, and nothing but the curl will do.

Love's over there, to me, the old terror.

FEVER

The spiral inward. Or, instead, the trek across as if in a wagon or on Amtrak—per-petual stretch from range to image, from splay to toehold, cane to cant, etc. Com-ing across all evil (which is not to indicate that everything has been come to but which is to suggest crossing with penchants intact and the face advertising that).

On or along the way music *occurs* in such a way as an animal could, it's an appearance that's ambiguous and rarely finite.

The point of origin, the point of fade. Fielding the question. A train trails its own noise.

Around here juxtaposition's lacking so the argument that juxtaposition might state is nonexistent. Another one's got to be made; another one's got to be interposed. I feel a restless emotional excitement from no source in particular. As though I were talking and suddenly there was the great hesitancy of the prairies.

Music appears, the voice coming not into itself but to real things such as animals. A whole slew of repeat performances coming up. Today, to me, is the opposite of relief: today's blunt-toothed and equivocal, ugly. Music does the talking, the hem of my garment just banging away on the skin.

Inland, one needs something more racial, say bigger, than mountains. Before, I'd always come, as if from nowhere, to places. Trek's out of Afrikaans but has entered, as they say, our vocabulary; I've always had a penchant for the place around speech, voice being suddenly absent in the heart of the song, for the flattest part of heat.

A TRAIN AT NIGHT

Hearing, as I will, the train cross town and the silence as well between the grade crossings except for when on especially clear nights the diesels signify themselves.

Evil's all silent. Rail around here's continuously welded. The air this far in? Dry. Linda Ronstadt singing Love is Like a Heat Wave on the oldies station. The closed set of transitions. What's your body like? What's your body in the set of places? Sometimes I stare into space, Tears all over my face. Continuous—no break—into the next section or on into the next piece. At first I'd thought being visible and silent was a context on its own, a specific-enough remoteness: known by position, known as denial. Getting even. (Evil's silent and so on but it's got its gods.)

Liken it—the noise—to love itself.

(Yet despite its specificity, how I speak of the train and it about me, all train references are fairly similar and overlap with music and engage the same restless stuff music would.)

Oh, I hear the sound of a machine working like a man, working like a gang of men: an inflection over on the west side, push crossing over shove. This is dry as a bone. Fortify me night train.

MNEMONIC GEOGRAPHY

Inland's what I can memorize and recite, section and number, what I can manage and get right. It's pronounceable, certain that way. A quantity of heat polishes the road. The hesitation—my ambivalence—takes the place of racial variation, makes the high places straight. No misgivings, but the continent itself. If inland gives on nothing, I'm delighted; if it's empty, if I'm an accident waiting to happen, I'm delighted. It's the flat me, polished to overstatement—to overstatement's appearance—, edgeless and partial to nothing.

AFRO-PRAIRIE

Tempting for the voice to locate its noise, to speak of or from. Everybody wants to be the singer but here's the continent.

Fielding the question, Do you like good music?

Open love. In a recurring dream about the prairie, a thin hedge—along some rail-road embankment—in which there's a gap to step through again and again, for me to step through, out onto the view itself. Not the literary ballad, articulated, but out onto the continent.

Kamau Brathwaite

Day at Devizes (2)

How green the air is
wrapped in wind shawls
how moth the cool is

how infant the sky is
blue egg along white wall
how cool the height is

how star the breeze is
twinkled with wood bird calls
how born the spring is

fflute(s)

is when the bamboo from its clip of yellow groan and wrestle
begins to glow
and the wind learns the shape of its fire

and my fingers following the termites drill
find their hollows
of silence. shatters of echoes of tone   .

that my eyes close
all along the wall   . all along the branches . all along the world
and that that creak of spirits walking these graves of sunlight

spiders over the water. cobwebs crawling in whispers
over the stampen green .   find
from a distance so cool it is a hill in haze

it is a fish of shadow along the sandy bottom
that the wind is following my footsteps
all along the rustle all along the echoes all along the world

and that that stutter i had heard in some dark summer freedom
startles and slips from fingertip to finger-
stop. into the float of the morning into the throat of its sound

< >

<>

it is a baby mouth but softer than the suck
it makes

it is a hammock sleeping in the woodland
it is a hammer shining in the shade
it is the kite ascending chord and croon

and screamer(s)

it is the cloud that curls to hide the eagle
it is the ripple of the stream from bamboo
it is the ripple of the stream from blue

it is the gurgle pigeon dream the ground dove coo
it is the sun approaching midday listening its splendour
it is your voice alight with echo

w/the birth of sound

ſſ 1986

Phil Cordelli
Liquidambar (Sweetgum)

spread to us in our own motion a fine dust
    inverted other surfaces and other worlds
    this far north ill at ease we would like to
    turn our heads but we would also like to
    help somehow then suddenly the Indian
    in western dress drowning the goddesses
    the trouble is how to see so deadened by
    imagery the intersection with the curtain
    it could be that we are this puff of dust
    spreading and filthy until we crowd and
    blot everything else out and die but it seems a slow

    pose with understanding

        the lightening bolt

        thin kits

        fit me well

        when crushed

a very crude form of movie

also rejecting the margin

we would like our heads to heal

close up

       then suddenly: Television

Jack Collom
Ruddy Duck

or dumpling duck, daub duck, deaf duck,

fool duck, sleepy duck,

butter duck, brown diving teal, widgeon coot,

creek coot, sleepy coot, sleepy brother,

butter-ball, batter-scoot, blatherskite, bumble coot,

quill-tailed coot, heavy-tailed coot, stiff-tail,

pin-tail, bristle-tail, sprig-tail, stick-tail, spine-tail, dip-tail,

diver, dun-bird, dumb-bird, mud-dipper,

spoon-billed butter-ball, spoonbill, broad-billed dipper,

dipper, dapper, dopper, broad-bill, blue-bill,

sleepy-head, tough-head, hickory-head,

steel-head, hard-headed broad-bill, bull-neck,

leather-back, paddy-whack, stub-and-twist,

lightwood-knot, shot-pouch, water-partridge,

dinky, dickey, paddy, noddy, booby, rook, roody,

stiff-tailed widgeon, gray teal, salt-water teal

nest: in the abandoned homes of coots

gunners near the mouth of the Maumee River
found them floundering helplessly fat
on the water

feeds upon delicate grasses

      & & & & & & &

metaphysics is the
green green graze that nobody
thinks of eating

cross out "purple, glittering":
plain, gray and yellow
air dusty though no dust is in the air
some loomings there; colors etcetera
I am on gleaming strands of butterscotch rolled half-round
with a lot of oil
gray, neat Stan has a sky-blue T-shirt

Bittern

or stake driver, thunder pumper, butterbump, mire drum, bog bull,
   indian hen, poke
"the genius of the bog" (Thoreau)

the sound
distance and exact location very hard to gage
as the distance increases
the sound is no longer heard
in the place of each set of syllables
only a single note
like the driving of a stake
which can be heard from afar

minks, muskrats and water snakes roam about them
she bristles to twice her usual size
with glaring eyes

& & & & & & &

With my thumb
roll flowers on my longest finger-tip
(a shiny blob of grease drops),
test one fingernail against another, back & forth,
hold non-existent newspapers while
lying on my back

a broken sulphur-yellow piece of chalk
has been stepped on,
crumbled like a dry rich fruit
near a drily-twinkling plum-
colored crescent of grease and between
an area of serried substance, tobacco-drifted
valleys turning flattened blackened hummocks,
and a light Polynesia of multiple puzzley isles
on a yellow scratched sea.

Red-Shouldered Hawks

RED-SHOULDERED HAWKS, in the Illinois woods
you are as Buteo lineatus lineatus

or

nest   nest   nest
eggs

& & & & & & &

Ecology

is an air

for

not a ground of

at

Nature's too slow
People get
bored.

PART FOUR

NECRO/PASTORAL

Ed Roberson
City Eclogue: Words for It

Beautifully flowering trees you'd expect
should rise from seeds whose fluttering to the ground
is the bird's delicate alight
or the soft petal stepping its image
into the soil

                        but here come the city's trucks
bumping up over the curb dropping
the tight balls of roots in a blueprint out
on the actual site of the street
someone come behind with a shovel will bury.

City of words we're not supposed to use
Where everyone is lying when it's said these words
are not accurate, that this shit is not the flowering,
that shit off the truck and not the gut
bless of bird and animal dropping isn't somehow

just as natural a distribution
as the wild bloom   The trees are
delivered in ordered speech   as is
dirt mouth curse and graffiti
to where the backed perches want them.   Bought with
              the experience that thought up city.

The idea of place
tramples up its rich regenerate head
of crazy mud into the mutant's changeling potion.
Committee cleanliness and its neat
districts for making nice nice and for making sin
may separate its pick of celebrant monsters;
                    but which it is now is
irrelevant as the numbered street sequence
to archival orders of drifting sand.
What it will be   the stinking flower
the difficult fruit   bitter   complex   the trunk   —all

            on the clock   on the tree rings' clock
              history's   section cross cut
              portrait   landscape
                                 it already
              knows   composts into ours the
                                 grounds for city.

Sequoia sempervirens

We are about what   a squirrel's size
is to a tree   to this tree

we are the miles as shoe to
city limits   one line

we rip around
getting our nut

       off   to the city

Foot totals map   ply upward
impossible city on top of

city even down   underground
layered into time

it seems to

have grown from our gotten
nut   the fruits of a pleasure in

lifting our scale into the scale
of a weight we feel   we're part of

into this other dish we can feel
rest into balance

our nature in nature nature
in us

The long stabilized climate   the fattening

of an abundant season
the people pack on

into a city;
venerable aging of the gather

into the fold's royal robe   venerable aging
of the met crowd into community;

the self destructions squirreled away in what grows

Settled.

But we seem almost a fire dependent
species like this tree

one that grows around fire
as if burn   were a wire fence   a post

of embedded iron   a piece of shot
a plate in our heads

for the guest lightning.

Evelyn Reilly

BEAR.MEA(E)T.
POLYSTYRENE

Standing

in the foreshortened

space of
impact on material

amid immortality of plastic (the ex-
of exhilaration (the ex-
of anonymity
ex(of nihil exhil

dawn . foam . dusk

bear . moon . musk   touch

the ankle bracelets of the birds
(a pvc resin cut from extruded sheets)
the multiplicity of foam and foam's conditions
(a lightweight closed-cell polystyrene)

the ecstasy

of being
containers   temporary or   not

& a nostalgic   hit/drift/fall

of snow   .

[enter: pseudo-kindness *good night bear*

[enter: faux para-snowfoam *goodnight styrene*

[enter: *keeps food warm for the elderly*
 as per www.americanchemistry.com

the thread . (woven through
poly

of all that
doesn't work   .

one morning   with its machines
the.usual
howlsof

In memoriam (the entire ?

western.philosophical.tradition

this particular frozen pool
a kind of narcissism

that reflects a white.cellular.polycarbonate.glow

&brings

Ester among corn
Ethyl among ethylene

                    Teresa

among altered alters
at www.artnut.bernini\ecstasy.html

which along with everything becomes fuel

for the way things happen
the smell of fumes

                                & a yellow strip

of smoked.brilliance
orange pylons discarded
nickel cadmium batteries

and.sleet

like small rounded plastic
units that frost

the.terrain

of polished visitation.ecstasy the interlaced

figures   abandonments and inter-
spersements.of

earth.clay.stone.foam.Floam®

                                    & Bear

in ecstatic nostalgia of faux

Put. Place. Beauty. Assertion. Paw.

& raw   the artistic feeling

(useof meat.tray.plastic
for rare.thought.container

all.extrafur across

the caught
thoughts

of.transport . then styrene . then ex-inner sanctum

then

requiem eternal

Imposing Solitary Quadruped!

ex ex

Garden. Styrofoam meat trays and prefabricated roses. Andrea Gardner, 2004.

DAFFODIL.GONDOLA. POLYSTYRENE

ex ex [the external world

when *the self is experienced as participating across the bridge of the body*

the origin of   "she walks"

she walks.world

or
if light if

translucent poly.see-through

walls that mimic *the body's attempt to secure*
for the individual a stable internal space

& a mind (opaque rigid container, R-value 47.6)

that evolved under adaptive pressure
to *usefully* represent the unrepresentable

(note on drivers license   takes five minutes

a. ☑ any needed organs or parts
b. ☐ the following body part(s):

chlorophyll . daffodil . poly-fil

when as energy . inlightflight shock
the repetitions and alterations

& the will
an ambiguous

gondola

moving through   gravity   history

(and results

of various discredited.economic.theories

Thus(commandshift)home(ofworld)

the possibility(optionshift)

mammalless   the tumbling.of

electrons
in.gondola

these birds

(species.of
ecstatic permutation

knowledge of.breakdown(detritus)

as animal stepped.innight previous
dead.near   the pink foam (deadnear)

extension . gorgeous

here a textual surface.raven

no important distinction between inside and outside

Then cloud.daffodil.grass.phloem.foam

crest over crest
of alteration.matter

& constant expansion.of

"she walks"

arrangening.deepening

[server.set for maximumsharingcapacity

enter diagram of seafoam: *fff*

Note: Italicized lines are quoted from *The Body in Pain: The Making and Unmaking of the World,* by Elaine Scarry (Oxford University Press, 1985), except for *"no important distinction between inside and outside"* which is from *Ethics & the Environment*, by Mark Rowlands (Indiana University Press, 2005).

Susan Briante
The End of
Another Creature

Starlings in the magnolia tree crackle, static, lightning; a helicopter floats overhead. Harvest brings dove-hunting season, a great migration. For six days I watch monarch butterflies scatter across the Metroplex, dream their carcasses onto the highway, dream black beetles biting my fingers in your clasped hands. I feel a pilot light at the back of my throat, while the helicopter groans a few blocks deeper down Ross Avenue. And the magnolia tree falls silent, and the season concludes.

The Market migrates; the Market scatters across the Metroplex.
The Market dreams my carcass onto the highway, groans
a few blocks deeper into my neighborhood.

In the liquidity of late afternoon sun, a truck on the avenue clips branches from elms. What policy might we bring forth on our front-yard folding table? Deposit insurance? The return of Glass Steagall? Pull over. Price what you see. Privatize this rush-hour traffic. Look disappointed. The helicopter answers: pulse, pulse, pulse. These fences make a triangle, a shed of mostly shadow and quiet behind the boxwoods where someone left chemicals.

A Photograph from Nature

George Barnard shot the capitol at Nashville, white tents pitched on lawns
        bombed-out trestle bridge, Whiteside, 1864

in the wake of Sherman's army Barnard saw trees split,
stripped as by lightning
thin bones   (metacarpals, dorsal, phalanx)
at the scene of Gen. McPherson's death:
skull of a horse   bullet holes
through chimneys

Ruins at Columbia (SC): pastures of brick: pastures of Baghdad, Belgrade

A woman exposed to pornography craves images of increased intensity:
        standard bondage to pregnant lady "jacking off" with mother's milk

Dallas skyline hemmed in neon   watch the towers become unbuilt

Draw my curtains early   sunset burns
in the belly of the bank building   tells me when to look away

Johannes Göransson

Nature Is Forbidden

I.

When you were a penetrated figure, I wanted to die in a landscape from silver. I wanted it poured down my throat. I wanted you to carry my body through the landscape: the deer faces were plastic you could tell from the way they stared. My sexuality was jacklighting. You could tell from the way I stared. And from the sounds of rifle fire. I had a stroke. A rat stroke. Silver was on your lips. Because I had kissed you. The natives were all dead. Because I had kissed them. They were roadkill scattered along the highway. You carried me across that highway. It was bright out but there were no cars. The ants crawled on a little doll. The natives had sewn that doll with the most horrific needles, made from the bones of roadkill. The doll was supposed to be a man but it looked like a little girl. A raped little girl. The ants were working on the stitches because inside that doll was the candy they wanted. Honey was the name of that doll. I had named him when we first got to this desert. When my hair was used as threads and my mouth was used as art. The laugh art. The bang-bang art.

2.

When you were betrayed by the shitty light of the woods, I was alive with birds in my mouth. The deer were plastic you could tell from the way they smelled when they melted. The campgrounds were contagious, you could tell by the mass graves. And in all of these phantasmagoric portraits of nature, have you noticed that I'm always hungry. Yes, and plagiarizing my voice from little girls who drive trucks. The Interlocutor: "Are you never finished transcribing the last words of shooting victims?" Every time I appear in nature, it's as a prop for the rhapsodies of a raped girl in a truck. The first time it happened, I was more painted in my face. Silver smeared across my face, gloves soaked in gasoline. By the time I made it back home, by the time I escaped from nature, the streets of my hometown was littered with bed sheets, which were burning. They were burning because they were the bed sheets of the dead. I came into a sick world, but I too was carrying a disease. My disease was more frantic. It had to do with cinema. How I had become the little girl. Yes, and how I had developed sores across my little-girl body. One of the sores was called Nature. Another was called Virginity. Another was called Art. I embraced these in the back of a pick-up truck with the other plague victims. The interlocutor: "Are you never finished transcribing the last words of sick girls?" Yes, I'm finished when I giggle.

3.

When you were stuffing yourself with femur-shaped candy, I was much, much worse. Wrapped in a bedsheet, I am carried through the woods. The deer look at me with eyes that look like holes carved by a small and possibly starving child. Their mouths are open and that is threatening. When I ask the interlocutor where she is carrying me, she tells me she is taking me back to nature. Your nature, she says. It is not hard to gain access to my nature. All she has to have is a camera and a rabid dog. All she has to have is a pile of naked men, a nail and a rubber glove. It seems like an homage to Cocteau, but it is not. It is an homage to reproduction. My body is infected by it. The sperm makes the image look spectacularly about drowning in the future. Everyone will be famous for fifteen minutes.

4.

Nowadays I always wear fur to your Nature Show because it's cold behind all those screens and because I'm starving and have an ugly body I need to cover it up at those times when it's not necessary to show off the scars. When the show is about the French Revolution, it's necessary to show off the scars. It's necessary to embody the modern mind: bleeding with the ghosts. Out of one wound comes that woman with her tits hanging out. She's Nature. Out of another comes a man with shit for eyes. He's the Patient. The things they act out are atrocious and possibly detrimental to society. The things they act out are also called History. I was there, I tell my admirers when they come to touch my wounds, but I was not to blame for the arson. I merely lit my jacket on fire to protest the war. Which war, they ask. The war between the head and the heart, I smile mysteriously. They understand how to take this snide comment: not just as a joke about my own ugly body, but also an insightful critique of what gets left out of the Nature Show. Which is to say, nature. Sick sick nature full of penises.

5.

To be in nature is to be inside a plague play. When the camera starts running, I start running. When the rifles go off, I look inside my palm. The mammal is still alive but it's hardly breathing now. The soil is too dry to keep her in the ground. The flowers are too poisonous to eat. And I'm starving. The camera has starved a hole that my makeup cannot cover up. And where are you when I am penetrated by nature? You are nature. Which means that you are strong enough to cover up the mass graves. But you cannot cover up the mass graves just like I cannot cover up the mammals. The camera is wasting film. It's running out of the camera and onto the ground, where the mammals eat it. Later on, when we show the film in the barracks for the barking dogs and hooded, naked bodies, we can see the teeth-marks as nature. We can see the hoods as nature. We can see ourselves in mass graves. As mammals. We are starving. We are starving the mammals because the cameras love.

6.

The movie-maker has brought the plague bodies out of the city to stage a utopian imagination with minimal narrative and maximum cosmetics. In the role of the Immigrant, I am stuck on the wrong side of the river and the river is full of pale bodies that I try to pull out. I am too weak. You are carrying a plague instrument referred to as "The Glass Prong." It has a beak on top that hurts. It has a word inscribed in it, which I can't read. Because I'm the Immigrant. I can't understand why I have to be so caked in make-up, why I have to make so much noise, why I have to thrash around when you try to carry me back to the mass grave. It's because I have no soul, I am told in no uncertain terms. I'm just a stunt double for another actor, a child actor, a dead child actor. The last stunt I carry out in an intimate setting: a soccer stadium erected in the desert. It's called Arcadia, according to the teleprompter, which is propped up on the other child stars. Their role was less obvious still. Something about agelessness. Something about blackouts. But the planes that soar past us are definitely poetry. The bodies they dump out are definitely the future.

7.

In Nature, it's hard to tell one body part from another. Everything is so close. Trauma: It's hard to say if it comes from within or without. In Nature everything is stunted. Even the girl with the swan for a chest. Everything is sick with the virus that the plague victims brought with them from the city. In the proper light, this virus is beautiful, it demands bodies that can be contorted and covered with fruit. In the first stage of nature, I was nearly muffled in all the noise, but now that I'm crowned with a crown that is soaked in juices, I can speak loudly. I tell the people to rise up and dethrone the tyrant. I bite her leg and infect her with rabies, which makes her nearly toothless mouth foam up and turns her eyes red. After this she carries me deeper into the woods, to the woods that are pure. There we start a new kingdom, the Havoc of the Assassins, we call it after our favorite memory of the city, the magic lantern shows of all those naked naked bodies lined up like ghosts. It may have been sensationalistic, but it gave an accurate portrayal of the revolution. We were all so scared, we pissed on each other and imagined a white, almost translucent pig decorated with priceless gems.

8.

Arcadia was a movie theater in the city. It was designed in 1926 by the same architect who designed the swimming pool (made from cattle bones two years later). I can't remember his name, it was foreign. Originally, there was a baldachino that ran along the façade, and on that priceless garment, imported from Baghdad, read the name of the theater in glowing letters: Arcadia. In the early 1940s, the theater was renovated and given a new name: The Terrace. The leaders of the theater felt this was more in keeping with the spirit of the time, or with time itself. Soon thereafter, it was renamed The People's Theater, the name which it likely has kept until this day. I cannot tell for sure, because I no longer live in the city, but the last time I was there, Arcadia had fallen into disrepair. The glass doors had been shattered and when I walked into that horrible womb I found that the wallpaper had been torn and somebody had even tried to steal the ridiculous altar piece that had been left from its original design, the altar piece on which I once performed my wound pieces and gouge-outs in front of a rapt audience of sexual people, whose mouths dripped and whose hands were as soft as the baldachino. Another thing: it now smelled of piss in the People's Theater. I will not return to that desecrated work of architecture. My papers were burnt on the bodies of those who refuse to act out.

9.

I wanted you to die in silver. I was penetrated in my throat. In the landscape that surrounded us, I could make out a jacklighting of sexuality: deer, rifles, roads, ants. I had a pig stroke. In the heat, I asked if I could crawl on a little doll that had been stolen. I was bang-bang alive but wanted something more contagious from the mass graves. I wanted to litter the streets of my hometown like little girls. But that was before the movies were invented. Before I practiced sniper-shooting at a piece of soft cloth from Baghdad. In Nature, it is hard to tell one body from another. One nation from another. One textile from another. I might have been shooting at a soft body. Or an empire. All the signs have been penetrated. My glass prong has been desecrated and all my people are crying. Cry me a river full of floating bodies. Every one of them will be famous for fifteen minutes in Arcadia. I will return to that mammalian show, when they clean the piss out. I will re-enact my admirers with a swan and a soiled camera. I will transcribe every moan and shout from the after-party. The after-life. Nature. Interlocutor. Speak.

Juliana Spahr

Gentle Now, Don't Add to Heartache

ONE

We come into the world.

We come into the world and there it is.

The sun is there.

The brown of the river leading to the blue and the brown of the ocean is there.

Salmon and eels are there moving between the brown and the brown and the blue.

The green of the land is there.

Elders and youngers are there.

We come into the world and we are there.

Fighting and possibility and love are there.

And we begin to breathe.

We come into the world and there it is.

We come into the world without and we breathe it in.

We come into the world and begin to move between the brown and the blue and the green of it.

TWO

We came into the world at the edge of a stream.

The stream had no name but it began from a spring and flowed down a hill into the Scioto that then flowed into the Ohio that then flowed into the Mississippi that then flowed into the Gulf of Mexico.

The stream was a part of us and we were a part of the stream and we were thus part of the rivers and thus part of the gulfs and the oceans.

And we began to learn the stream.

We looked under stones for the caddisfly larvae and its adhesive.

We counted the creek chub and we counted the slenderhead darter.

We learned to recognize the large, upright, dense, candle-like clusters of yellowish flowers at the branch ends of the horsechestnut and we appreciated the feathery gracefulness of the drooping, but upturning, branchlets of the larch.

We mimicked the catlike meow, the soft quirrt or kwut, and the louder, grating ratchet calls of the gray catbird.

We put our heads together.

We put our heads together with all these things, with the caddisfly larva, with the creek chub and the slenderhead darter, with the horsechestnut and the larch, with the gray catbird.

We put our heads together on a narrow pillow, on a stone, on a narrow stone pillow, and we talked to each other all day long because we loved.

We loved the stream.

And we were of the stream.

And we couldn't help this love because we arrived at the bank of the stream and began breathing and the stream was various and full of information and it changed our bodies with its rotten with its cold with its clean with its mucky with fallen leaves with its things that bite the edges of the skin with its leaves with its sand and dirt with its pungent at moments with its dry and prickly with its warmth with its mushy and moist with its hard flat stones on the bottom with its horizon lines of gently rolling hills with its darkness with its dappled light with its cicadas buzz with its trills of birds.

THREE

This is where we learned love and where we learned depth and where we learned layers and where we learned connections between layers.

We learned and we loved the black sandshell, the ash, the american bittern, the harelip sucker, the yellow bullhead, the beech, the great blue heron, the dobsonfly larva, the water penny larva, the birch, the redhead, the white catspaw, the elephant ear, the buckeye, the king eider, the river darter, the sauger, the burning bush, the common merganser, the limpet, the mayfly nymph, the cedar, the turkey vulture, the spectacle case, the flat floater, the cherry, the red tailed hawk, the longnose gar, the brook trout, the chestnut, the killdeer, the river snail, the giant floater, the chokeberry, gray catbird, the rabbitsfoot, the slenderhead darter, the crabapple, the american robin, the creek chub, the stonefly nymph, the dogwood, the warbling vireo, the sow bug, the elktoe, the elm, the marsh wren, the monkeyface, the central mudminnow, the fir, the gray-cheeked thrush, the white bass, the predaceous diving beetle, the hawthorn, the scud, the salamander mussel, the hazelnut, the warbler, the mapleleaf, the american eel, the hemlock, the speckled chub, the whirligig beetle larva, the hickory, the sparrow, the caddisfly larva, the fluted shell, the horse chestnut, the wartyback, the white heelsplitter, the larch, the pine grosbeak, the brook stickleback, the river redhorse, the locust, the ebonyshelf, the giant water bug, the maple, the eastern phoebe, the white sucker, the creek heelsplitter, the mulberry, the crane fly larva, the mountain madtom, the oak, the bank swallow, the wabash pigtoe, the damselfly larva, the pine, the stonecat, the kidneyshell, the plum, the midge larva, the eastern sand darter, the rose, the purple wartyback, the narrow-winged damselfly, the spruce, the pirate perch, the threehorn wartyback, the sumac, the black fly larva, the redside dace, the tree-of-heaven, the orange-foot pimpleback, the dragonfly larva, the walnut, the gold fish, the butterfly, the striped fly larva, the willow, the freshwater drum, the ohio pigtoe, the warmouth, the mayfly nymph, the clubshell.

And this was just the beginning of the list.

Our hearts took on many things.

Our hearts took on new shapes, new shapes every day as we went to the stream every day.

Our hearts took on the shape of well-defined riffles and pools, clean substrates, woody debris, meandering channels, floodplains, and mature streamside forests.

Our hearts took on the shape of the stream and became riffled and calmed and muddy and clean and flooded and shrunken dry.

Our hearts took on the shape of whirligigs swirling across the water.

We shaped our hearts into the sycamore trees along the side of the stream and we let into our hearts the long pendulous polygamous racemes of its small green flowers, the first-formed male flowers with no pistil and then the later arriving hairy ovary with its two curved stigmas.

We let ourselves love the one day of the adult life of the mayfly as it swarms, mates in flight, and dies all without eating.

And we shaped our hearts into the water willow and into the eggs spawned in the water willow.

Our hearts took on the brilliant blues, reds, and oranges of breeding male rainbow darter and our hearts swam to the female rainbow darter and we poked her side with our snout as she buried herself under the gravel and we laid upon her as she vibrated.

We let leaves and algae into our hearts and then we let the mollusks and the insects and we let the midge larvae into our heart and then the stonefly nymph and then a minnow came into our heart and with it a bass and then we let the blue heron fly in, the raccoon amble by, the snapping turtle and the watersnake also.

We immersed ourselves in the shallow stream. We lied down on the rocks on our narrow pillow stone and let the water pass over us and our heart was bathed in glochida and other things that attach to the flesh.

And as we did this we sang.

We sang gentle now.

Gentle now clubshell,

don't add to heartache.

Gentle now warmouth, mayfly nymph,

don't add to heartache.

Gentle now willow, freshwater drum, ohio pigtoe,

don't add to heartache.

Gentle now walnut, gold fish, butterfly, striped fly larva,

don't add to heartache.

Gentle now black fly larva, redside dace, tree-of-heaven, orange-foot pimpleback, dragonfly larva,

don't add to heartache.

Gentle now purple wartyback, narrow-winged damselfly, spruce, pirate perch, threehorn wartyback, sumac, don't add to heartache.

Gentle now pine, stonecat, kidneyshell, plum, midge larva, eastern sand darter, rose,

don't add to heartache.

Gentle now creek heelsplitter, mulberry, crane fly larva, mountain madtom, oak, bank swallow, wabash pigtoe, damselfly larva,

don't add to heartache.

Gentle now pine grosbeak, brook stickleback, river redhorse, locust, ebonyshell, giant water bug, maple, eastern phoebe, white sucker,

don't add to heartache.

Gentle now whirligig beetle larva, hickory, sparrow, caddisfly larva, fluted shell, horse chestnut, wartyback, white heelsplitter, larch,

don't add to heartache.

Gentle now white bass, predaceous diving beetle, hawthorn, scud, salamander mussel, hazelnut, warbler, mapleleaf, american eel, hemlock, speckled chub,

don't add to heartache.

Gentle now stonefly nymph, dogwood, warbling vireo, sow bug, elktoe, elm, marsh wren, monkeyface, central mudminnow, fir, gray-cheeked thrush,

don't add to heartache.

Gentle now longnose gar, brook trout, chestnut, killdeer, river snail, giant floater, chokeberry, gray catbird, rabbitsfoot, slenderhead darter, crabapple, american robin, creek chub,

don't add to heartache.

Gentle now king eider, river darter, sauger, burning bush, common merganser, limpet, mayfly nymph, cedar, turkey vulture, spectacle case, flat floater, cherry, red tailed hawk,

don't add to heartache.

Gentle now black sandshell, ash, american bittern, harelip sucker, yellow bullhead, beech, great blue heron, dobsonfly larva, water penny larva, birch, redhead, white catspaw, elephant ear, buckeye,

don't add to heartache.

Gentle now, we sang,

Circle our heart in rapture, in love-ache. Circle our heart.

FOUR

It was not all long lines of connection and utopia.

It was a brackish stream and it went through the field beside our house.

But we let into our hearts the brackish parts of it also.

Some of it knowingly.

We let in soda cans and we let in cigarette butts and we let in pink tampon applicators and we let in six pack of beer connectors and we let in various other pieces of plastic that would travel through the stream.

And some of it unknowingly.

We let the run off from agriculture, surface mines, forestry, home wastewater treatment systems, construction sites, urban yards, and roadways into our hearts.

We let chloride, magnesium, sulfate, manganese, iron, nitrite/nitrate, aluminum, suspended solids, zinc, phosphorus, fertilizers, animal wastes, oil, grease, dioxins, heavy metals and lead go through our skin and into our tissues.

We were born at the beginning of these things, at the time of chemicals combining, at the time of stream run off.

These things were a part of us and would become more a part of us but we did not know it yet.

Still we noticed enough to sing a lament.

To sing in lament for whoever lost her elephant ear lost her mountain madtom

and whoever lost her butterfly lost her harelip sucker

and whoever lost her white catspaw lost her rabbitsfoot

and whoever lost her monkeyface lost her speckled chub

and whoever lost her wartyback lost her ebonyshell

and whoever lost her pirate perch lost her ohio pigtoe lost her clubshell.

FIVE

What I did not know as I sang the lament of what was becoming lost and what was already lost was how this loss would happen.

I did not know that I would turn from the stream to each other.

I did not know I would turn to each other.

That I would turn to each other to admire the softness of each other's breast, the folds of each other's elbows, the brightness of each other's eyes, the smoothness of each other's hair, the evenness of each other's teeth, the firm blush of each other's lips, the firm softness of each other's breasts, the fuzz of each other's down, the rich, ripe pungency of each other's smell, all of it, each other's cheeks, legs, neck, roof of mouth, webbing between the fingers, tips of nails and also cuticles, hair on toes, whorls on fingers, skin discolorations.

I turned to each other.

Ensnared, bewildered, I turned to each other and from the stream.

I turned to each other and I began to work for the chemical

factory and I began to work for the paper mill and I began to work for the atomic waste disposal plant and I began to work at
keeping men in jail.

I turned to each other.

I didn't even say goodbye elephant ear, mountain madtorn, butterfly, harelip sucker, white catspaw, rabbitsfoot, monkeyface, speckled chub, wartyback, ebonyshell, pirate perch, ohio pigtoe, clubshell.

I replaced what I knew of the stream with Lifestream Total Cholesterol Test Packets, with Snuggle Emerald Stream Fabric Softener Dryer Sheets, with Tisserand Aromatherapy Aroma-Stream Cartridges, with Filter Stream Dust Tamer, and Streamzap PC Remote Control, Acid Stream Launcher, and Viral Data Stream.

I didn't even say goodbye elephant ear, mountain madtorn, butterfly, harelip sucker, white catspaw, rabbitsfoot, monkeyface, speckled chub, wartyback, ebonyshell, pirate perch, ohio pigtoe, clubshell.

I put a Streamline Tilt Mirror in my shower and I kept a crystal Serenity Sphere with a Winter Stream view on my dresser.

I didn't even say goodbye elephant ear, mountain madtorn, butterfly, harelip sucker, white catspaw, rabbitsfoot, monkeyface, speckled chub, wartyback, ebonyshell, pirate perch, ohio pigtoe, clubshell.

I bought a Gulf Stream Blue Polyester Boat Cover for my 14-16 Foot V-Hull Fishing boat with beam widths up to sixty-eight feet and I talked about value stream management with men in suits over a desk.

I didn't even say goodbye elephant ear, mountain madtorn, butterfly, harelip sucker, white catspaw, rabbitsfoot, monkeyface, speckled chub, wartyback, ebonyshell, pirate perch, ohio pigtoe, clubshell.

I just turned to each other and the body parts of the other suddenly glowed with the beauty and detail that I had found in the stream.

I put my head together on a narrow pillow and talked with each other all night long.

And I did not sing.

I did not sing otototoi; dark, all merged together, oi.

I did not sing groaning words.

I did not sing otototoi; dark, all merged together, oi.

I did not sing groaning words.

I did not sing o wo, wo, wo!

I did not sing I see, I see.

I did not sing wo, wo!

Note: "Gentle Now, Don't Add to Heartache" owes a number of debts: to a writing workshop at Goddard College in the winter residency of 2004, to a hypnotherapy session with Michelle Ritterman, to *A Guide to Ohio Streams* (published by the Ohio Chapter of the American Fisheries Society), to *The Path of the Rainbow: The Book of Indian Poems* (edited by George W. Cronyn), to Gail Holst-Warhaft's *Dangerous Voices: Women's Laments and Greek Literature* (thanks to Allison Cobb for reference to this book). The "gentle now" was stolen from Ibn 'Arabī's "Gentle Now, Doves" as translated by Michael A. Sells (collected in *Stations of Desire: Love Elegies from Ibn 'Arabī and New Poems*).

Mathias
Svalina
Metal

I .

It's reassuring, really, how a body at rest simply corrodes. The muscles atrophy &
one person is new-born as another. The chemical star new-born as a field. Sunlight
hits the earth in agitations & then the earth is warm & then the floors need sweep-
ing.

Would a person want to know what fields know of the snakes? Is there mercy in
movement? There are certain promises I made, when there was nothing else I could
do. There were walls & there were floors & there was wood & there was metal.

The rain makes a river to wash the chemicals into the canal. Television continues
when the television is off. The marble statues dissolve into lumps. When I think of
myself in the past I see myself as an entire field, what the stop bath means to the
man in the photograph.

2 .

The birth of images will solve the future problems & make it easier for friends, or
for the plastic bags of lavender flowers, filled yet clear. Drag plastic bags of white
rice through the metal fields, drag plastic bags of lavender, of water & drop them
at the ground-in grass.

Between the sulfur smell of roses with the stars & the innocent, we imagine the birth of images to be a problem. Wheel with a father, green & brown eyes & glory, our stars of rolling stones & transfer. Our stars of chemicals & agitation.

O you canals & cobblestones, this stream is not the same thing today, was not related to recall. Days without sleep? Lotus flowers? The fields of metal stretch across the canal. The bulls only breed at the mercy of chemicals. The bulls only founder in mercy & compassion, & the rain & drowned.

3.

When metal then metal. When water then field. When field then field. Metal on lotus, lotus on mercy, on metal field. When lotus then lavender down. When field then field. Mercy burnt the metal field. In lavender lotus, in lotus field. In field, mercy, metal on lotus, mercy, lotus, lavender, field. When metal in down on lotus, then field. On metal when metal, then metal, then field. New-born found in field. New-born found in the metal field. Metal on lotus, when lotus then field.

Then on burnt metal, then on metal lavender field. Mercy in metal in field. Metal, metal lotus chemical field. Mercy, metal, metal, field. Mercy, burnt metal, burnt chemical, field. Mercy, metal, chemical, field. Metal, metal then field. Metal lotus lavender metal, metal, metal on chemical. When field then mercy. Metal, metal, metal on mercy. Burnt lavender chemical. Burnt metal in lavender, burnt metal, field.

Metal lavender on burnt lavender. When metal chemical on burnt lavender then metal, metal on mercy, burnt lavender, field. Burnt lotus in burnt metal. Chemical, metal, metal, field. Chemical mercy then chemical field. When burnt lotus then metal, mercy, field. Metal on metal, metal chemical. When burnt chemical, mercy on metal. Metal chemical on chemical mercy, field. New-born found in the metal field.

4.

Lorem ipsum to the reclining bones. Lorem ipsum to the wash of chemicals across the metal face. Lorem ipsum to the empty shelves where the specimens once stood.

And it came of the God that will see thee, my hand; & on his heart, & wilt thou art my new-born that thou shalt bring to Jehovah. And she said, Before thee, sit & with all that sat over the land of the sea, & there was with me. One law shall be that thy servants are no children, & weep. And the land of Gomorrah, like his wife, which turned trembling, hid them at first. Behold the days of the bricks. Behold the mornings that line the well. Take a dream & thou shalt speak.

Grass was going to get him & the relief when the forge, & asked him vagrants of everything, everything is detestable in some flowers, that unexpected manner of still rooms, any small bundle of anything. In the works of Madonna, a predominant concept is the distinction between destruction & creation. There's a voice that keeps on calling me. We were like dumb-bells.

Certain of field, put the chemical instrument to the metal. Pretend to see cordially the you. Weeks, quiet, vex the fields of lavender, fields of chemical. Morning arrives through a cable or through the walls, new-born each day, sloughed into developer then fixer. There are certain promises I made, when there was nothing else I could do. Where you go, I go. Kiss me. Kiss me.

5.

Morning arrives new-born on time through the cables in the plaster wall, through the itch of frayed wiring, through the tacit pull of chemical skin. I wake to red spots, I wake to voices, to memory remixed as architecture. Noise spills through the window. Noise is the bones beating themselves in the body. Morning is an open field onto which one conceives the day.

One goes to sleep on fire & wakes up ash. One goes to sleep a willing victim & wakes up a teacher. The moon is new-born as corrosion, agitation new-born as a field. What reassures me is how the period holds the sentence & the sentence is spoken by someone else, how I revise my memory into the pluperfect. This is the miracle: the cannibal field new-born as a body, floating horizontally above the canal, making a bed of corrosion in the moonlight of memory.

Catherine Wagner

FROM "Mercury Vectors: A Romance"

Clair (Lucy, Lair)—in public relations

Damaris (Dam, Damn, Tamarisk)—in public relations

Proctor—executive

Gambol (Gamble)—executive

Noman (Nomad)—a god

Various security guards and revolutionaries

Others TBA

MERCURY VECTOR I

Crisis management women   working for

Proctor [*sic*]

 who watches over us &

Gamble

        working for Cingular flying to

    the mercury disposal site

inside an enormous airfilled sac of mercury.

Their plane doesn't have to look like
a real plane, it can be an existence-plane.

  The mercury cursors in their portables
  repelled by the sac in their likeness
      try to fidget free

      which motion
  powers the plane

          silver uterine delivery servix
      crankshaft hooks up to the cerver.

        *   *

        *   *

Damarisk and Clair public relators
preparing for the crisis management seminar
are unable to control
the information they are given

mercury cursor
    trying to get away from itself

"try to click when it is on something
useful! it's on crack!"

             says Damaris
to Clair   who is also
      called Lucy.   Lucy is

   all the way black and Clair is
   all the way white, they are
     the same person.
   A crack along the line btw
     Clair and Lucy is public
   Lair.

   Damn clicks on the cingular
   square-moving orange person—like a
   standard MAN-symbol

   has head detached   can't *CING* through that

      sings a song from the middle
   of the x

   In a human the arms and legs
   don't meatcross at center

   In the cingular figure
   the engine heart is
   missing   but not the action
   when the xinger cings

moving square/rooted in the server

* *

* *

To get out of the mercury plane
they climb into the
   crack in Lucy/Clair.

              "LucyClair"
                 \ /
                 / \
  "Lye Air cc:"   = "scrubclear air carbon copy"

LucyClair turned inside out =

Lair

addresses them in low-cut
  intestine dress

at the crisis management event

in a different plane   CASINO-PLANE

. . . all the men and women around the craps table, I
thought it was a boardroom table
but of course they are gambling.

Present: Gambol, Proctor, Cingular executors, Damneris,
Lair

dressed perfectly
 in her crap dress.

Now one of the crap they are throwing:

"They won't buy a green phone"

 (means an expensive cell phone
    with no mercury in it)

Damn says "1/5 of you colorblind

(1/5 of men are colorblind)

"will look at that green phone and
    see a blood phone

"sell it as a blood phone and they
will
the colorblind men

"buy a green phone"

Here we have a suggestion

that colorblind people
      want violence, will pay for violence.

Well they will, everyone does.

The lair will now have her period.
Lie air carbon copy full stop.

   * *

   * *

In another room, the Proctor sings
   a song   a jingle. Maybe
     he sings a commercial
  jungle

I am breathing in
The takers of this test
They have forty minutes
Nothing here but creepers
Creeping on the creepers

No roots or sky
A tumble jungle
Winding on its vines
Birds in nests
And monkeys in cartoons

Lair: My address is moving
    Peristalsis

Are you done Proctor?
The Proctor is a representative
   of absent authority

Proctor:

They—store collapse
Fly into the regibee
The jungle flew on
satellite tracked

   * *

   * *

"Will it work as a commercial jungle?
  will it persuade people of aught?

"is it a catchy jungle?"

"Maybe they will mute it, and not buy
        anything."

 "Oh I love the jungle
It's where the medicine comes from"

*   *

*   *

It's not unusual to be loved by anyone
I can pass the time in a flood of anyone
When I push your eyes with my thumbs
    the blood it comes.   I saw it in a zombie flick
da da, da da da da da

I cannot blame you all foh-ore
   be-he-hinge alive.
It's not unusual—   Any jungle

gets Smaller and smaller, it's a

Rattlecage   hanging On a leather

String from my ceiling—   What's that?

It was a jungle.   O my god,

I've never seen one of those before.
  May I touch it?   Sure, sure
it's mine
What's mine is yours
when you're staying in my house.

PASTORAL INTERLUDE

  Scum interlards
the pastoral interval:
Proctor&Gambol [*sic*] scum

in the forest by the creek?

The foam's probably natural.
Rot acts as surfactant.

Bubbles form atop the dead

  in turbulent water.
1% of river foam is dead/pollute. The rest is air.

Standing in the foam, a god-boy

Clair and Dam watch him

He's chest-only out of the water

Not possible, the stream's
six inches deep.

He's a god.

He's black, not brown-skinned
or dark-skinned—

like a hole in the forest, convex.

His edges have a green lamé-sheen

the shadows under
the musculature of his chest

set off the sheen, otherwise barely
visible in full sun

the blackwinged damselfly
lands on him and is absorbed

He's rising from the phosphorescent
foam.

Dam lying on a fallen log

not sure what she's seeing—"Clair!"

—"I see him," squats by the foam,

moves a stick lackadaisically

through him.

If this is to be a narrative,
characters must do things.

—"He's building himself of burst foam
momently"

 says Clair

observing fervently the border

of his body and the small island

of foam near and aside from the Dam.

A sheeny lowering of lids

 crashflutter as of wings

 he turns his head
to her.

He's a god.   That's what he's

doing.

Emerges feet, all of him
  hard to look at him, human-shaped
god-sized

hole in the forest, moving around

speaks as a vibration of

the all-around, inside-out

stereo woofer

verberant.

Clair and Dam by the creek

have
  each put a hand inside

the hole man.

    The nothing shirrs around
      their wrists.

Inside   no inner walls or

organs.

Clair reaches in
up to her armpit, flails her
arm where she thinks

his ribcage would be, reaches for
  his pubis, there's nothing

space. Aroint! she brushes past

Damn's hand,   loud wet warm

has *form*, buzzes at its

edges, Clair reaches after it

  grasps it, she and Dam outside

the nothing, arms disappeared

inside it, look at one

another; their hands are ringing.

Damaris ecstatic reaches in
  her other hand, grasps Clair's;

hands mouthing Clair's

porcupine-prickle sun-up

aftershock pleasure hand

Damaris pulls herself in

    entire, she's gone,

            Clair
pulls her hand out to her chest

    shocked gazes

at the nonman

    he's   with Damneris

watching   Dam float

nowhere to put

    the étagère.

(Clair beside the no-man will fuck him
eventually.

This was pastoral interlude—

Return to mercury plane and various

crisis-stops)

A Form
for Verse

Master,
make me collage it.

Do you see that you are
      adequating?

I refuse to be adequate
 to the day
hold it in
contemp.

"Recycle language
for a greener consciousness"
—That's easy.
Everyone's always done it.
We must be getting greener
by the hour.

Amy King
A Geography
of Pleasure

An orange star dying on my windowsill
—the sugared thing—is never a ship but a leisure.
Yes, to be allowed at least one leisure per life,
to sky someone in from the dispossessed
is to dispose of mind and body contents,
a bouquet of erotic breaths, the honeyed air
of a lover's lungs open as this planet, or the next
inhabitant: rabbit, blank face or bicycle man.
That banquet unknown, like manna torn
by the ridges of your tightening teeth.
How I wish one was matter
from one's own country, belly up
beneath the spell of geography, responsible only
to celluloid snapshots, neck turned,
half-smile of tight-cells tied by the growling oil green
of a bench on which sit figs, pomegranates.   —The markers of country,
Sunflower seeds shell the dirty asphalt.   corner fruit.
Square basement windows belch
a pack of cigarettes that flinch on star gas.
At dawn, a banknote's smile sucks us down,
frames a flock of sheep by the chimney's feet
that climb twelve more floors of syllabled steps,
the first piano view of a factory as nature.

Money the men. We nature whores.

Toes in black and white keys.

Depleting minor corpuscles and drain

the red serum from our skin graft's scales.

I have never found the neighboring sea

pretty, insert eyes that, instead, the lake frogs

and flies stretch over the cobwebs of me

in a bouquet of barrel trees: they spear through

vineyards, the airy earth too thick with painted vines

and footsteps up to the fronts of our wheelchairs.

Children's voices wash across a city terrace,

loudspeakers drown on our bottles of wine,

and a marching song comes rolling in

from the mountains of those who work to own

the luxury of bills, the leisure of beaches

and beaks that scramble along the attic walls . . .   —Plastic-filled entrails.

You go there, fondle that star,

and ache the race to kid-dom again.

The spectral vanishes with a rope painted chalk

to skew the sky apart. Cloud the weapons'

outlines that hopscotch us all where parallels meet.

A beak set to maw is only

a problem of vocabulary,

white syntax on paper, insofar unoccupied.

Comes the promise of boring bad weather.

Buy the pear tart at the kiosk raining

matchsticks from a pale sun and peer

through your dalai lama keyring. Your feet ache.

Heartbreak and sunset nooses evoke a theater,

but the three little dolls on the banks   —Trinity sprites.

of dying marshes smell like ellipsis.

An omission rests on what is certain:

not the germ of a story but the energy

to rope it, the events of sins that mar the wind

we peer through on sunny days we invented.

How do you find it? Down there, already

sober, droplets, the brakes and the valley are dirty.

I am sitting at a table by the little window.

Darkness falls into smoking. On a dictograph

even the imperfect valley sings holes over hills,

waiting to fill, pre-Spring. An afternoon passes quiet tulips

between these four lungs. Cribbage. A game

of tea and crumpets for perspective. The hour signals

a cloud of light, wayward in more-than-one place.

Something of protein we find ourselves

thinking *O warm wall*, wall of goats

moutainside, why won't you reveal what

rides beyond your reins, your plastic exterior,

why do you hide in the arteries of this planet's

metal and concrete static? The hearts' satchel thrum?

Who else can hide these arteries of small smiles

and tired-but-true handquakes?   —Diffusing the body electric.

The portrayal of space is an inner door,

an interior decor. A monologue we think

to share aloud leaves us seeing in three dimensions only.

That myth of the ten percent, our omen.

A proverb is also nature petrified.

Meets the eye with ferocious greens and mineral trees

holding a molecular structure. We energy, we sculpture

immortal, the skull of the valley falls perfectly ochre.

A frog sways its posture in the choreography
of agriculture. Genetic discouragement, DNA infects   —What is Africa to me?
the blight that warts imagination. Smoothes it so far.
We other inhabitants, not-frogs or DNA gospels
retain opaqueness, a "crazy" tag
on the toe of our corpses. That lasts before dawn
and all the rage. I have never had anything
to say in the face of such prisons. I'm open. My conversation
is a play on the stage of vanity, the who I fuck
and the why I am no boy, how I erase the space
of his mouth's residence from my skin, how I was never
a room to his marriage plans. I meticulously color out
the ease of nonchalance, the temptation to settle
into permanent housing. Good fences make good cages
and good cages teach patience. Or so the ides of childhood
sell those skeletal portals. I always wanted
escape into dwelling but never held the map's location.
I beheld the misprints. And ate that choreography.   —The living by osmosis.
Each key is the footprint escaping,
muting its position's maker.
That was what I wanted, a wandering gypsy Band-Aid,
one that would wait out the American Dream
to regroup and hold-in-court its listeners. For none who hear
can stand the ephemeras' absence. The passing boy   —Other, then the self.
clasps and delights in a fiasco sketch, undoes
the necklace in mime and offers us his baggage.
Which preoccupation will carry his lantern, aid him
in the mystery of no puzzle to produce and no employment
to escape him? He is the perfect pin-up of cliché
kitsch and which way did the wind go in this economic sidebar.

He will make good news someday. And that is a bet
you can write home about, if telling stories becomes your mattress
and the line that tows your part. Sometime milk cows,
sometime red boned, sometime go to Ireland
or a part of the sea you've never witnessed. Where makes
the smallest difference except the part you drop
the hold on newspaper heights and monstrous instruments
from your diction wand. Hitchhike the gates
to heaven's latest, a boy in the clutch of untold stagehands
narrating a bouquet of neighborhood proportions:
narrator-perfect enjoys the fission,
though his intentions seemed the grosser sketch
despite a capsized portrait, we accepted the route
with country-manners and storehouse-sales.
Azure smoke is a baby-turns-child,
small chin of the adult face designated color   —Graphing the fetal position.
of fire curling from God's promenade zone.
Cut from the same cloth,
or so we're told by those who wish to own a partial print
at the end of a gun. The right end. That leaves love
enough to suck drag from a cigar stem and hit the pavement
for the next burlesque. The real romantic is the woman who hangs
up, sighs and lights her pipe on the windowsill, looking
past any world, Ah-choo. Not the divinity of a Last Supper
painting but more of a Kahlo blemish, defunct or sky-colored
Cerulean. We move beyond bones now,   —Slant light, a housekeeping.
epoch editors of evolution, the one that avoids progression
but, like any old woman worth her weight in wax,
she can bite a nail in two and suck the iron
for plutonium, our next best energy bet. The waft of smell

reminds us that at one time northern ladies stood

beneath a carried-on horizon reciting, I am posture and toe,

content with a fake-fog stage, gazing into an overhead sea

with intense turtle blues reflecting my eyes

by the well of your loneliness, not a shadow in sight

of our simple undying, this Mediterranean

world is a beauty we beat, a submission salted

for a backyard beautician who leans us in short chairs

and laughs at the lack of yard and an unwashed sense

that liquid oxygen creeps up our knees, nipples and gasps . . .

We lash heads back for the laugh, clear throated

in the length of this cabin, fitted with

corpses it produces and the babies too, we suck them

in like so many beer cans tipped, sun-up

and still. The waves roll toward the backdoor   —The generative incest.

as sure as the sea is a sense making,

whether full of oil or hard-bodied salmon

that think like peopled brain waves,

a plastic goodbye where we place rocks gently

in trench coats and begin the bottom-up journey,

that planetary part that remarks

we're inadequate as shells but insist on the vault

of human endeavor and mischievousness we sink to enter.

The ash trees across the neighbor's yard yell

before we go that so much depends on the conjugal visits

of a million stellar forks and hands:

crashing voices, mobile Venus, Zephyr café days,

this marble embrace, the eagle cry of populations in stasis,

the loosely knit scarf of dusk around the souls' last

murmurs and snaking vines, Eve's lizard-shaped back,

the way we curl smoke into air,

how everything takes shape back into space,

the animated ancient, gods borne from almond-white holes

we dive to descend, how we leap the divide

where nothing is alike, make stone decorations, attend an invisible,

. blame the range of antelope, mothers, televised brands

and folk nomads for anything after anarchy:

this land is our land, the god guts and glory plan

goldens our wooden tables and glass franchises, the roads

that pave this way as if we're choices, our selves　　　　　—In always, again.

in unbridled pleasures, map quest replays and lover strategies,

somewhere that isn't, the false starts in bed

an always drawing nearer, as often the evermore begins.

Gabriel Gudding
ILLINOVOR-NEVERIVERNOIS —Ivne—MMX

River, definition of. Its busy nature. How does it differ from glue—its difference from glue. River water—ponds composed of. Scoliosic power thereof, its ranch of drowning. Motions of whirls—theory of their function. Water a coagulate of sunlight—its application as solvent; its method of action, propensity to spawn thunderbolts. Harmonic principles of boats. The nature of canoes. The nature of kayaks. Their methods of riding waves. Waves on river, how composed. The nature of inner tubes. The nature of rafts.

The Illinois River—is it finite? Dimensions of Illinois, square footage. Hiparchus. Comets falling on. Variates in radiation. Number of elms. Number of wedding rings found in. Number of meteorites striking in. Spinal column: their number and kind; number of hibernal vertebrates on the Illinois; those of quadruped, those of biped (bird, primate). Is there a burning field, disruption of children by industry. Varieties of thermal garments worn on rivers; what river water does to potions; the history of zipper construction in relation to river usage. Steamboats, nostalgia for. Positive effects of nostalgia: conservation. Negative effects of nostalgia: delusion, denial in face of dire change. Modern barge traffic. The Illinois River: its weight in tons. Infestation by invasive fish.

Islands—their cozy nature. Dams, global worry regarding, history of.

Mud—its relation to muck, its shape; varieties of its motion; its unnecessary retentions of organic matter; reason for its name; that it hardens to shale—shale as petrified mud. Kinds of muds. Mud—its relation to slurry; similarity to clabber. Its role in sedimentation; as a repository of entropy, example thereof; ubiquity on river banks; use in the construction industry. Ceramics, essential uses of. Lutites—visual similarity to pastries. The ducks—their nature. Floods—reasons for. Varieties of towns in Illinois. Immigration—its contributions to racism. Rivers—their reason. Regular effect of rivers. Irregular rivers. Rivers, their constant agitation and seeming quiet nature. Some persons think that rivers are everlasting. Rivers, their preposterous nature. Flowing water—its relation to fire; its mesmeric quality. Monotheism, its evils. Jesus as a violent influence. Love corrupted as a tool and method of violence. Kindness corrupted as a mask and habituation of violence. Religion as a means of utilizing and surreptitiously wielding evil rather than opposing or expunging it. Canada; metís culture; the French and canoe construction. Extinct towns on the Illinois. Thistles, insistence on carrying. Owls who look like headmistresses. A sad little gully seen and lived near. Tiskilwa watershed, its contour farming. Thunderbolts, what Illinois counties are immune from them and why. Ancient retreat of sea, where occurred? Ubiquity, its presence; the role of rivers in the making of notion of ubiquity. Tart smell of farts over river water. Woodsmoke felted in damp woolens. Seeds, curtseying through air. Spring.

Warmth, human fascination with. Mammalian fascination with. Depredation of human on mammal, given nakedness of former, for the purposes of acquiring the insulative coats of fur-bearing creatures. These in Illinois are only fourteen. They are the badger, coyote, weasel, least weasel, long-tailed weasel, the fox, the gray fox, the red fox, muskrat, the bobcat, the beaver, the otter, the river otter, the minks, the raccoon, striped skunk, the opossum. These furbearers, forbearers. Of these are protected only the bobcat, the river otter.

What is this rich river, rubber and unreal, on which I somehow have limbs, long and sustained event of lumber. Seems itself to act, rises bent from elasticity bunched in the hills, great motile lesson, gravy of serpent, lid of pounding, the beavers dead in you could fill a hundred buckets, the river encumbered, polluted in trade, lined by orange wood, laced in bright pith, applied with dials, parts of car dashes, a complexity at the shoe. I strained on the river my only shoulders.

The ocean — its unorthodox nature; the sea, a complicated doily of forces at the center of the universe. The need of marriages. Why we live, not infrequently, among dried jellies, why the sun semaphores inside its own alphabet, why the floor of the pond was hoisted onto the grease of the solar system.

Our illiterate jovial relations with the earth, development of. Labia, function and prettiness of. Labia, development through time: how the labia of your ancestor may become the jowls of yr grandchild. The need for a prosperous, if desultory, trade-agricultural world.

Greetings, their function. Greetings to your overlarge vehicles. Yr Buick Enclave, yr Cadillac Escalade, yr Chevrolet Avalanche, yr Suburban Glacier, yr Tahoe, yr GMC Yukon, yr Hummer, yr Headwater, yr Grand Cherokee, yr Jeep Commander and Compass, yr Wrangler and Liberty, yr Land Rover Range Rover, yr Lincoln Navigator, yr Mercury Mariner, Mitsubishi Outlander and Endeavor, Mercury Mountaineer, Toyota Sequoia, yr Subaru Forester, yr named of ships named of, named like ships named of, yr named of maps named of, yr mountains, yr seas, named of tribes named of, named of trees who are named of native. The gathering also of your corpulent gluttonous ass, your filth plinth, the gathering of our car supports our buttcunt, our carbuncle, our gristle shitsqueez ass bun holder that is your car, which is your passive fusscoffin. Your genitals are the vehicles of warts. They are as everything. The river —its blunders; its eels and bells under it, as a native organ of a hill, long and old, how it lengthens toward whatever seems to block it, its fecal tongue, as alphabet and aliment at once in a helix thru the weeds, reaming everywhere its agglutinous gewgaws.

Outside—its nature. What is "to be outside"; partly to expose the dermis at sensations caused by moving air, damp from rain, dew patina, biofilm and sunpound, impact of small object borne by air current, the subjection of those membranes that produce mucus (mucus —a viscous colloid containing antibiotic enzymes) composing and surrounding the eyeball, nose, mouth, sometimes anus and genital, to the webwork of twigs, boughs, muds, animal leavings, the rusting of filaments, foisting of hair, threat of bodily attack, exposure to dust, inhalation risk, pollen fume, the floating of genetically modified spores, is to feel the world without a house or other anchored or otherwise heavy climate-controlled integument containing seats, beds, desks such as building or vehicle into which we otherwise insert our bodies individually or en masse.

How there is no end of beds in the solar system, magniscient waters swaddled in cambium and chained with antic, esculent meats who collect the chunky impediment called food. We imagine the landscape as an asymptote filled with ejected things. How geese sound like pleasant and anxious dorks. Dissolution, its nature: how most corn, weather, cow, comes at us in pieces, how rain, divided to thousand of pieces, coalesces to one piece of river, water mass of liquid distended to cohesive slab of rain slipping through hillside in which is suspended a brambledom of dissolving animals. Floors—their destiny in the solar system; let floors be hoisted into the solar system. Ayn Rand—her retarded nature. Immunohistoriver, cell rill, Twain and the demise of river life. The wrecking of Illinois by supermarket. Supermarkets—their relation to monoculture agribusiness; their relation to Sunday school. The old kosmos of the river— its absence; *"non flumen, sed orbis,"* panta rhei. Rays— demise of; Bradbury, Sugar, Charles, sun. Meat as condensed sorrow. Sorrow, its proximity to rivers. The river as essay. The river as Montaigne. The stupidity of the river as Montaigne.

[congratulations on being here]

Celeb.ration "is"."se
lf.res.traint, is a
t.ten.tiveness, is qu
est.ioning, is medi
tating is a
waiting" is a per.son
's .body a[t] large, [a] mob.ile collect.ion of molecule. We congratulate th.is
id.ea.of.body.

That "a wo.rld is wor.lding,"
rehearsing in fact .that we a.re."here."
We congrat.ulate "th.at the.re a.re be.ings at all"
th.e not.ion of hereness, of here.

A, boulder,'s a large, part.icle. We congratulate, this accident, of boulder.

We congratulate a Vermilion, River. We kayak. We congratulate, a bridge, thanks,
you carry, us, the bridge, for holding, I saw them the, mo.ving babies, we mean, it
even today, the Mill St, bridge at Pontiac. Illi.nois. And, that guy, who honked, you,
honked, your honk, reverberating on the dam wall, thank you, we're in y.our,
mid.st.

All, of the daughters, in the waters, all, of the brothers, with the, others: you, are
con.gra.tulated: thanks.for h.old.ing love,s tho, you, do.n't, think of it, like that,
maybe, my youths I, congrat.ulate, you, for, depositing my selves, in this, "time
place," I congratulate, the waters, of Evergreen, Lake, Co.mlara's Park for support-

ing, the gramanoid weights, of for.aging hundred, and then thousand, of our, medium geese, crissum, crown and occiput, who are, little little, meat boats. We congratulate, the geese, thems.elves, for having, such little he.arty legs. You're all, scaly and nude, and knobby legged, you pinioned, you squamous senators. And Yo.ga, because, yo.u are, in this whirled, I congratulate, you, and all your, lo.vely te.[ache].rs. I congrat.ulate ants, for being cut.e, I have never seen, an ugly ant, even up, close, in those photographs, by E. O., Wilson.

I congratulate Clio, Byrne-Gudding, d[a[we][la]ughter of G.ab[e]riel Gud.ding, a.nd, Ma.iréad Byrne, you have done, so well, in yr 15, yrs, sis.ter, of Mar.ina, Byrne-Folan, for you, as we.ll, as Ma.rina, a.re a, ch[isle]ld, of letters, of ladders, child of answers, of elbows, child of apples, of bellows, child of rivers, of otters, child of sunspecks, of waters: child of tendons, thin, springing, both the tendons, of her ankles, and the tendons, of the allosaur: I congratulate, Clio and the arrange-ment, of things, that made her. You, are a child, of that cloud and that cloud and that cloud. You, are a sister, of that chicken and that chicken, you are a sister, of a sister. You, are a child, of fat and wheat and wide fish. You are, in no way, related, to any dogs, but all cats, at once. Child of purple, child of cool canal.

For Clio, and the distance to her, the ac.cident, of her, the int.ention of e.very mindhe.art that ma.kes, we congratulate J.ohn Mui.r, the *pays d'en haut*, mud as a colloidal fruit, the river as a lung barn, angry people, seven little bit, seven clam river, theoretical hull speed, that we clean the toilet, the mantle, the honey cell, the ladle, a columnar crown, the fouled animal, bird work and culvert fuss, bilge arts, bioaccumulate, echinodermata your sister. We hoist Clio. We hoist house and un-house: your unreadable library. "All that is beloved must be changed, separated, severed." Whatever causes the weapons to sparkle. It is remarkable there are stu-pid ladies. Camp on the muddy feather. Be sad as in a zoo. As in a leaving outward. Potamalalia, outmouth. The horses touch our gravel. Riparian accipiters. Franz Joseph rifle. Accepting misfortune cheerfully in the pleasant saloon. All of it. Peri-stalted.

The globe
a fruit, a hive
of pity : inviting
to demand, peppered
in moth, smeared
in wind

The globe a fruit + a hive of pity
: lacquered in sun, stitched in genital
against destruction

where living
w/ brightened mind
is enough
an exit for sorrow

so congratulate
the worx
of compassion

what is this basket   of horses?

[if a world]

what is this bedaisy'ed
casket of gristle, stowed
in skin?

[if a body]

if we, are each, a novice and continue to sleep

our days a stream of morals, a string

of what use is this childhood
if we just assemble love
around us

        to die from it
        or watch it die?

Dana Levin

Spring

Forensic Anthropology Center, University of Tennessee, Knoxville

I

The sun, in shafts and spades.

Through the pine and birches, little breeze setting off
      the leaves—

Their golden green increase.

Pollen to the air, its colonial dream
      of a new imperium of trees—

Snap against the wrist-skin.

And then you press down on the tongue with your gloved thumb
      to let the honey-bee show you the way.

2

The dark tunnel paths from light to light.

Flay the face and scoop out the eyes—you'll see.

3

Bees in a cloud round your hand.

Egg-herder, your smell
          synonymous with treasure—

Shining a light at the back of the throat:
          blowflies
in liquid pearls
          the bees murder to eat—

And all at the lips and nose a yellow dust, pollen
          they have
delivered—

You scrape it into a little sack.

4

Ripple and snap.

Bend to the O of the rigored mouth—listen:

Plastic bags, like souls, caught in trees.

5

What to harvest
        from the sloughed-off suits of the dead.

Like sea-shells cupping the ghost-tongue of the sea,
        their black mouths speak—

You crouch to the hum with a bag and a blade. You

the god it sways.

Marthe Reed
Chandeleur Sound

A categorical exclusion, birdfoot deltaic lobe sprawling (   ) eastward. "No significant adverse impacts are expected," planned for. A lapse, this: piping plover habitat, brown pelican nursery. Caspian and Sandwich terns diving against sludge. Catastrophe too "unlikely" no (additional) mitigation measures necessary. Though urgency obligatory (revenue management), abrogating safety and environmental— Oil "plume" blanket, mantle smothering spongefields, corals, remnant cordgrass meadows. A lapse and a rush, field of rushes fouled.

Barrier islands braceleted in orange. Royal terns, laughing gulls glide above (oiled) surf. Pelicans, given to loafing on shoals. Shelter dolphin, turtles: haven, refuge, home. This: investment portfolio, what's really at stake. Residual marsh toxicity, pompom booms mimicking widgeon-grass. A regulatory regime cut-to-fit Big Oil, profit, thirst of our idealized machines. Fill in the blank. "No clear strategic objectives"—tern estuary, soak, seat—"linked to statutory requirements." What is required?

Profit, 93 million dollars a day. "No adverse", not. Part of the scheme. Copepods grazing on corexit, this (   ) web feeding squid, sperm whales, dolphin. MMS, like BP, leashing science to production, acquisition. *Yield.* Meaning to take, harvest. Accumulate, at the bottom of things. Wealth. Counting our blessings and breathing in fumes. Larval bluefin, swordfish, this (   ) hydrocarbon nursery. "adverse impacts" cannot be expected. Or imagined. Preparing the bottom line. Thousands of frigatebirds roosting amid black mangroves stabilizing the coast.

No detailed environmental analysis. Necessary, the exigencies of greed. Keeping us grounded. Coral reef, widgeon-grass meadow another. Pipe dream. Illusion. Feeding on (corexit and oil suspension) dreams. Shrimp bed, oyster bed. Better this: cheap petrol. Trading covenant, land, law, our "good intentions". What we want: jobs-in-the-industry. The industry. Selling. Out. Road going everywhere nowhere. Down and— Kissing it good-bye. Chandeleur Sound, a categorical exclusion.

Michael Dumanis

The Woods Are Burning

I. THE CEASE-FIRE

I thought there was a war on. I was wrong. To think the war
was over me! The war was over. No: the war was over
there, the other side of the barbed wire enclosure
from our side, warless, where we fidgeted and held
each other's hands as though they were the last
we'd ever think to hold, all the while keeping
strict tabs on the body count covering the soft
field of lamb's ear, beside the nasturtiums,
it's just a field, merely an empty space
between the hydrangea bushes. The war was not over
the bushes, who, like the lamb's ear, the boy-gardener,
and the flowers, became the war's first casualties.
Because there was no cause for war and none of us
were sure there was a war for us to win, the newspapers
named it The Casual War, The War That's Not Really
a War, The Don't Mention It War, The What War,
The There Isn't a War War, The War Over Nothing,
and (on the day the papers were shut down) The War
The Authorities Ban Us From Covering. I,
as I have told the Truth Commission, didn't think

there was a war, nor spread the vicious rumor,
until the ground shook and I saw you fall, until I took
the survivor's cracked mouth into my open mouth,
tried giving the survivor my last breath, and in the smoke
and cannonfire confusion of the war, mistook
his breath for mine, and pulled (I didn't mean to) his
last breath into my healthy mouth and watched him not
survive—

        but this is not about me. I have testified.
Lay prostrate on the courtroom floor. Went down
before the Justice of the Peace on my trick knee.
Reached for the lavender-scented sleeve of her black robe
in her secluded chamber. Swore I knew nothing of
the Schlieffen Plan, the Bay of Pigs, the secret pact
we struck to fan the cease-fire's flames until it burned
itself out of existence, as she turned to me and ran
her satin hands over my eyelids, toward my lips.
Knowing the war would never end, we kissed.

Am I the one who suffered? Was I there?

This is not about me, Trojan Horse.

2. THE INSURRECTION

My students are angry. Biting their lips at me, brushing stray eyelashes off with one
hand's middle finger. I made them read the entirety of *Death of a Salesman* out loud
while I watched them. Each time the student playing Willy Loman would say, "The
woods are burning," I would stop her and ask, "What woods? Why burning?" She
said Willy was one crazy son-of-a-bitch spouting gibberish mixed with self-pity.

Said his family should be relieved and grateful that he killed himself, spared them additional anguish, more maudlin burning forests of self-pity. I asked my students what it means for somebody to say the woods are burning. The consensus was, maybe it doesn't mean anything. Until another student, the one playing Happy, said he was in a forest fire once, on the periphery. "It's hard to get out of the woods when they burn," Happy told me. "It's not like a house fire, where you have sprinklers and smoke detectors, windows and ladders. You can't contain it. Winds decide its course. Once it starts, there's no stopping it. Often you don't find what started it. And when you do, it's something insignificant, a cigarette thrown down at the wrong angle, a heap of twigs during a dry hot season." "This play is horrible," said Willy Loman. "Maybe in the old days, people could relate to it. But nowadays how could you feel sorry? I had several options: I chose not to take them. I cheated on my wife. I lived a lie. I'm just a loser: I deserved to die." She is a beautiful woman with bands wearing a baby blue baby-T. She works the night shift at the Emergency Ward, has to leave every class period a few minutes early so she can check the wounded in on time, call the appropriate insurance companies.

The wounded come on time to be checked in.

The wound in opposition
                    to the idea of the wound.

The woods are burning.

3. THE CINEMA

I had two options at the movie theater:

1) Footage of people being blown to pieces.
2) Footage of people being blown.

4. THE WOODS

either:

It's Pilsner Time at the Palace of Tines
in Palestine, along the Seine,
where Paul Celan, that Philistine,
where Paul Celan, in pale soutane,
or someone else I once saw drown
(it was this summer, in the Seine)
is passing time. Or pausing time.

or:

don't know
downtown
don't now
tone down

gauze gaze Gaza ghazal gazelle Giselle guise guess gasp grasp graze grace
glossary glacier glazier glass lipgloss galoshes goulashes gouaches Gauloises
valse triste the valises of Lillian Gish

gaze, gaze, Gazelle
at Gizelle's disguise

a striking resemblance
to Lillian Gish

she is in Gaza now
gasping through gauze

go, go, Giselle
through Gaza's gossamer

applying your lipgloss
and grasping at air

dance, veiled Giselle
dance the valse triste in Gaza

while the gazelles, they graze:

something like grace
that one would not call grace

your gaze assuages
I am not a carpenter

no one in my family or yours
has ever been a carpenter

Giselle, disguised,
find something in your glossary

of gazes to assuage
each gasp in Gaza

each gasp is a palette of grays

4 ½. THE INSURRECTION, CONTINUED

I don't remember things the way I used to.

Words disappear: I asked my students what apartheid was.

All of them knew,
except the ones who were black.

None of my students were black.

I asked my students what Jim Crow was.

None of them knew, except the students
who were black.

I tried comparing Jim Crow to apartheid,
but that's like saying that the circumstances of my sister's murder
were like the circumstances of your sister's murder.

I have no sisters.

True or False? Lillian Gish

True or False? Paul Celan

Fatty Arbuckle? I ask my students.

They don't know.

They, who know everything.

Are the woods burning?

What time is it anyway?

No, I have hundreds of sisters.
Most of them died in the war.

5 . THE EULOGY

these are the only
remains of your circus

fat dwarves emerging
from the thin hour

this dancing camel and his
indiscernible strings

this photogravure
of the wild man of borneo

this is your borneo
this backwoods laughter

you've bent over backwards
you're stilted on stilts

you're highly unlikely
inside this enclosure

this ring is the zero
sum game of your passion

this maudlin this dusk
this unpurchased concession

this leotard's seam tear
this falling of limbs

this cobweb the only
thing veiling your laughter

this would-be obscured
trap of doorway and these

various passions of clowns
along with them the memory

of riding a train
through a forest on fire

then passing the fire
and seeing the platform

and leaving the train

K. Silem Mohammad

FROM "The Sonnagrams"

OUNCE CODE ORANGEADE (I EYE WOODY)

If mutant vultures chew the stretchy hides
Of old Athenian stooges (ugh, the thought),
They figure better meat therein resides
Than can from any newer corpse be got;

If kitten fur became the new chinchilla
Some folks would get a tiny bit upset,
Though not as much as when they find vanilla
Is made from chewed-up wads of Nicorette;

If little tattooed strumpets of thirteen
In crusty navy taverns pitch their tent,
What's shameful isn't where these girls have been;
It's what they sang in Latin as they went.

Must queer Horatian beer hymns echo so
In every Roman cathouse (*yo, yo, yo…*)?

[Sonnet 15 ("When I consider every thing that grows")]

WWW (I HEIL MY, MY, MY HITLER;
I HEEL MY WHINY CUR; I WRAP MY
RUEFUL VULVA IN MY LIMP, UNHOLY FUR)

You few non-nude and many naked elk,
Who, in your ludic pastures over yon,
Fear not the mad Behemoth's flailing whelk
That abrogates our fretful Helicon:

You indolent nude teens who always flee
Redactions of a crude antithesis:
The symmetry of progress yet must be
The progress of a symmetry (like this).

If ponies value nudity, they do
As Puritans do patriotic rap;
You hear this said, and know it to be true,
As if it were a boner in your lap.

For nudity is only true in porn;
For why was Woodrow Wilson ever born?

[Sonnet 16 ("But wherefore do not you a mightier way")]

Author's note: Each Sonnagram, including its title, is an anagram of a standard modern-spelling version of one of Shakespeare's Sonnets, containing exactly the same letters in the same distribution as the original. The title is composed last, using whatever letters are left over once I've assembled a working sonnet in iambic pentameter with an English rhyme scheme.

Standard
Schaefer
The L.A. River

smog typhoid celery like a ghost splashing out of a beaker
comes a dot off the ridge to cancel the orthography of
bramble and pine the abyss fits in the parenthesis
fragrance of isotherms route numbers and the glint of chrome
that hits the vein each day more prophylactic
than the exit wound of pragmatism and public work but with a plush silence
has no preference though if pushed hedges with performance
dim pleats in the slovenly limits of custom, obligation, and verve
works the work of the major languish against slobber, skin,
and any serviceable language of submission and proposal
come and gone in spars and shafts part e-flat part pleas
twelve chords of gray ash until sixty watts offshore,
it does nothing, but at least it does it consistently, despite shortness
of breath and the liver's long career of whispering yes

Arielle Greenberg

Tour of _____
Morning Farms

The round   (hours)   tucked in each   iron   bell
        worn by goats   (wormed, hoofed):
a lie & a lust.   Nightmare knockings
      of shoehorn testicles against the clapboard door,
neighbor   (trampy)   horse, shaking her head no no no.
The boys   (white-haired, hockey)   are allergic
  to that which   is not shit,   not that spray of hayseed,
             not rubber boots upturned all through the loft,
    lost spaniels splaying their tongues.
Two trays of soap (on the counter):   olive   rosemary
      various saps & seeds,   starved marble.
The tight face the sun makes.   We pull out
    from the hormones of fresh cheese,   from solar panels
grinding dimmer & dimmer roots,   the cellar
& its jars of Mason,   whatever,   fraternal;
    (disorder this skinned life carries)
towards the edge of organic,   plunge into
     a brisk & clear shot of filament,   process,   spasm.

Erika Howsare
& Kate Schapira

FROM **The Waste Project**

FLORIDA

// *s* + *s* // —

The wastenaut is cattle strolling among stands of palmetto.

She is gulls at the dump, a dead cat in the road, one sick tree in an orange grove.

She is a boat hauled by trailer down 95.

She is a broadcast breaking up near Saturn.

She is the Flying J.

The peel. The tower. The engineered island. The traffic island.

Her seat pushed back so far it looks like no one's driving.

"Steak on the buffet every night."

"Slow down."

"Hort Lab." Stems in her pocket, her slides clouding, dew in her hair.

She is rounding the bend in the outer lane.

// *s* + *s* // roads and driveways like sutures,

Coming down over the poison blue tiles of dream houses, circuitry of streets over more acreage, uneasily stitched to palmetto-stuffed undergrowth. Who sleeps in this room? Who unlocks this gate? If I leave it, will wealth leak out, freon, bills, the dreamlife? Is this water wasted? When something here is not human, it grows thick, it appears from the air. The pumps reiterate. Also, my parents have a much huger pool than this.

//*s + s*// When something here is not

As the metaphor goes, we have intestinal problems because we are consumers. As the metaphor goes, we eliminate toxins. The water receives them.

//*s + s*// human, over

Stinking canal. Ants gather on half a squirrel.

//*s + s*// Palm. Absolution.

I am the viper in your bosom, the alligator in your water trap. I eat quietly from pocket to pocket of enforced cool air, more water than I can drink in, I say, "Buffets are kind of wasted on me."

//*s + s*// sweating, knowing

Cracked cap on the sprinkler—no, everything works perfectly, nothing is worse, nothing interrupts but little ponds of bone disease or little ponds of cancer. The pond's a color that drives fish downhill from fertilizer lawns. Inherit unkindness and feel its salt burn your tongue, change your ways, place the bins in the right order. Place wastes, in a way. Sprinklers the sidewalk, the lights, the A/C, the pool filter, the computer. Sometimes we waste opportunities to educate. Sometimes we run our mouths.

//*s + s*// what we pour and pour ourselves.

We drive down to the school in Boca for the worms. A/C on in the empty building. The worms in a bucket with shredded newspaper, papaya that someone forgot to use before it went bad, and their own castings. Too many worms for the bucket, less movement, fewer babies. They've slowed down their living. We take them out into the shaded patio, a rush of cooled air as we open the door. R loves the worms— digging through the bucket to see them dive, finding babies, wetting down the paper she just shredded from the copy room, putting lettuce and peas into the top.

The worms should be able to live well in the confines of the system if their food, castings and water are kept in right proportion to their own numbers. And they're beautiful, a wine-red color, not too big. A lingering smell of compost under our nails after we've sifted the castings and set up the new bucket. On the drive R and I talked about money, babies and jobs. Maybe we'll get pregnant around the same time. Maybe we'll be able to paint a line around our kid to keep the bad habits out.

// *s* + *s* // carelessly there's too much.
Do you recycle stuff like this—flat cardboard? No. I'll take it back inside. No, give it to me, I'll throw it away. As long as I'm here.

// *s* + *s* // (People good enough to do
Some plantation connotation. Some deluge. Eat some cereal, listen to the dishwasher's song, bathe in the monitor glow. Windshear and troubled weather: "It's a drought. Conserve! Learn how at watermatters.org" says a stick-in-the-ground sign near the golf course in the wet grass. A wasteland of judgment and disapproval spreading like skin cells.

// *s* + *s* // a contrail of cultural
Graze on chips and cheese before dinner.
Drive to the nursery to buy a lime tree.
Call R or S to pick up sour cream at Publix on the way.
Drink rum while swimming.
Kiss the oldest member of the family when she arrives.
Flick our eyes past condo towers on the horizon, their balconies empty.
Go to bed early.
Text a picture of the baby.
Fiddle with spyware. Rearrange the plants. Power-wash the patio.

//*s* + *s*// and unwanting,

The mind that consigns humans, animals, plants or terrain to waste for the usual reasons is more than a gated compound whose screen door I can close and lock behind me, its garbage collected at the end of a day. Pizza congeals in the fridge; we pull pieces off the atmosphere. Look at the dark water: resting or decaying?

//*s* + *s*// waste according to a way of thinking.)

He hates mango because·he spent his childhood walking through fields of rotting mangoes.

//*s* + *s*// what other people don't want to do, wanting

Extravagantly the species wade, spear, nest, tunnel and sleep all over the peninsula. From everything sliding past to everything lined up on shelves, message and coins, the clerks behind plexiglass in one small town and unprotected in the next. And when we arrive a feeling of something between us and everything else.

//*s* + *s*// jetsam, We eat

Where are you? I'm on the other side of the world-wall, reading fat thrillers; the pool filter's choked with sadistic bullshit. I'm still thinking of me. "69 Acres Available"—dense, interlaced, resistant, full of creatures, "Now Leasing," pits of half-dug gravel. I'm a passenger. Palms and an empty billboard. Pat blames himself for the tension dispersing itself in the streets of unknown neighborhoods, then switches to ceramic batteries. In Florida, when you·build a subdivision, you have to keep a certain percentage of your land as water: "They're trying to move toward an environmentally safe golf course." Fans blow cook grease out the back. Families mean it kindly. Places are available.

//*s* + *s*// baked and scraped dirt. placed with no

He runs the gas-powered edger along the unused sidewalk, the driveway, the bougainvillea—under his long-sleeved shirt and heavy pants, what must boil, must run down . . . when they get through the last cul-de-sac in the last subdivision they go back to the first. Sun higher. A paycheck. The gates open slowly like toys. What's inside is none of your business. What's outside isn't worth it.

// s + s // away lay turf over
Microorganisms baffle at every turn: why won't you dampen? Why won't you break down? What about the kind of waste you don't collect, that's too late the minute it exists as waste? Filter this out: threat levels in excess produce more fear than we need, than the open system of the airport needs.

// s + s // hamburgers and talk about
There are dangers—fire ants and alligators. Her jewelry was stolen from her bedroom despite the gate. Lizards in the bathroom despite the screen that encloses the patio. Everything you see looks a bit darker because of it. Fine mesh of protection. The A/C laboring to stop the mold. Turn down the thermostat. "Then maybe you shouldn't live there."

// s + s // ambiguity. We idle in
She asked for the tapes from the day of the robbery and never got a call back. They must be sitting in someone's den, the association president, probably. We say "hola" as we squeeze against the truck to let him pass with his machine. Or maybe we said "hello."

// s + s // the car, waiting
The fake lake is big, with big dragonflies. The golf balls are hidden by venomous fake grass.

// s + s // for the camera to register our presence
She closes the French door every single time she enters or leaves the house. It's a heavy sliding thing and you can hear it making a seal when it shuts. Tiles cool un-

derfoot in the kitchen. We bring home a tray of ziti in the cooler but have too much fresh produce to get through, so we end up freezing it. That's OK. Our freezer is new. It won't break down.

//*s* + *s*// of the orange blanket hanging,
But the heat is coming in.
It lies on the sand.
It bubbles through coral.
It invades the white wall.
It reverses the season.
It sprays itself through hoses.
It draws pictures of trees.

//*s* + *s*// Awareness pools on
We got engineered into this deal with property and love. It cycles on and off. They patrol at 12 o'clock, 2 o'clock, 4 o'clock, 100 villas, 300 single families exploit what's inside. In the "town center", no one's outside but men hacking the grass on the verge with picks. When people praise disorder they mean disruption of this order, they mean this order as a kind of Saran wrap. What can you safely use on the broken skin of a sealed, scrubbed place, excluding by extra, much extra, three men walking by the window with lawn tools and sweating.

//*s* + *s*// will dry it shining
A couple of limes on the neighbors' lime tree have become diseased or galled, swelling yellow, corrugated and triple the hard green ones' size. "He said my uterus was like cottage cheese."

//*s* + *s*// like a restaurant lamp.
Behind the house is a vista of water. First the pool, then the lake. Between them a flag. An unused sailboat. One house on the other side keeps its shutters on the win-

dows all year—heavy steel, for hurricanes. On the western horizon is one of the only hills, behind a school. It's an odd-shaped thing, long and square. On its top white-shirted men trundle golf carts in a ferocious sun.

//s + s// through it

Hold the small soft round and tender healthy clean baby, the little demand in the air, on the ground, little suckling, little drain. Everything inside a baby should be elastic, distendable, prone to accumulation. Suckle the airport's electric. Live off the fat of the land, the grease of the water, carrots, potato chips and coffee, I say to myself, look at your sloppy self, the great shadows of animals passing under your bristles—what reaction could take place in you of value, in secret, in darkness, trawling up your guts, asking for your opinion, blogging furiously and sinking into the accusation of working *toward* nothing, you conduct yourself, reacting, collapsing, the chronic pain taste in your mouth waking up, dully, after hours, like a prophet of ruin and water—inefficient ground cover, like a tract of sticky carpet where people sit with their computers like little islands in a fertilizer bay, watching movies about pollution. The river choked with greens in patterns like lightning.

//s + s//—

It's made of garbage. It's message material from houses offices and haircut and bagel shops, gathered one blade at a time, bagged up, coated, flung, pressed, interred, vented for methane, doused, drained, pooled, and planted with sharp, uncomfortable grass. Hole in one. This is the protrusion on a table-flat state. This is the writing on the map, the end of the view, the line. Hold your hand at arm's length and count the fingers between sun and horizon. Each one is 15 minutes until sunset. Waste makes it sooner.

Robert Fitterman

LULU (Locally Unwanted Land Use)

Juice
cartons
395,1.85%.
Tickets, **ATM**,
vending 323,1.5%.
Abe**rc**rombie &
Fitch **3**88,
1.43%.

Nike 391
12.04%. Com-
mercial **pa**ckaging
and bo**xes**,1.13%.
Ham**me**rmill 728,
1.13%. Plastic
to-go **8**11,
2.04%.

Juice
cartons
395,1.85%.
Tickets, ATM,
vending 3**rc**1.5%.
Abe**rc**rombie &
Fitch 388,
1.43%.

Nike 391
12.04%. Com-
mercial **pa**ckaging
and bo**xes** 19,
Ham**me**rmill 728,
1.13%. Plastic
to-go 811,
2.04%.

Zoomburb

Ecko, Enyce, Phat Farm, AMUS, AMD, Timberland,

Coleman, Shady, FUBU,Nike, Maxtor,

Lite-On, Armani Exchange, Mecca, Lugz,

Prada,
Enermax,
Bebe,
Phat Farm, Guess, Rockawear, Puma, Polo, ABU

Garcia,
Levi's,
Chippewa, Delta, Mac, Staley,

Black Hawk, Converse, Betsey Johnson,

Craftsman, Gerber, Listerine, Columbia, Von Dutch, Oakley, Hummer, Abit,

Old Navy, Buffalo, GB, Nike, Deisel, Shox,

North Face, Iceberg, Ecko, FCUK, Lugz, Polarflow, Ocean Pacific, Nine West, Oilily, Old Navy, Adidas, Kenneth Cole, Prada,

Phat Farm, Ch **ap s** tick, Puma, Crest, Advil, Tokoyo Mauri, Hummer, Fossil, Mac, Origins,

Champion, Dove,

Coke, Pixar, Dr Pepper, Taylor, Fender,

Ocean Minded, Dove, Dial, Playboy, Minded, **Dial,** Playboy,

Audio- Tech**nica** **Pum**a, Izod, Giga, Sprite, Marlboro,

Vantec, Microsoft, Frye, Giorgio Brutini,

Audio- Technica, Puma, Izod, Giga,

Lian–Lu, Light-On,

Kate Spade, Polo, Hope, Intense, Axe, Atomlab, Red Wing, Guess,

Antec, Thompson,

Eastland, Ralph Lauren, Weight Watchers,

Dangerden, Coca-Cola,

Sprite, PolarFlow, Florsheim, Vantec, Microsoft,

Frye, Giorgio Br **um** m er, Abit,

Lian–Lu, Light-On, Deisel, Lacoste, **ea** Nauti

Seg a, Rock Shox, Red Wing, Guess, North Face, Iceberg,

Polarflow, Ocean Pacific, Nine West,

Oilily, Old Navy, Adidas, Eastland,

Ralph Freed of London,

Izod, Old Nav **y**, Quicksilver, Adidas, Lacoste, Nautica,

Apple, Uggs, Duracell,

Old Friends, Axis, Quicksilver, Maramot,

Lauren, North Face, Geox,

Kenneth Cole, Prada, Weight Watchers,

Phat Farm, **ang** Champ Stick, Deisel Freed **er** of London, Axe, Atomlab, Puma, Crest, Advil, Tokoyo Mauri, Hummer,

Light-On, Antec, Thompson, Lugz,

Polarflow, BMW, Old Navy, Ralph Lauren,

Champi on, Barilla, Pez, Hope, Chips Ahoy!,

Old Friends, Axis, Fender, Old Navy, Buffalo, Polo, Coach, Intense, GB, Puma, Deisel, Hanes, Honda,

Lacoste, Na **u** tica, Fruit Sega, of the Loom, Shady, FUBU,Nike, Maxtor, Quicksilver, Armani Exchange, Mecca, Lugz,Prada,

Fossil, Mac, Origins,Guess,

Rockawear, Puma, Dewalt, Apple, Data, **Data, Mac,**

Staley, Champion, Dove,

Reebok, Oakley, Fender, Ocean Pacific, **Pepsi, Nokia, Everlast,**

Ben & Jerry's, Wilson,

Polo, Hope, Intense, Adidas,

Western Digital, Ban,

Polo, ABU Garcia, Park-Tool, Hummer

Black Hawk, Converse, PolarFlo, Florsheim,

Maybelline, Mac, Nike, Black Hawk, Maxwell House,

Sega, Rock

Saucony,

Izod, Old Navy,

Levi's, Chippewa, American Eagle

Betsey Johnson, North Face, Ge

Tony Trigilio
Rainforests for Boneshakers

Jerk, you sat in charcoal. Raincoat tiles, stalagmite boulevards.

The blowtorch never quite washes out.

Each scrubbing cloves a bigger clue.

Early mortgage near the great lamentation.

Tsars in starlight among the raincoats. Other perch shaped like cruets . . . .

The wean, smug yellow meets your trademark.

Everyone's going somewhere . . . .

Lollipop dirty as newsprint, yakking into nightlight.

These napkins. Get a grocery on it.

You are so many yes-men ago.

Hundreds of militia where your jerk-ass sophistry came from.

I remember that nightlight, the startle you swear you saw.

Shore startles for Nostradamus. Pipeline startles for *tinctura physicorum*.

The pedal startles horizontally. An imbroglio of carbuncles.

You're due from Warsaw at 4 p.m., so bailiff I stand tingled.

Oh, lean and perfect abroad, the suitcase and greenfly for the grapevine.

Just one consignment, man. One mandible.

Jane Sprague
Politics of
the Unread

the directions maintain
fragments of "this"

pure pine pile up
sulfur rattlers bark

cut sharp with slant "L"
askance/the gaze/cut

to known pronoun/proverb/pro let aire
there is no other than that which already within you

but the bittern bark
the blades trace

path from ocean
sullied under coast

packed in like rats
shouldered up to one fine clatter manse

with no lawn

no nature

to speak of

        *

but to maintain directions—
impropriety of no one

my child comes running
pier side/dry dock/ canal stink
lip
"sharks! big fish!"
and I too late for the glimpse

though having seen them too
the histories of fishes
blunt cut any path to narrative
or narrativity
voices/voiceless
swim

        *

the way of it
the way

the place here
place of pronouns supple reach

place shark empty
place rays anchovy black jellies
pale listing to red tide

wetland reclamation space
they moved the highway

they built this island
they dredge the creamy
seamless
coast

to water to wetland to
piles to pinging depth charge
naval seal ship bevied
levied with fear
fear grips
who's the bigger dark lurker now?

         *

these days
my materia medica
some bittern arsenal
some tern-like commission
to sneak in/pull yield

they're making nests for the killdeer
sapling white pelican lesser grebe
spoonbill skimmer sea hare

dainty mole crab
with her fine fiddler freight
orange roe cake
a sample for sale

response—an utterance
what words do rise up in iris
flipped gaze the mimic
to stutter arctic—or just tic
a long thigh a long thick
finger of grease
spill leak from something
these monstrous yachts
doth offend thee oh evermore
than any Ulsan oil seep

gutter to stillness
or smother the grunions
left offspring
eke out a living at the edge of such
opening gaps

layers of oil
one shiny magenta yellow blue
not distinct
indeterminate pure petrol
absolutely bad flow
fills my neighborhood

water artery wet streets
and us no boat to row—
so the watcher, come looker
what choice her
fine foot/tucks/sidewalk to city
beach
fine picking litter—the effronter
of dunderheaded gargantua
this bottle cap
condom
cup
and again

repeat into stillness

this weekend, next—what dates
what matter
again and again we do it

bend spines to the earth
our littoral zone

White Footed Mouse

In the days of apocalypse wind blows clean and lovely

In the field of the barn wheat sways gentle under

In the line of forest mice grow stout and handsome

In the days of our remembered

In the fur of the mouse the rider

In the rider the small disease

In the disease the spirochetes snapping

In the scratching

come in

In the light of the night sky

In the memory of constellations

      *

the white footed mouse SHALL INHERIT THE EARTH the meek opportune arachnid
INHERENT THE GRANDEUR the male deer stamp in velvet BADGER FUR our thick
chambered heart HOLLOW BONE WHISTLE we of diminished consequence
TEMPEST MADE OF MOSS trampling the holy EVERY SINGLE EAGLE PART

when they went down to grassland KAOLIN CLAY FOR PREGNANT some say to
subdivide LITTLE BACKYARD LANDFILL some trap the menace deer NEW
SCIENCE PROTOCOL some wonder at their sperm count STERILE DOES ARE DEAR
some miss their hybrid hosta INSURANCE CLAIM TEN THOUSAND and cars
    and cars
and gears

there was a way, a western way
a history of lawns.
there was a place, an england place, the staid and landed gentry

below the rolling hills
below the groundlings stye
below the manor trappings

surround surround hemmed in by lawn by leaf our trifles
lawned in by grass no beasts of burden bedlam feasting
their trifle garden collection

once become betray we beckon
see them steal them mimic best
our noble tweedy classmen

herbs of the temple PURPLE LOOSESTRIFE garden herbs of hothouse toolshed
JAPANESE KNOTWEED medicine of the doorstep GOLDENROD
rip and treadle snap and treacle butter for to fat you VIRGINIA CREEPER
knifing needling vines WILD PURPLE GRAPE choking chiming threading binding

*an etymology of plants: PURPLE LOOSESTRIFE: to lose strife. to peaceful to sweeten to
bind. fragrant herb for strewing. tacit tool for gall. stones. back in the day. of laudanum
lauds. before our fine tuned landfills. we tread upon such ground.*

they plant seed instead. four hectares. four types of standard needle grasses.
lush livid limpid luxuriate languish languid languorous
our green triumph disorder

THE LEGACY OF MICE

in the apocalyptic time in the new and dawning dark time our sacred books will make
clean and ample homes for rodents. if only we had such teeth.

in the end the survivors will be the white footed mice. the ticks. the white-tailed deer. and
cockroaches. they can be trusted with our leavings. WHAT ENDURES. LASTS.

the bedcovers will be put to good use. grass will not be beaten. these few will use it well.
feed to seed and cover. KAOLIN CLAY. sparse and shallow places.

*

KENTUCKY BLUE

CRAB

FLAME

RICE

WHEAT

BAMBOO

JOHN BARLEYCORN

KAOLIN CLAY

SPIROCHETES
TICK
TICK
TICK
TICK

*

Long teeth. Curved edge. Vulnerable to hawks.

haws
brambles
berries

such small and human hands

a small place

is all

white footed mouse

white tailed deer

deer tick

these cycles

contiguous to . . . a meadow . . . contiguous to forest . . . contiguous to in the
winter . . . contiguous to the deepest winter . . . contiguous to they tunnel under
snow . . . contiguous to the drifts blow . . . connection treacherous to larger . . .
    connection to a
dog will nose in deep . . . contiguous to a doe will keep her shape . . . connection to a
thaw . . . connection to all it takes for insects . . . connection to arachnids will move
in . . . contiguous to their corpses in the freezer . . . connection to nestled into
skin . . . connection to we soaked them long in lye baths . . . contiguous to it was
    not long
enough.

connection from connection. contiguity from contiguity.

on NPR. a VOICE. a FEMALE voice. a SCIENCE nimble master.
a MOUSY girl. she's BOOKISH.

the white footed mouse will inherit the earth. no way to eradicate. tenacious and
steadfast. the suburb is their homeland. their avenues of lawns. on the mice, the ticks, in
the ticks, disease. in the grass, the mice. on the grass, the ticks. who comes loping? our
hybrid suburb deer. on the deer, the grass. in the deer the grass. on the deer the ticks. in
the blood the spirochetes. tick. when they went down to grassland. where we shot them
there. where we took off all their skin. where we found a prize. tick is an arachnid. in the
spirochetes, at the full moon, they stimulate, they wriggle. one afflicted feels this. in the
blood. in the heart. in. they've come in. and look at us: we've let them.

WHAT WE DO WITH TRIMMINGS

we soak the hide in lye. a solution of 3 parts lye to more parts water. this should loosen
off the fur. the hide of a male deer. we remove his testicles we wonder at their smallness.

their remarkable attachment. we think of his other parts and wonder where the antlers. a candelabra. or mounted in a cabin. and covered up with spiders. where is all his velvet. the lye is not working. we haul out his hide we scrape it with a blade. we do this alone in nighttime. every angle of its wrong.

in between the floors. in buckets in the garden shed. in between the walls. an anarchy of rodents.

we hear them run their long trails. we find their slatted lodge.

TO THE HIDE THE TICKS
A HUNDRED OF THEM, MORE

we give up. we lose faith in scraping. our weight is not enough. we dump the liquid poolside. the hide returns to deep freeze. it lingers there for years.

WHAT TO DO WITH WASTE

what was the cover a deer a mouse what once was congeals or turns to dust
in the GARDEN shed. a mouse. she turns to DUST in a freezer a BUCK he's stiffened
out in ice. some PART what was him. his other parts GONE DOWN to GRASSLAND.

WHAT LINGERS AT THE DOORSTEP

in the mice so cute and sweetly. an england lady, little beatrice the spinster.
these lovely little books

turning to dust dusting to turn the covers of
tucking in tightly down from the goose cotton from texas simple homely pie.
police patrolled streets exterminators cuteness tipping the newsboy stopping up drains.

and

'goodnight mummy'

and

'lights out son'

Laura Mullen

The White Box
of Mirror Dissolved
Is Not Singular

("White for diluting dreams": CY TWOMBLY*)*

Sun or eye or boat or stiff reeds on a small island rising out of their own reflection

A surface alluded to these ambiguous traces seeming to undulate like a spill of cloud against cloud or a pale drift net deep in a white ocean

These airs made of what remains of a repeated gesture

To begin with nothing

I won't tell anyone what you say here the water promises and the reeds take it up as a whisper which reaches at last the very ears gossip discovers

A reiterated *not* makes at once as surface as if removed and as modulated its horizon too high a landscape the auditor is led always deeper into and shut out of lead on lead

You'll tell I know you will

A "counter-love . . . the reflection of the love he inspires

Asleep among the stirred swirl of sweet white blossoms asleep or passed out

Felt

The impasto parents

Reading the repeated mark no ear for that

Sun or out-stretched hand or boat or empty crown spiky as a battered flower

These airs made of traces of the first repeated gesture "and a cloud came by and it broke apart on the tower. A small piece of it came in my window and floated across the room

No ear for that music

Even now I can barely talk about the erasure what should have been pleasure the sense of something lived through the horizon line over my head shame a stiff weight parts

Under a thick white sky the impasto parents the edge loss

I sought on surfaces too fragile to breathe on almost the signs of trauma they endured

Orographic

Flat sky light as elsewhere light as reference to light to look up later coming in with
a vague idea of the meaning what you meant by what was meant

Nothing to trust
but the repetition

Long silences ("I have," he said, flatly
"No interiority.")

Only the charm and thread
Alphabet

Rustling of pages rustling of cattle rust

High thin featureless clouds in fact
Contingencies
Conversations about what to pack

What is good enough *intelligence*

As glowing discovering edges layers in what seemed featureless light as what you
meant to say the switched because you forgot or found as you were speaking an-
other better word for it

Exactly light that

"I'm working too hard right now," he said, "no time for . . ."
Why not change it
Intended

The book is thick, the woods are thick, the plot

Or back
Inflict thicket

"Only a fear of death which keeps me up at night."

"First faint haze of green"
Stuck interpellant

In what sense
In every sense

Joyelle McSweeney

Arcadia, or, Anachronism: A Necropastoral Effigy

1. The radio told me about the death of Billy the Kid.

2. The Martians told me.

3. Something [Or, Art] is always in media, in medias res.

4. In transit. Sick Transit.

5. Radio Arcadia: the membrane becomes inflamed. Begins to signal. A medium for media. Stigmatas, sarcomas: floods the scene with Art.

6. "Blood was its Avatar and its seal—the redness and the horror of blood. There were sharp pains, and sudden dizziness, and then profuse bleeding at the pores, with dissolution. The scarlet stains up the body and especially upon the face of the victim were the pest ban which shut him out from the aid and from the sympathy of his fellow-men. And the whole seizure, progress, and termination of the disease, were the incidents of half and hour." "The Masque of the Red Death: A Mask."

7. In which the courtiers flee the plague for the countryside, bringing the plague with them. And maketh of the countryside a horror show, a mise-en-abyme, a masque of the fuckedup city, a wrecked and bleeding eye.

8. Radio Obscura. Now I is a camera, bleeds through walls. An eye that doesn't see but leaks.

9. Thy theme park is Death, and Death thy entrance fee.

10. "[The Velvet Underground] won't replace anything, except maybe suicide." —Cher, 1966

11. Et in Acadia Ego.

12. Arcadia, Or, Death. A fluid and a shunt. A permanent and spasming dilation. Radio Arcadia: Sur la Plage. While the King dozed on his beachtowel at Juan Le Pins, his bathing togs striped like a gently breathing tent, the Nazis marched down the Champs Élysées; necrotically; the narcotic poison poured in through the ear. The ear drum saturated, spasming with fluid, struck the brain with a permanently resounding noise. *Tintinnabulation.* This clangor means *catastrophe*, and this swoon means *syncope*. The radio told me: A contraction of the market. A slit and shuddering eye. Just wants to make a hole in itself and flood out of its own side. A diaphragming market: flexes concave,convex. Strikes (itself) like a bell. Like a tarn, a tear or tear in which is reflected a non-identical double. Through some freak of light. An evil eye, a wound shedding difference. Uncontrollable bleeding of debt and time. Steeped in hemorrhage: Arcadia. Hematomic Arcadia. Or Art. Or

13. Arcadia, or Anachronism. A Golden Age, a prehistory somehow concurrent with the present tense; a presumptively sumptuous version of the afterlife, sharing its Elysian geography, weather, and customs. A Velvet Underground.

14. An expensive shopping street, a high rent district: Elysian Field.

15. Exorbitance, expenditure: growing at an exponential rate. Doubling, and more than doubling. Rising and digging: a paradox. A convulsing sublime.

16. She wanted to be die, and to live in Paris. So she ran up unsustainable debts (deaths). *Mort*gages. Expenditures. So then she took a purgative. It dissolved her tooth enamel like the whitest, smallest shoon. Like the Pope's shoes, so admired by Petit Richard.

17. Purple spots on a thigh; sarcoma; or, purple prose: the clean form glutted with genre. To succumb in several months to a disease old men lived with for several decades. To be glutted and junked. Genre, Or Anachronism, Or Illness, Or, Death.

18. "Who wants to be famous? Who wants to die for Art?" —Divine, Baltimore.

19. The Afterlife: A Necropastoral. There scum will be superstars, but the stars won't rise. The uppers shall be downers. In slime. A convulsive sublime.

20. I wrote a pastoral about a girl suicide bomber from Chechnya. Snub nosed, she posed with a snub nosed pistol (mise en abyme). Draped in a veil, and draped around her young dead husband's shoulders, she blew up the terminal line. She blew up the terminal (the underground). It was in all the papers (electronic edition).

21. Letters on a wet black bough.

22. Germinal.

23. Broadcast.

24. Springtime. With hise Shoures soot. The radio told me:

25. Silence goes faster backwards. I repeat:

26. I had an *at home* experience.

27. I shoop me into shroudes as I a sheep were.

28. I built a *hameau* there. At Versailles. (Turned eye. Wink, wink. Do you know me? (applause)) I had to get away from the fountains like eyes with plugs in their sockets. From the mirror halls with their cycles on repeat: an eye for an eye. Mise en scene: Mise en abyme. (applause) I tried to short the circuit by plugging into another time. And so to my idyll, my waste of time. I slipped on my wig like a head of steam. Adorned with miniature sailing ships, cotton and chattel. But once I reached my *hameau*, it came off. The dial set to idle. My frock, plain cotton. Did you know I invented the shift as outerwear? *Pop makes the outside the inside and the inside the outside*—Rousseau. The cows were cleaned of their cud, grime and defecant, and the churns were made of porcelain imitating wood. O hameau, O seasons! I sank into my rustic Arts, and I never emerged; that is, I never emerged intact. In the opera, I sat in the bowl of the eye, macular in my maquillage, I was the apple of each raised lorgnette, a carefully painted apple, they called me La Lunette, for the hole in the throat where the guillotine winks. No guillotine, wrong scene. To return to my hameau, my theme: What happened next made every eye stand up on its stalk like, citoyens! Those grounds were grounds for my conviction: I lost my head. For the movie trailer, the trailer which precedes, I ran backwards through the nouvelle popsong without a thought. Bleeding from the neck like a farmyard animal. Ahem. A hen. Or singing through my own throat like a pig. Then I found my head, packed up all the blood in my trunk. The film began again. Anachronism: a counterfeit bill I could spend. It made me feel/like the only girl in the world.

29. Chechyna: certainly that's a pastoral. Those people just have nothing but suicide.

30. History? We'll all be dead.

31. As in, Bomb them back into the *stone age*.

32. "I'm tired of looking like a shepherd boy," Robert said, inspecting his hair in the mirror. "Can you cut it like a fifties rock star?" Though I was greatly attached to his unruly curls, I got out my shears and thought rocakabilly as I snipped. I sadly picked up a lock and pressed it in a book, while Robert, taken with this new image, lingered at the mirror.

33. Simon was infected with cryptosporidium, a parasite that normally inhabits the bowels of sheep.
   "What do you do with sheep that get this? he asked eagerly.
   "There is no treatment," the expert said. "We shoot them."

34. Mourning in America. Again:

35. "It only took a slightly metaphorical imagination to transform the Seine into the river Lethe; because the phantasmagoria were principally located on its banks, there was not one quai . . . which did not offer you a little phantom at the end of the dark corridor or at the top of a tortuous staircase." 1790.

36. "When the subject blacks out, it is always possible that he might find himself elsewhere in another form." Et in Arcadia Ego. "If brass wakes up a trumpet, it's not its fault."

37. We had to find a way to cross the blood brain barrier, just like the virus could. Otherwise the virus would go into hiding the brain, just like an aristocrat fleeing the plague, just like a parasite fleeing *Citoyen Medicine*. So we put it in a spike, shot it right up into the spinal fluid. Like,

38. Alma shot up into her forehead. Like

39. The radio told me, "The real work will be your metamorphosis into your evil twin."

40. "Grace had changed. Four years earlier a meeting of occurrences had precipitated, or suddenly there was a man who had been a marine dead who was in her. She would be running out, it would be him running. [. . .] He'd been Special Forces, an assassin when he was alive; she hadn't known him but she would feel the presence of his activities, 'ghosts of actions she had done' which were apparently his, or hers."

Enviolenced. Persophoned. Impersonated. Possessed by Media. Transported to the Velvet Underworld. [Art]. Shooped into shroudes.

41. There dilating, like Janet Leigh's eye. There relaxing in my iridium. In my rainbow room/shroud.

42. Weeping wound. Shedding copies of itself.

43. Counterfeits. Each flaw in the iris: blown up. Recounts the tale. The same but different. Anachronism.

44. Eye's issue. Floods and drains. Floods elsewhere, drains again.

45. Et in Vertigo ego. Dot dot dot. Anachronism: the retrovirus. Blow Up: the sequel. The sequestered, long-anticipated prequel. Now running on several screens at The Oasis. Le Mirage. Sur le plage, the necrotic landscape convulsing with germination, supparating time. The necrophilic cloud goes bulbous over the white and powdered boys. The pedophilic cloud admires their draped and wasted forms. The narcissistic cloud begins to flake likes the cheeks of the sleeping boys . Mise en abyme: Opaque and dissolute mirrors. Flawed copies.

46. Now I am another.

NOTES

Jack Spicer; Poe; Cher; Madame Bovary; John Waters, *Role Models* (FSG, 2010); Andy Warhol; Patti Smith, *Just Kids* (Ecco, 2010); Randy Shilts, *And the Band Played On: Politics, People, and the AIDS Epidemic* (St. Martin's, 1987); Terry Castle, *The Female Thermometer: Eighteenth-Century Culture and the Invention of the Uncanny* (OUP, 1995); Leslie Scalapino, *Dahlia's Iris: Secret Autobiography & Fiction* (FC2, 2003); Catherine Clement, *Syncope: The Philosophy of Rapture* (U. of Minnesota, 1994; trans. Sally O'Driscoll and Dierdre Mahoney); Alice Notley. Rimbaud.

Stephen Collis

Blackberries

thrust out backward bramble common

no visible fairyland utopian terse

my companion and I along

blue wall sudden as children

throwing the baby in red

dress frozen the quilted thrush

no other interest save pecuniary

voluntary huckle berry party affect

the hedgerow the light dissolving

onto mercury flash paper prints

the owl the sod the

soft gravelly banks elastic nature

confounds vagrant meandering river wrecks

strew bottoms rivulet shrubs nuthatch

thither all birds in woods

spring nights and chickadee lisps

especially for aldermen and epicures

do not feed the imagination

as study out of doors

let alone your garden cease

I am astonished quenching click

focus on bramble berry dell

over against self window us

a vision compelling in part

scattering a legion about one

my companion whispers between berries

the glory of architecture grows

many an unnoticed wild berry

vespertinal habits the walking of

which the springs of life

growing imaginary alternatives to chainlink

marginalia of suburban texts rubus

remains august edges improvements converts

leaves gentrified junk swagged with

fruit taking to the fences

points unjoined canes lines spreading

indefinitely spreading lines curving fruit

centres circumference euclid arcs radius

all right angles are incongruent

infinitely many intersecting commons coil

to find wind sudden together

along roadside untended curving canes

walk fields wood since selves

those which you have fetched

yourself carry us thither baskets

shake off village return senses

prospect harmony radius never quite

familiar of all large trees

people would begin mere objects

to the state burning fences

a rare red low being

where it grows prickles sparingly

this sound information in fives

sides of canes and leaves

fifth berry of the year

trundled amongst trees to offer

form to swallows songs or

robins trying to recognize the

shape of a nest amongst

tangle of twigs and bramble

found in emerson antennae and

stamina fuller dial rejected downcast

delight and interjected this else

solitary and clear perception was

no apples theft from others

orchard each fruit wild and

independent of any other though

many taken together make a

better tart or with cream

as his almost constant companion

to monopolize the little gothic

window then did I use

with eyes upturned the clouds

to wander in rich drapery

that I might peep a

truant hawk or write a

brief obituary as to what

of the beautiful it had

lived election amongst the plants

feeding all kinds of pensioners

everything miracle spore sated geometry

found equinox thrusting words having

no connection into all parts

of every sentence boot jack

for instance taking liberty nothing

and no place ventured gained

to whit the berries abundance

how could any contain scarcity

this many hands picking sense

to gather scrutiny shared provenance

in moist woods and thickets

shoots tinge the earth crimson

my liberty is in wandering

to what nothing owns but

blackberries tangle throughout the fringe

up to the town in

trinkets beyond nature's own growth

the fruit which I celebrate

growing everywhere we cannot purchase

leaning into the dark cluster

scituate wandering lines in cool

atmosphere frothed linen sweet attire

the pleasure of gathering together

the wreaths of black fruit

cottonwood smell ripe hawks' truancy

to call crows clatter we

see so much only as

we already possess jointly together

a pronoun a basket bushel

collected selves between no others

thursday they awoke their tents

in a corn barn abandoned

friday dawned clear sunday and

monday devoted to mountains awoke

to find autumn continuing rapidly

downstream wind through haze of

memory purchased an apple pie

nature under a veil there

in town or beaten common

the neglected bramble tangles property

I hear of service berries

poke weed juniper vines dross

the creaking of the earths

axle where the beauty is

in mosses along dry leaves

or lifting the leaves the

meadow mouse has slept in

the mutter of aperture saying

we only to themselves alone

another memory of strained light

stood clasped in brother's scarlatina

consolation a visiting daguerrotypist dawn

burnt chemical pyre watchful of

nurses and friends goodbyes nimble

the nuthatch unlocked his health

on fences forgotten between properties

the very roadsides a fruit

garden all culture aims to

secure though I've heard of

pickers ordered out of fields

october tinged poetry confound change

leaves with withered ones ensued

island no concord runs a-blur

look ma no hands triumph

so do leaves the pellicle

earth show of many fruits

which we ignore softening already

in shade till near end

of august thick enough to

pick as some idler's folly

I understand nothing of illness

what grows out against our

other springings this spent thistle

sending its spores adoring leaving

as only a short excursion

look this is a print

of the night sky unfolding

look these are my loved

ones uttering chaos I only

see the beginning of bereavement

earliest reddening woodbine the lake

of radical leaves hickory beautifully

flecked turn over its leaves

and through oaks and aspens

spotted leaves gloaming brakes of

purple grasses red maple elm

fallen sugar scarlet patches glow

I begin to see children

the first ripe blackberries thereabouts

scarcely rising above the ground

lookout shadowy boxers lineage palimpsest

vogue mixt with twillberry oft

picked haversack full of berries

gone to saunter and free

to culture flint the forest

filled on long peduncles lifted

in the shade of pines

different variety from the common

counting berries five a fist

plenty sprung on unwanted easements

built subtle shack on common

turned back clock solitary nary

chipmunk dug borrowed mowed berried

thrift silent merchant spent days

mellowing this captioned self gave

banks mud warmed winged life

those large and late low

whortle spur snare buck prune

run over common dense clusters

clammy acid taste countless variety

true flavor never purchased obtained

lost with the bloom become

mere provender thus finished errand

miles off midst endless berries

nowhere states seen history prisons

amidst sweet fern and sumac

or growing more rankly in

low ground by rich roadsides

what no one owns shared

thus our blackberries remnant commons

Chris Green
A-Pastoral

; more
plotless   (the pregant swale—   vega);
—babes nevergreen   —   *Unfoldment*   is   grown
        so radix.

        Dear ear of corn,   I
        hose your auricle, whisper styl(o)-   or
        megasporophyll.

        Jungly, overgrown,   I   legume—
why so weedy,   cocci-;   ?

Macbeth
for Everyone

Hurlyburly: *hurly-*
burly
hurlyburly.

Nature is
          weird
: be not so happy.

Joshua Corey is the author most recently of *Severance Songs* (Tupelo Press, 2011), which won the Dorset Prize and was named a Notable Book of 2011 by the Academy of American Poets. His other books are *Selah* (Barrow Street Press, 2003) and *Fourier Series* (Spineless Books, 2005). He has recently completed his first novel and lives in Evanston, Illinois with his wife and daughter and teaches English at Lake Forest College.

G. C. Waldrep's most recent full-length collections are *Archicembalo* (Tupelo, 2009), winner of the Dorset Prize, and *Your Father on the Train of Ghosts* (BOA Editions, 2011), a collaboration with John Gallaher. His most recent chapbook is "St. Laszlo Hotel" (Projective Industries, 2011). He lives in Lewisburg, Pennsylvania, where he teaches at Bucknell University, edits the journal *West Branch*, and serves as editor-at-large for *The Kenyon Review*.

Emily Abendroth is a writer and artist currently residing in Philadelphia, where she co-curates the Moles not Molar Reading & Performance Series. Her print publications include: *Exclosures {#1-8}*, forthcoming from Albion Press; *Toward Eadward Forward* from Horse Less Press; *Property : None / Property : Undone*, a broadside and multi-media collaboration with TapRoot Editions; and an extended excerpt from the book-length work-in-progress "Muzzle Blast Dander" in *Refuge/Refugee* (Vol 3 of the ChainLinks book series).

Will Alexander is a poet, novelist, essayist, playwright, philosopher, aphorist, and visual artist who has published over 20 books. His latest works include *Compression & Purity, Diary as Sin, Inside The Earthquake Palace, Mirach Speaks To His Grammatical Transparents,* and *The Brimstone Boat*. In addition to the above he remains visually active, drawing in both black and white and colour, while also instructing himself on piano.

Rae Armantrout is the author of eleven books of poetry, most recently *Next Life; Versed* (which won the 2009 National Book Critics Circle Award and the 2010 Pulitzer Prize for Poetry); and *Money Shot,* all published by Wesleyan University Press. Her work has appeared in many anthologies, including *Postmodern American Poetry* (Norton), *American Women Poets of the 21st Century* (Wesleyan), *The Oxford Book of American Poetry, American Hybrid* (Norton), and *The New Anthology of American Poetry 3: Postmodernism to the Present* (Rutgers). She teaches writing at the University of California-San Diego.

Eric Baus is the author of *The To Sound,* winner of the Verse Prize (Verse Press/Wave Books, 2004), *Tuned Droves* (Octopus Books, 2009), and *Scared Text,* winner of the Colorado Prize for poetry, selected by Cole Swensen (Colorado State University Press, 2011), as well as several chapbooks. His commentary column on poetry audio recordings, *Notes on PennSound,* recently appeared in *Jacket2*. He lives in Denver, where he co-edits Marcel Chapbooks with Andrea Rexilius.

Dan Beachy-Quick is the author of five books of poetry, including *Circle's Apprentice* and *Spell*. He is also the author of two collections of prose, *A Whaler's Dictionary* and *Wonderful Investigations*. He teaches in the MFA Writing Program at Colorado State University.

John Beer is the author of *The Waste Land and Other Poems* (Canarium, 2010), which received the Norma Farber First Book Award from the Poetry Society of America. He is currently at work on a book-length fake translation of Friedrich Schlegel's 1799 novel *Lucinde*; in addition to the selection included in this volume, a portion of the work in progress was published in 2012 by Spork Press. A former drama critic for *Time Out Chicago*, he currently lives in Portland, OR, where he teaches in the MFA program at Portland State University.

Mei-mei Berssenbrugge was born in Beijing and grew up in Massachusetts. She is the author of twelve books of poetry, including *Empathy* (Station Hill Press), *Nest* (Kelsey Street Press), and *I Love Artists, New and Selected Poems* (University of California Press), and *Hello, the Roses*, forthcoming from New Directions. A collaboration with Richard Tuttle about communicating with plants will open in the Munich Kunstverein, fall 2012. She lives in New York City and northern New Mexico.

Sherwin Bitsui is the author of two poetry books, *Flood Song* (Copper Canyon, 2009), and *Shapeshift* (University of Arizona Press, 2003). His honors include a 2011 Lannan Literary Fellowship, a 2011 Native Arts & Cultures Foundation Artist Fellowship for Literature, a 2010 PEN Open Book Award, an American Book Award, and a Whiting Writers Award. He is originally from Baa'oogeedí (White Cone, Arizona on the Navajo Nation). He is Diné of the Todich'íi'nii (Bitter Water Clan), born for the Tł'ízíláni (Many Goats Clan).

Kamau Brathwaite, born in Barbados in 1930, is an internationally celebrated poet, performer, and cultural theorist. Co-founder of the Caribbean Artists Movement, he was educated at Pembroke College, Cambridge and the University of Sussex in the U.K. He has served on the board of directors of UNESCO's History of Mankind project since 1979, and as cultural advisor to the government of Barbados from 1975–1979 and since 1990. His many books include *The Zea Mexican Diary* (1993, a *Village Voice* Book of the Year), *Middle Passages* (1994), *Ancestors* (2001), and *Born to Slow Horses* (Wesleyan, 2005), which won the International Griffin Poetry Prize. He is currently a professor of comparative literature at New York University, and shares his time between CowPastor, Barbados, and New York City.

Susan Briante is the author of *Pioneers in the Study of Motion* (Ahsahta, 2007) and *Utopia Minus* (Ahsahta, 2011). Her chapbook, *The Market is a Parasite that Looks like a Nest*, part of an on-going lyric investigation of the stock market, was recently published by Dancing Girl Press. She is an associate professor of literature and creative writing at the University of Texas at Dallas. She lives in east Dallas with the poet Farid Matuk.

Oni Buchanan's poetry books include *Must a Violence* (Kuhl House Poets, 2012), *Spring* (National Poetry Series, published by the University of Illinois Press, 2008), and *What*

Animal (University of Georgia Press, 2003). Buchanan is also a concert pianist, actively performing across the U.S. and abroad, as well as founder and director of Ariel Artists, a Boston-based management company which represents a national roster of classical and contemporary-classical musicians pursuing visionary performance projects.

Heather Christle is the author of three poetry collections: *What Is Amazing* (Wesleyan, 2012), *The Trees The Trees* (Octopus, 2011), and *The Difficult Farm* (Octopus, 2009). She has taught at the University of Massachusetts, Amherst, and at Emory University, where she was the 2009–2011 Creative Writing Fellow in Poetry. She is the Web Editor for *jubilat* and frequently a writer in residence at the Juniper Summer Writing Institute. A native of Wolfeboro, New Hampshire, she lives in western Massachusetts.

Stephen Collis is the author of four books of poetry, the most recent of which, *On the Material* (Talonbooks, 2010), was the recipient of the 2011 Dorothy Livesay Poetry Prize. Forthcoming books include *A History of Change (vol.1): Dispatches from the Occupation* (Talonbooks, 2012) and *To the Barricades* (Talonbooks, 2013). He teaches poetry and poetics at Simon Fraser University, where he is a 2011/12 Shadbolt Fellow; since October 2011 he has been involved in Occupy Vancouver, writing for occupyvancouvervoice.com.

Jack Collom was born in Chicago in 1931 and spent much of his youth birdwatching in the Illinois woods. A Coloradan since 1947, he's had 25 books and chapbooks of poetry published. He has abundantly evoked creative writing from children of all ages and teaches Eco-Lit and Community Outreach at Naropa University. His experimental prose and poetry hybrid *Second Nature* is forthcoming from Instance Press.

Phil Cordelli is or has been a poet, editor, translator (amateur), filmmaker, painter, farmer, gardener, teacher, carpet cleaner, dishwasher, waiter, surveyor (one who passes out surveys), Marine (by mistake), marine biologist (also by mistake), courier, activist (for one day), and probably a few other things along the way. He currently resides in the hilltowns of western Massachusetts. He is the author of *New Wave* (Blazevox, 2008), *Book of Letters/Book of Numbers* (Agnes Fox, 2010), and *Manual of Woody Plants* (forthcoming from Ugly Duckling Presse).

Theodore Zachary Cotler is the author of *House with a Dark Sky Roof* (Salt, 2011) and *Sonnets to the Humans* (Ahsahta, 2013), winner of the Sawtooth Poetry Prize. He is a founding editor of *The Winter Anthology*.

Brent Cunningham is a writer, publisher, and visual artist living in Oakland, California. He has published two books of poetry, *Bird & Forest* (Ugly Duckling Presse, 2005) and *Journey to the Sun* (Atelos, 2012). He currently works as the Operations Director at

Small Press Distribution in Berkeley. He and Neil Alger are the co-founders of Hooke Press, a chapbook press dedicated to publishing short runs of poetry, criticism, theory, writing and ephemera. Since at least the Clinton administration he has been working on a novel.

Canadian poet and essayist **Christopher Dewdney** is best known for his work engaging the landscape of his native Ontario. Winner of the 2007 Harbourfront Festival Prize, he is the author of fifteen books, four of which were finalists for Canada's Governor's General Award (three in poetry and one in nonfiction). He lives in Toronto and teaches at York University.

Timothy Donnelly is the author of *Twenty-seven Props for a Production of Eine Lebenszeit* and *The Cloud Corporation*, winner of the 2012 Kingsley Tufts Poetry Award. He has been poetry editor of *Boston Review* since 1996. He has served as the Theodore H. Holmes '51 and Bernice Holmes Visiting Professor at Princeton University's Program in Creative Writing and Lewis Center for the Arts and is on the permanent faculty of the Writing Program at Columbia University's School of the Arts. He lives in Brooklyn with his wife and two daughters.

Michael Dumanis is author of *My Soviet Union* (University of Massachusetts Press, 2007), winner of the Juniper Prize for Poetry, and coeditor, with poet Cate Marvin, of *Legitimate Dangers: American Poets of the New Century* (Sarabande, 2006). From 2007 to 2012 he served as Director of the Cleveland State University Poetry Center. In 2012 he joined the literature faculty of Bennington College.

Camille T. Dungy is author of *Smith Blue, Suck on the Marrow,* and *What to Eat, What to Drink, What to Leave for Poison;* editor of *Black Nature: Four Centuries of African American Nature Poetry;* co-editor of *From the Fishouse: An Anthology of Poems that Sing, Rhyme, Resound, Syncopate, Alliterate, and Just Plain Sound Great;* and assistant editor of *Gathering Ground: A Reader Celebrating Cave Canem's First Decade.* Her honors include fellowships from the National Endowment for the Arts, the Virginia Commission for the Arts, Cave Canem, and the Bread Loaf Writers Conference; a 2011 American Book Award; a silver medal in the 2011 California Book Award; and two Northern California Book Awards. Dungy is currently a professor in the Creative Writing Department at San Francisco State University.

Marcella Durand's books include *Deep Eco Pré,* a collaboration with Tina Darragh published by Little Red Leaves in 2009; *Area,* published by Belladonna Books in 2008; and *Traffic & Weather,* a site-specific book-length poem written during a residency at the

Lower Manhattan Cultural Council in downtown Manhattan (Futurepoem, 2008). She lives with her husband and son in New York City, where she is a student of natural urban systems.

Lisa Fishman's five books include *FLOWER CART* (Ahsahta, 2011), *Current* (Parlor Press, 2011), and *The Happiness Experiment* (Ahsahta, 2007). Her chapbooks include "at the same time as scattering" (Albion Books, 2010) and "Lining" (Boxwood Editions, 2009). She lives in Orfordville, Wisconsin, where she and her husband, with the help of friends, have farmed 11 acres (orchards, berries, vegetables) for thirteen years, selling the produce and unpasteurized cider at farmers' markets and a few restaurants in Madison. They plan to convert to working with horses instead of a tractor over time.

Robert Fitterman is the author of twelve books of poetry, including *Metropolis,* published in four volumes. Other titles include *Holocaust Museum* (Veer, 2011), *now we are friends* (Truck Books, 2010), *Rob the Plagiarist* (Roof, 2009), and *Notes on Conceptualisms,* co-authored with Vanessa Place (Ugly Duckling Presse, 2009). He is the founder of *Collective Task,* a collective of over twenty artists and writers. He has collaborated with several visual artists including Tim Davis, Nayland Blake, Dirk Rowntree, Cheryl Donegan, Penelope Umbrico, and Klaus Killisch. He teaches writing and poetry at New York University and Bard College's Milton Avery School of Graduate Studies. http://homepages .nyu.edu/~rmf1

Forrest Gander was born in the Mojave Desert but grew up, for the most part, in Virginia. He has degrees in geology and English literature. His recent books include *Core Samples from the World* and (with John Kinsella) *Redstart: An Ecological Poetics.* His most recent translations include Pura López Colomé's Villaurrutia Award-winning *Watchword* and (with Kyoko Yoshida) *Spectacle & Pigsty: Selected Poems of Kiwao Nomura.* A United States Artists Rockefeller Fellow, Gander is recipient of fellowships from PEN, the NEA, the Guggenheim, Howard, Witter Bynner and Whiting foundations. He is the Adele Kellenberg Seaver Professor of Literary Arts and Comparative Literature at Brown University.

Merrill Gilfillan was born in Ohio in 1945. He has lived in the American West since 1980, Colorado for the most part. When he tunes his zither, coyotes howl. Recent books include *Undanceable* and *The Bark of the Dog* (poetry) and *The Warbler Road* (essays).

C. S. Giscombe was born in Dayton, Ohio. His poetry books are *Prairie Style*, *Giscome Road*, *Here*, and *Postcards*; his prose book—about Canada—is *Into and Out of Dislocation*. *Prairie Style* was awarded a 2008 American Book Award by the Before Columbus

Foundation and *Giscome Road* won the 1998 Carl Sandburg Prize, given by the Chicago Public Library. He is the 2010 recipient of the Stephen Henderson Award in poetry, given by the African-American Literature and Culture Society. His writing has appeared in several anthologies—the *Best American Poetry* series, the *Oxford Anthology of African-American Poetry, Telling It Slant: Avant-Garde Poetics of the 1990s, Bluesprint: Black British Columbia Literature and Orature, American Hybrid,* the *&Now Awards/ Best Innovative Writing* series, etc. He teaches poetry at the University of California, Berkeley.

Peter Gizzi is the author of *Threshold Songs* (Wesleyan, 2011), *The Outernationale* (Wesleyan, 2007), *Some Values of Landscape and Weather* (Wesleyan, 2003), *Artificial Heart* (Burning Deck, 1998), and *Periplum* (Avec Books, 1992). His honors include the Lavan Younger Poet Award from the Academy of American Poets (1994) and fellowships in poetry from The Howard Foundation (1998), The Foundation for Contemporary Arts (1999), and The John Simon Guggenheim Memorial Foundation (2005). Recent editing projects include *My Vocabulary Did This to Me: The Collected Poetry of Jack Spicer* (2008, Wesleyan) and serving as Poetry Editor for *The Nation* (2007 to 2011). In 2011 he was the Judith E Wilson Visiting Fellow in Poetry at Cambridge University. He lives in western Massachusetts and works at the University of Massachusetts, Amherst.

Jody Gladding's most recent poetry collection is *Rooms and Their Airs* (Milkweed Editions, 2009). She has translated many books from French, including Jean Giono's *Serpent of Stars* and Pierre Michon's *Small Lives,* which won the 2009 French-American Foundation Translation Prize. She lives in East Calais, Vermont and teaches poetry in the MFA in Writing Program at Vermont College of the Fine Arts. These are her first translations from Bark Beetle.

Johannes Göransson is the author of several books—including, most recently, *Entrance to a colonial pageant in which we all begin to intricate* and *Haute Surveillance* (forthcoming 2012)—and the translator of several books of Swedish poetry, including most recently *With Deer* and *Transfer Fat*, both by Aase Berg. He is the co-editor of Action Books and writes for www.Montevidayo.com. He teaches at the University of Notre Dame.

Chris Green is the author of two books of poetry: *Epiphany School* and *The Sky Over Walgreens*. His poetry has appeared in such journals as *Poetry, Verse, Court Green, North American Review,* and *RATTLE*. He edited the anthology *A Writer's Congress: Chicago Poets on Barack Obama's Inauguration,* and he is co-editor of *Brute Neighbors: Urban Nature Poetry, Prose & Photography*. He teaches in the English Department at DePaul University.

Arielle Greenberg is the co-author, with Rachel Zucker, of *Home/Birth: A Poemic* (1913 Press, 2011), and author of *My Kafka Century* (Action Books, 2005), *Given* (Verse, 2002) and the chapbooks *Shake Her* (Dusie Kollektiv, 2009; to be republished by Ugly Duckling Presse in 2012) and *Farther Down: Songs from the Allergy Trials* (New Michigan, 2003). She is co-editor of three anthologies: with Rachel Zucker, *Starting Today: 100 Poems for Obama's First 100 Days* (Iowa, 2010) and *Women Poets on Mentorship: Efforts and Affections* (Iowa, 2008); and with Lara Glenum, *Gurlesque* (Saturnalia, 2010). In 2011 she left a tenured position in poetry at Columbia College Chicago to move with her family to a small town in rural Maine. She now teaches out of her home and writes a regular column on contemporary poetry and poetics for the *American Poetry Review*.

Richard Greenfield is the author of *Tracer* (Omnidawn. 2009) and *A Carnage in the Love-trees* (University of California Press, 2003). He was born in Hemet, California, spent his early childhood in Southern California, and later lived in the Pacific Northwest. He is currently a professor at New Mexico State University in Las Cruces.

Sarah Gridley is the author of two books of poetry: *Weather Eye Open* (2005) and *Green is the Orator* (2010), both from the University of California Press. Her poems have appeared in *Crazyhorse, Denver Quarterly, Gulf Coast, jubilat, New American Poetry*, and *Slope*. Poems included in this collection also appear in her third book, *Loom* (Omnidawn, 2013). She is an assistant professor of English at Case Western Reserve University.

E. Tracy Grinnell is the author of *Helen: A Fugue* (Belladonna Elder Series #1, 2008), *Some Clear Souvenir* (O Books, 2006), and *Music or Forgetting* (O Books, 2001), as well as the limited edition chapbooks *Mirrorly, A Window* (flynpyntar press, 2009), *Leukadia* (Trafficker Press, 2008), *Hell and Lower Evil* (Lyre Lyre Pants on Fire, 2008), and *Humoresque* (Blood Pudding/Dusie #3, 2008), *Quadriga* (a collaboration with Paul Foster Johnson: gong chapbooks, 2006), *Of the Frame* (Portable Press at Yo-Yo Labs, 2004), and *Harmonics* (Melodeon Poetry Systems, 2000). She has taught creative writing at the Pratt Institute, Brown University, and in the Summer Writing Program at Naropa University. She lives in Brooklyn, New York, where she is the founding editor and director of Litmus Press.

Gabriel Gudding is the author of *Rhode Island Notebook* (Dalkey Archive, 2007) and *A Defense of Poetry* (Pitt, 2002). His essays and poems appear in such periodicals as *Harper's Magazine, The Nation,* and *Journal of the History of Ideas* and in such anthologies as *Great American Prose Poems, Best American Poetry*, and *&Now: Best Innovative Writing*. His translations from Spanish appear in anthologies such as *The Oxford Book of Latin American Poetry, Poems for the Millennium*, and *The Whole Island: Six Decades of Cuban Poetry*. His essays and poems have been translated into French, Danish, Vietnamese, and Spanish. He teaches poetics, ethics, literature, and poetry writing at Illinois State University.

Joshua Harmon is the author of two books of poems—*Le Spleen de Poughkeepsie* and

Scape—and a novel, *Quinnehtukqut*. His writing has received fellowships from the National Endowment for the Arts and the Rhode Island State Council on the Arts. He lives in western Massachusetts.

Nathan Hauke was born and raised in rural Michigan. He is the author of *In the Marble of Your Animal Eyes* (Publication Studio, 2012), and the chapbooks *SEWN* (Horse Less Press, 2011) and *In the Living Room* (Lame House Press, 2010). His poetry has been published in *American Letters & Commentary, Colorado Review, Denver Quarterly, Interim,* and *New American Writing*, among others. He is co-editor of Ark Press.

Lyn Hejinian is the author of numerous books, including *The Book of a Thousand Eyes* (Omnidawn, 2012), *The Language of Inquiry* (University of California Press, 2000), and *The Wide Road,* written in collaboration with Carla Harryman (Belladonna, 2010). In Fall 2012, Wesleyan University Press is republishing her best-known book, *My Life,* in an edition that will include her related work, *My Life in the Nineties.* In addition to literary writing, editing, and translating, she has in recent years been involved in anti-privatization activism at the University of California, Berkeley, where she teaches.

A graduate of the Iowa Writers' Workshop, **Mary Hickman** lives in Iowa City where she runs Cosa Nostra Editions with Robert Fernandez and makes artist's books with the Center for the Book.

Brenda Hillman is the author of eight collections of poetry, all published by Wesleyan University Press, the most recent of which are *Cascadia* (2001) and *Pieces of Air in the Epic* (2005), which received the William Carlos Williams Prize for Poetry, and *Practical Water* (2009). With Patricia Dienstfrey, she edited *The Grand Permission: New Writings on Poetics and Motherhood* (Wesleyan, 2003). Hillman teaches at St. Mary's College in Moraga, California where she is Olivia Filippi Professor of Poetry.

Kevin Holden is the author of two books, *Alpine* (White Queen) and *Identity* (Cannibal Books). His translations of poetry from Russian and French have also been published, most recently in *Pyramid* and *Aufgabe.* He received an MFA from Iowa in 2008, where he also taught. He currently studies and teaches at Yale, and is working on a book about meaning in poetry, focusing especially on the work of Paul Celan. He is the editor of the journal *Heliograph.*

Paul Hoover is the author of numerous poetry books, including *desolation: souvenir, Sonnet 56, Edge and Fold,* and *Poems in Spanish,* as well as *Fables of Representation,* a collection of literary essays. He is co-translator of *Beyond the Court Gate: Selected Poems of Nguyen Trai;* the anthology *Black Dog, Black Night: Contemporary Vietnamese Poetry;* and *Selected Poems of Friedrich Hölderlin,* which won the PEN-USA Translation Award. He is also a past winner of the Frederick Bock Award from *Poetry* and the Jerome J. Shestack Award from *American Poetry Review*. Professor of Creative Writing at San Francisco State University, Hoover is editor of the anthology *Postmodern American Poetry* (W.W. Norton, 1994/2013), and co-editor—with Maxine Chernoff—of the literary magazine *New American Writing*.

Erika Howsare's work has appeared in *Fence, Verse, Denver Quarterly,* and elsewhere. She is the author of the chapbooks *Elect June Grooms* and (with Jen Tynes) *The Ohio System*, a journalist, and a co-editor at Horse Less Press. She writes and teaches near Charlottesville, Virginia.

Brenda Iijima is the author of five collections of poetry, most recently *Early Linoleum* (Say it With Stones, 2012). She is the editor of *The Eco Language Reader* published by Nightboat Books. She lives in Brooklyn, where she publishes books under the Portable Press at Yo-Yo Labs imprint.

Sally Keith is the author of *The Fact of the Matter* (Milkweed, 2012) and two previous collections of poetry: *Design,* winner of the 2000 Colorado Prize for Poetry, and *Dwelling Song* (Georgia, 2004). Recipient of a Pushcart Prize and recent fellowships at the Virginia Center for the Creative Arts, the Ucross Foundation, and the Fundación Valparaíso, she is a member of the MFA faculty at George Mason University. She lives in Washington, D.C.

Karla Kelsey is author of the chapbooks *3 Movements* (Pilot Press) and *Little Sliding Doors in the Mind* (Noemi Press) and two books of poetry: *Knowledge, Forms, the Aviary* and *Iteration Nets* (both by Ahsahta Press). She edits and contributes to Fence Books' *Constant Critic* poetry book review website and has had essays on poetics published in literary journals and anthologies. A recipient of a Fulbright lectureship, Karla graduated from the Iowa Writers' Workshop and the University of Denver. She teaches at Susquehanna University.

Amy King's latest is *I Want to Make You Safe* (Litmus Press). She is preparing a book of interviews with the poet Ron Padgett. King co-edits *Esque Magazine* with Ana Bozicevic and teaches English and Creative Writing at SUNY Nassau Community College. More at amyking.org.

Melissa Kwasny is the author of four books of poetry: *The Archival Birds, Thistle, Reading Novalis in Montana,* and *The Nine Senses.* She is also the editor of *Toward the Open Field: Poets on the Art of Poetry, 1800-1950* and co-editor, with M. L. Smoker, of the human rights anthology *I Go to the Ruined Place.* She lives in western Montana.

Brian Laidlaw is a poet and songwriter from Northern California and a graduate of the University of Minnesota MFA program in poetry. His poems have appeared or are forthcoming in *New American Writing, Volt, The Iowa Review, Handsome, No Tell Motel* and elsewhere, and his lyrics have appeared in *American Songwriter Magazine*. He often works in a multimedia format, composing music as a thematically linked counterpart or "soundtrack" to his poems. The newest such project, *wolf wolf wolf*, was released by Yes!Lets Records in 2011. Laidlaw currently teaches songwriting at McNally Smith College of Music and continues to tour nationally as a folksinger.

Maryrose Larkin is author of *Book of Ocean* (ie press), *The Name of this Intersection is Frost* (Shearsman Books), *Darc* (FLASH+CARD), and *Marrowing* (airfoil). Her next book, *The Identification of Ghosts,* is forthcoming from Chax Press. She is a member of the Spare Room Collective, as well as a co-editor of Flash+Card press. She lives in Portland, Oregon, where she attempts to move through the procedural into the unknowable.

Ann Lauterbach is the author of eight books of poetry, several collaborations with visual artists, and an essay collection, *The Night Sky: Writings on the Poetics of Experience*. Her most recent book, *Or to Begin Again* (Penguin, 2009) was a finalist for a National Book Award. An essay, *The Given and the Chosen* was published as a chapbook from Omnidawn in 2011. She is Ruth and David Schwab Professor of Languages and Literature at Bard College, where she is also co-directs Writing in the Milton Avery Graduate School of the Arts. Among her awards are a Guggenheim Fellowship and a MacArthur Fellowship. She lives in Germantown, New York.

Karen An-hwei Lee is the author of *Phyla of Joy* (Tupelo, 2012), *Ardor* (Tupelo, 2008), and *In Medias Res* (Sarabande, 2004), which won the Kathryn A. Morton Prize and the Norma Farber First Book Award. Her chapbook, *God's One Hundred Promises,* received the Swan Scythe Press Prize. The recipient of a National Endowment for the Arts Fellowship, she lives and teaches in southern California, where she is a novice harpist.

Paul Legault is the co-founder of the translation press Telephone Books and the author of three books of poetry: *The Madeleine Poems* (Omnidawn, 2010), *The Other Poems* (Fence, 2011), and *The Emily Dickinson Reader* (McSweeney's, 2012).

Sylvia Legris' most recently published collection, *Nerve Squall* (Coach House Books), won both the 2006 Griffin Poetry Prize and the 2006 Pat Lowther Memorial Award, given for the best book of poetry published by a Canadian woman. Her work has appeared widely in journals, including *New American Writing, Conjunctions,* and *The Capilano Review*. "Almost Migration" is from a small collection, *Pneumatic Antiphonal,* forthcoming from New Directions.

Dana Levin is the author of three books of poetry, most recently *Sky Burial* (Copper Canyon,

2011). A recipient of fellowships and awards from the Rona Jaffe, Whiting, and Guggenheim Foundations, Levin is on the faculty at Santa Fe University of Art and Design.

Eric Linsker's poems have recently appeared in *Hi Zero* and *Lana Turner*. He co-edits *The Claudius App* (www.theclaudiusapp.com).

Alessandra Lynch is the author of two books of poetry: *Sails the Wind Left Behind*, winner of Alice James Books' New York/New England Prize, and *It was a terrible cloud at twilight*, winner of Pleiades Press' Lena-Miles Wever Todd Award. She has received fellowships from the Macdowell Arts Colony and the Corporation of Yaddo. Currently, Lynch teaches at Butler University and lives near an Indianapolisian canal.

Aaron McCollough is the author of five books of poetry. His fourth, *No Grave Can Hold My Body Down,* was released by Ahsahta Press in September 2011, and his fifth, *Underlight,* will be published by Ugly Duckling Presse in November 2012. His other books include *Little Ease, Double Venus,* and *Welkin*. McCollough is the Librarian for English Language and Literature at the University of Michigan's Hatcher Graduate Library. He lives in Ann Arbor.

Joyelle McSweeney is the author of *The Necropastoral* (Spork Press, 2010), an artist's book featuring essays and poems by McSweeney and collages and design by Andrew Shuta; the volumes *Percussion Grenade* (poems and necropastoral farce, 2012), *The Commandrine* (poems and nautical verse play, 2004), and *The Red Bird* (poems, 2001), all from Fence Books; the lyric novels *Flet* (sci-fi baroque; Fence, 2008) and *Nylund, the Sarcographer* (baroque noir; Tarpaulin Sky, 2007); and the forthcoming collection of a play and seven stories, *Salamandrine, 8 Gothics* (Tarpaulin Sky, 2012). She is a co-founder of Action Books, teaches at the University of Notre Dame, and is a founding contributor of montevidayo.com, a collective blog for hi, lo, pop, and microbiological cultures.

J. Michael Martinez's *Heredities* was awarded the Walt Whitman Award, and he is pursuing a Ph.D. in Literature at the University of Colorado at Boulder. He is a contributing editor at *The Volta* and a poetry editor for Noemi Press.

Nicole Mauro's poems and criticism have appeared in numerous publications. She is the author of seven chapbooks; one full-length poetry collection, *The Contortions* (Dusie, 2009); and is the co-editor of an interdisciplinary book about sidewalks titled *Intersection: Sidewalks and Public Space* (with Marci Nelligan, A'A' Arts, 2008). Her second full-length collection, *Tax-Dollar Super-Sonnet Featuring Sarah Palin as Poet,* is due out in Fall 2012 from Black Radish Books. She lives in the San Francisco Bay Area with her husband, Patrick, and daughters Nina and Faye. She teaches rhetoric and language at the University of San Francisco.

K. Silem Mohammad is the author of several books of poetry, including *Deer Head Nation* (Tougher Disguises, 2003), *A Thousand Devils* (Combo, 2004), *Breathalyzer* (Edge, 2008), *The Front* (Roof, 2009), and *Monsters* (forthcoming, Edge Books). In his current project, "The Sonnagrams," Mohammad anagrammatizes Shakespeare's Sonnets into all-new English sonnets in iambic pentameter. He is also a co-editor of the forthcoming *Flarf: An Anthology of Flarf*, editor of the poetry magazine *Abraham Lincoln*, and faculty editor of *West Wind Review*. He is an associate professor in the English & Writing program at Southern Oregon University.

Laura Moriarty's books include *A Tonalist*, an essay poem from Nightboat Books, and the novels *Cunning* and *Ultravioleta*. *A Semblance: Selected and New Poems, 1975-2007* came out from Omnidawn in 2007. *Who That Divines* is forthcoming from Nightboat. She is the author of ten other books of poetry going back to 1980. She won the Poetry Center Book Award in 1983, a Wallace Alexander Gerbode Foundation Award in Poetry in 1992, a New Langton Arts Award in Literature 1998, and a Fund for Poetry grant in 2007. She has taught at Mills College and Naropa University, among other places, and is Deputy Director of Small Press Distribution. For more, see the blog A Tonalist Notes.

Rusty Morrison's *After Urgency* won Tupelo's Dorset Prize and is forthcoming in 2012; *The Book of the Given* is available from Noemi Press; *the true keeps calm biding its story* won Academy of American Poet's James Laughlin Award, the Northern California Book Award for Poetry, the Alice Fay DiCastagnola Award from Poetry Society of America, and was published by Ahsahta as a Sawtooth Prize winner. *Whethering* won the Colorado Prize for Poetry from the Center for Literary Publishing. She's Omnidawn's co-publisher and lives in Richmond, CA.

Canadian poet and essayist **Erín Moure** has published seventeen books of poetry plus a volume of essays, and is also a translator from French, Spanish, Galician, and Portuguese, with eleven books of poetry translated by people as diverse as Nicole Brossard, Andrés Ajens, and Fernando Pessoa. Her work has received the Governor General's Award, the Pat Lowther Memorial Award, the A.M. Klein Prize (twice), and was a three-time finalist for the Griffin Poetry Prize. Moure also holds an honorary doctorate from Brandon University. Her latest works are *The Unmemntioable* (House of Anansi), and *Secession* (Zat-So), her fourth translation of internationally acclaimed Galician poet Chus Pato.

Jennifer Moxley is the author of five books of poetry: *Clampdown* (Flood, 2009), *The Line* (Post-Apollo, 2007), *Often Capital* (Flood, 2005), *The Sense Record* (Edge, 2002; Salt, 2003) and *Imagination Verses* (Tender Buttons, 1996; Salt, 2003). Her memoir, *The Mid-*

dle Room, was published by subpress in 2007. Her translation of the French poet Anne Portugal's *Absolute bob* appeared in fall of 2010 from Burning Deck. In addition, she has translated two books by the French poet Jacqueline Risset, *The Translation Begins* (Burning Deck, 1996) and *Sleep's Powers* (Ugly Duckling, 2008). She works as an Associate Professor at the University of Maine.

Laura Mullen is on the MFA faculty at Louisiana State University. She is the author of six books: *The Surface, After I Was Dead, Subject* and *Dark Archive* (University of California Press, 2011), *The Tales of Horror,* and *Murmur.* Her work has been widely anthologized and is included in *American Hybrid* (Norton) and *I'll Drown My Book: Conceptual Writing by Women. Undersong,* the composer Jason Eckardt's setting of "The Distance (This)" (from *Subject*), premiered in New York and Helsinki and was released on Mode records in 2011. Mullen's seventh book (*Enduring Freedom: A Little Book of Mechanical Brides*) is forthcoming in June 2012.

Melanie Noel is the author of *The Monarchs* (forthcoming from Stockport Flats). Her poems have appeared in *Fine Madness, Filter, Weekday,* and on the audiomagazine *Weird Deer.* She's also written poems for short films and installations, and co-curated APOS-TROPHE, a dance, music, and poetry series, with musician Gust Burns and dancers Michèle Steinwald and Beth Graczyk.

Kathryn Nuernberger is the author of *Rag & Bone,* which was the winner of Elixir Press's Antivenom prize. She teaches at the University of Central Missouri, where she also serves as poetry editor of the journal *Pleiades.*

Peter O'Leary was born in Detroit, Michigan in 1968. His books of poetry include *Watchfulness, Depth Theology,* and *Luminous Epinoia.* In 2012, the Cultural Society will publish a new book, *The Phosphorescence of Thought.* As Ronald Johnson's literary executor, he has edited several volumes of Johnson's poetry, including *The Shrubberies* and *Radi os.* A new edition of Johnson's masterpiece, *ARK,* is forthcoming. Recently he also edited *Is Music: Selected Poems* by John Taggart. In 2002 his critical study, *Gnostic Contagion: Robert Duncan & the Poetry of Illness,* appeared. He lives in Berwyn, Illinois, and teaches at the School of the Art Institute of Chicago and for the Committee on Creative Writing at the University of Chicago.

Craig Santos Perez is from Mongmong, Guåhan. He is the co-founder of Ala Press, co-star of the poetry album Undercurrent (Hawai'i Dub Machine, 2011), and author of two collections of poetry: *from unincorporated territory [hacha]* (Tinfish Press, 2008) and *from unincorporated territory [saina]* (Omnidawn Publishing, 2010), winner of the 2011

PEN Center USA Literary Award for Poetry. He is an Assistant Professor in the English Department at the University of Hawai'i, Manoa.

Patrick Pritchett is the author of two books of poems, *Burn* and *Gnostic Frequencies* (Spuyten Duyvil, 2011). Scholarly work includes articles in *Radical Vernacular: Lorine Niedecker and the Politics of Place* (Iowa University Press) and *Ronald Johnson: Life and Works* (National Poetry Foundation). An exchange of letters on poetry and form with Kathleen Fraser is featured in *Letters to Poets: Conversations about Poetry, Politics, and Community* (Saturnalia Press). More recently, he has written on Michael Palmer and Rachel Blau DuPlessis for *Jacket 2*. He serves on the advisory editorial board of *Journal of Modern Literature* and is a Lecturer in the History and Literature Program at Harvard University and Visiting Lecturer in Poetry at Amherst College.

Bin Ramke's eleventh book of poems, *Aerial,* was just published by Omnidawn. He teaches at the University of Denver and occasionally at the School of the Art Institute of Chicago. For sixteen years he was editor of the *Denver Quarterly*.

Stephen Ratcliffe's most recent books are *CLOUD / RIDGE* (BlazeVOX) and *Conversation* (Bootstrap Press / Plein Air Editions), both published last year. His *HUMAN / NATURE, Remarks on Color / Sound*, and *Temporality* (three 1,000-page books each written in 1,000 consecutive days) are now up at Eclipse (http://english.utah.edu/eclipse/). A book of criticism, *Reading the Unseen: (Offstage) Hamlet*, was published by Counterpath in 2011. His daily poems-plus-photographs can be found on Facebook and on his blog stephenratcliffe.blogspot.com. He has lived in Bolinas, California, since 1973, and teaches at Mills College in Oakland.

Matt Reeck has published chapbooks from Fact-Simile, MIPOesias, and Other Rooms presses. His poetry won the 2010 *BOMB* magazine contest, judged by Susan Howe, and he was a finalist for the 2011 Nightboat Poetry Prize. He was a semi-finalist for the 2010 Princess Grace Award for playwriting, and his dramatic work has appeared in St Ann's Warehouse's Labapalooza Festival, in the Boog City Poetry and Music Festival and at Dixon Place in New York City. He won a Fulbright to India, and his translations from the Urdu, Hindi, and French have appeared in various magazines.

Marthe Reed has published two books, *Gaze* (Black Radish) and *Tender Box, A Wunderkammer* with drawings by Rikki Ducornet (Lavender Ink); a third book is forthcoming from Moria Books. She has also published three chapbooks, *post*cards: Lafayette a Lafayette* (with j/j hastain), *(em)bodied bliss,* and *zaum alliterations*, all as part of the Dusie Kollektiv Series. An essay is forthcoming in *American Letters and Commentary,* June 2012.

Evelyn Reilly's most recent book, *Apocalypso* (Roof Books, 2012), continues the dystopic reworking of nature poetry she began in *Styrofoam* (Roof Books, 2009). An image/text adaptation of "Wing/Span/Screw/Cluster (Aves)" from *Styrofoam* was displayed at the Center for Contemporary Art and the Natural World, Project Space, Haldon Forest Park, Exeter, UK. Earlier work includes *Hiatus,* from Barrow Street Press, and *Fervent Remnants of Reflective Surfaces,* a chapbook from Portable Press at Yo Yo Labs. Reilly has taught poetics at St. Marks Poetry Project and the Summer Writing Program at Naropa University, and has been a curator of the Segue Reading Series. She lives in New York City.

Karen Rigby is the author of *Chinoiserie* (2011 Sawtooth Poetry Prize; Ahsahta, 2012). Awarded fellowships and grants from the National Endowment for the Arts, the Vermont Studio Center, and the Greater Pittsburgh Arts Council, she is one of the founding editors of *Cerise Press,* an international online journal of literature, arts, and culture, as well as a member of the National Book Critics Circle.

Ed Roberson has published nine books of poetry including *To See the Earth before the End of the World,* which was a finalist for the *LA Times* Poetry Book of the Year 2011. His *Voices Cast Out to Talk Us In* was a winner of the Iowa Poetry Prize. *Atmosphere Conditions* (2000) was one of the winners in the National Poetry Series Competition and was nominated by the Academy of American Poets for the Lenore Marshall Award. *City Eclogue* was selected by the Atelos series in 2007 and *The New Wing of the Labyrinth,* published by Singing Horse in 2009. He has also received the Lila Wallace Reader's Digest Writer's Award and the Poetry Society of America's Shelley Memorial Award in 2008.

Lisa Robertson was born in Toronto, lived for many years in Vancouver, spent three years teaching in California, and now makes her home in France. Her first book was the 1993 pastoral *XEclogue; Debbie: An Epic,* and *The Weather* followed. Among her other books of poetry are *Lisa Robertson's Magenta Soul Whip, The Men,* and *R's Boat.* She has published two books of essays—*Occasional Works and Seven Walks from the Office for Soft Architecture* and *Nilling.* A frequent collaborator in the translation, visual and sound arts, her most extensive collaboration was with the late Stacy Doris, as The Perfume Recordist. She has no ongoing academic affiliation nor credentials, and supports herself as a freelance writer, critic and teacher, currently at Piet Zwart Institute in Rotterdam.

Elizabeth Robinson is the author of several collections of poetry, most recently *Three Novels* (Omnidawn) and *The Orphan & its Relations* (Fence). With Colleen Lookingbill, she has edited *As if it Fell from the Sun,* an anthology of women's poetry (Instance/Ether-

Dome). Robinson has been the recipient of grants from the Fund for Poetry, the Boomerang Fund, and the Foundation for Contemporary Arts. She has also been a winner of the National Poetry Series and the Fence Modern Poets Prize.

Leslie Scalapino (1944–2010) published some thirty volumes of poetry, experimental prose, plays, essays, and inter-genre work between 1976 and her death. She taught at Bard College, Naropa University, and at several schools in the San Francisco Bay area. She was twice a National Endowment for the Arts Fellow in Literature and in 1988 received an American Book Award for *way*. For almost a quarter century she directed O Books, the Oakland-based small-press publisher she founded in 1986.

Poet, essayist, and fiction writer **Standard Schaefer**'s first book of poetry, *Nova,* was selected for the 1999 National Poetry Series and published by Sun & Moon Books. His second book, *Water & Power,* was published by Agincourt in 2005. *Desert Notebook* was published in Italy and the U.S. in 2008 in limited editions. His poetry has been translated into Italian and anthologized internationally, most recently in *Nuova Poesia Americana* (Mondadori, 2005) as well as in Vol. 5 of *The PIP Anthology of World Poetry of the 20th Century* (Los Angeles: Green Integer, 2005). He has co-edited several literary and arts journals including *Ribot*, *New Review of Literature*, *Rhizome* and *Or*. He has taught writing and literature at Otis College of Art (Los Angeles) and California College of the Arts (San Francisco). His latest book of poems, *The Notebook of False Purgatories,* is forthcoming from Chax Books (2012). He lives in Portland with his wife and daughter.

Kate Schapira is the author of four books and seven chapbooks of poetry, most recently *The Soft Place* (Horse Less Press) and *Little Eva, the Insomniac from Mars* (dancing girl press). She lives in Providence, RI, where she co-organizes the Publicly Complex Reading Series and teaches writing to college students and fourth grade scientists.

Brandon Shimoda is the author of three books of poetry—*O Bon* (Litmus Press, 2011), *The Girl Without Arms* (Black Ocean, 2011), and *The Alps* (Flim Forum, 2008)—as well as numerous limited-edition solo and collaborative works. He was born in California and has since lived in eleven states and six countries, most recently Maine, Taiwan, and Arizona.

Eleni Sikelianos, a native of California, is the author of a hybrid memoir, a long eco-poem, and other books of poetry, the most recent being *Body Clock*. Forthcoming is *The Loving Details of the Living & the Dead* (2013). She has been the happy recipient of various awards for her poetry, nonfiction, and translations. A selected poems was published in France (translator Béatrice Trotignon, Editions Grèges) in 2007; *Le poème Californie* (trans. Trotignon, Grèges) and *Le livre de Jon* (translator Christophe Claro, Actes Sud) were published in 2012. In August, she performed parts of *The California Poem* with composer Philip Glass, set to his music, for his inaugural Days & Nights festival. Her work has been anthologized here and there, including in *American Hybrid* and *The Norton Anthology of Postmodern American Poetry*.

Jonathan Skinner's poetry collections include *Birds of Tifft* (BlazeVOX, 2011) and *Political Cactus Poems* (Palm Press, 2005). He founded and edits the journal *ecopoetics* (www.ecopoetics.org), which features creative-critical intersections between writing and ecology. Skinner also writes ecocriticism on contemporary poetry and poetics: he has published essays on Charles Olson, Ronald Johnson, Lorine Niedecker, Mei-mei Berssenbrugge, Bernadette Mayer, and on horizontal concepts such as the Third Landscape. Currently, he is writing a book of investigative poems on the urban landscapes of Frederick Law Olmsted, and a critical book on Animal Transcriptions in contemporary poetry. Skinner makes his home in South Central Maine, in the Merrymeeting Bay watershed.

Gustaf Sobin (1935–2005) was an American poet who moved to Provence in 1963 to study under French poet René Char. He spent the rest of his life in France, ultimately publishing some nine collections of poetry, five novels, three essay volumes, and several other books in the U.S., many with New Directions. His *Collected Poems* appeared from Talisman House in 2010.

Juliana Spahr edits with Jena Osman the book series Chain Links. She recently edited with Stephanie Young *A Megaphone: Some Enactments, Some Numbers, and Some Essays about the Continued Usefulness of Crotchless-pants-and-a-machine-gun Feminism*. She is writing with David Buuck a book about two friends who are writers in a time of war and ecological collapse. And she recently organized with Joshua Clover the 95 cent Skool and the Durutti/Durruti Free Skool.

Jane Sprague is the author of *The Port of Los Angeles, Belladonna Elder Series 8* (with Diane Ward and Tim Darragh), and numerous chapbooks; she also edited the collection *Imaginary Syllabi,* a book that explores utopian, fabulist, and actual innovative pedagogies in the disciplines of contemporary art and writing. Sprague has received grants from NYFA, NYSCA, and other organizations for her writing, teaching, and curatorial work. She lives with her family on an island in Long Beach, California and writes among Great Blue herons, Green Night herons, egrets, terns, sea lions, dolphins, whales, anchovies, sardines, and the occasional puffin, which eke out their lives in waters polluted by oil, human waste, red tides, and an endless flow of garbage. She feeds abandoned companion animals in the littoral zone adjacent to the Port of Long Beach, in addition to engaging in acts of advocacy and agitation on behalf of abused and neglected human and non-human animals.

Fenn Stewart reads and writes in Toronto, Canada. Her work can be found in *The Capilano Review* and *Open Letter*, and online at ditchpoetry.com. Her first chapbook, *An OK Organ Man*, was published by above/ground press in 2012.

Adam Strauss has three chapbooks out: *Nation-State* (BlazeVox), *Address* (Scantily Clad Press), and *Perhaps A Girl Elsewhere* (Birds of Lace Press). As well, he has a full-length manuscript, *For Days*, out with BlazeVox. One of the poems in this anthology, "Others Necessary," is from a manuscript titled *Classic*. The other two, "No Fathers Without Mothers" and "The Wild Carrot Taking The Field By Force," are from a manuscript titled *From Feminism*.

Mathias Svalina is a co-editor of Octopus Books and the author of one book of prose, *I Am a Very Productive Entrepreneur* (Mud Luscious Press, 2011), as well as two books of poetry, *Destruction Myth* (Cleveland State University Press, 2009) and *The Explosions* (Subito, 2012).

Arthur Sze is the author of nine books of poetry, including *The Ginkgo Light, Quipu, The Redshifting Web: Poems 1970-1998, Archipelago,* and *The Silk Dragon: Translations from the Chinese* from Copper Canyon Press. He is also the editor of *Chinese Writers on Writing* (Trinity University Press). His poems have been translated into a dozen languages, including Chinese, Dutch, Italian, and Spanish. He is the recipient of numerous awards, including a PEN Southwest Book Award, a Lila Wallace-Reader's Digest Writers' Award, a Guggenheim Fellowship, an American Book Award, a Lannan Literary Award for Poetry, and two National Endowment for the Arts Creative Writing fellowships. A professor emeritus at the Institute of American Indian Arts, Arthur Sze lives in Santa Fe, New Mexico and recently joined the Board of Chancellors at the Academy of American Poets.

John Taggart's most recent book is *Is Music: Selected Poems* (Copper Canyon Press, 2010). He lives in the Cumberland Valley of Pennsylvania.

Michelle Taransky's *Barn Burned, Then* was selected by Marjorie Welish for the 2008 Omnidawn Poetry Prize. Taransky lives in Philadelphia, works as Reviews Editor for *Jacket2,* and teaches in the critical and creative writing programs at the University of Pennsylvania. *Sorry Was in the Woods* is forthcoming from Omnidawn in 2013.

A former National Endowment for the Arts fellow, **Brian Teare** is the recipient of poetry fellowships from the MacDowell Colony, the American Antiquarian Society, and the Headlands Center for the Arts. He is the author of *The Room Where I Was Born*, *Sight Map*, the Lambda-award winning *Pleasure*, and *Companion Grasses*, forthcoming from Omnidawn in 2013, as well as the chapbooks *Pilgrim*, *?*, and *Black Sun Crown*. An Assistant Professor at Temple University, he lives in Philadelphia, where he makes books by hand for his micropress, Albion Books.

Tony Tost was born in the Missouri Ozarks in 1975 and raised in an unincorporated, abandoned mining town in rural Washington state. His first book of poems, *Invisible Bride* (LSU, 2004), was selected by C.D. Wright for the 2003 Walt Whitman Award. A second volume of poetry, *Complex Sleep*, was published by the University of Iowa in 2007 in their Kuhl House Poets series. A prose exploration of Johnny Cash's 1990s comeback and enduring mythology, *American Recordings*, was published by Continuum Books in 2011 in their 33 1/3 series. Tost now writes for the contemporary western television series *Longmire*, based on Craig Johnson's best-selling mystery novels, debuting on A&E in summer 2012. Tost's original television pilots are in development at Fox Television Studios, Fox 21 and Sony Pictures Television. He lives in Ann Arbor, MI with his wife Leigh and young sons Simon and Wyatt.

Tony Trigilio's books of poetry and criticism include, most recently, the poetry collection *Historic Diary* (BlazeVOX) and the critical monograph *Allen Ginsberg's Buddhist Poetics* (Southern Illinois University Press). With Tim Prchal, he co-edited the anthology *Visions and Divisions: American Immigration Literature, 1870-1930* (Rutgers University Press). He is a member of the core poetry faculty at Columbia College Chicago and is a co-founder and co-editor of *Court Green*.

Catherine Wagner's collections of poems include *Nervous Device* (City Lights, 2012) and three books from Fence: *My New Job* (2009), *Macular Hole* (2004), and *Miss America* (2001). Her work has been anthologized in *Norton Anthology of Postmodern American Poetry*, *Out of Everywhere: Linguistically Innovative Poetry by Women in North America and the UK* (second edition), *Gurlesque*, *Poets on Teaching*, *Best American Erotic Poems* and elsewhere. An anthology she co-edited with Rebecca Wolff, *Not for Mothers Only*, was published by Fence in 2007. She is associate professor of English at Miami University in Oxford, Ohio.

Jasmine Dreame Wagner is the author of two chapbooks: *Listening for Earthquakes* (Caketrain Journal and Press, 2012) and *CHARCOAL* (For Arbors, 2008). Her poems have appeared in *American Letters & Commentary*, *Aufgabe*, *Colorado Review*, *New American*

Writing, and *Verse*. A graduate of Columbia University and the University of Montana, Jasmine has received grants and fellowships from the Foundation for Contemporary Arts, Hall Farm Center for Arts & Education, Kultuuritehas Polymer, and The Wassaic Project. She lives in Connecticut where she teaches creative writing at Western Connecticut State University and makes folk and experimental music as Cabinet of Natural Curiosities.

Elizabeth Willis is the author of five books of poetry: *Second Law* (Avenue B, 1993), *The Human Abstract* (Penguin, 1994), *Turneresque* (Burning Deck, 2003), *Meteoric Flowers* (Wesleyan University Press, 2006), and most recently *Address* (Wesleyan, 2011). She has also written about 19th- and 20th-century poetry from Erasmus Darwin to the present, focusing on the intersections of public and private life, the effects of politics and technology on aesthetic production, and the relation of poets to their sources. Recently she edited a volume of essays entitled *Radical Vernacular: Lorine Niedecker and the Poetics of Place* (University of Iowa Press, 2008). She teaches at Wesleyan University.

Jane Wong received her M.F.A. from the University of Iowa and is a former U.S. Fulbright Fellow. She is the recipient of scholarships from the Bread Loaf Writers' Conference and the Fine Arts Work Center in Provincetown. Poems appear recently or are forthcoming in *CutBank, EOAGH, Mid-American Review, ZYZZYVA, The Journal,* and *Tuesday; An Art Project*. She has two chapbooks: *Dendrochronology* (dancing girl press) and the forthcoming *Impossible Map* (Fact-Simile). She lives in Seattle, where she is pursuing a Ph.D. in English at the University of Washington.

C. D. Wright is the author of more than a dozen books, most recently *One With Others: a little book of her days*, which won the National Book Critics Circle Award and the Leonore Marshal Prize. Her collection *Rising, Falling, Hovering* won the Griffin International Poetry Prize (2009). In 2004 she was named a MacArthur Fellow. She is married to poet Forrest Gander. They have a son, Brecht. She is on the faculty at Brown University.

Emily Abendroth: "evitative spool" previously appeared in the journal *Ecopoetics*. Reprinted by permission of the author.

Will Alexander: "On Scorpions & Swallows" previously appeared in *Compression & Purity* (City Lights, 2011). Reprinted by permission of the author and City Lights Books.

Rae Armantrout: "Long Green" previously appeared in *Money Shot* (Wesleyan, 2011). Reprinted by permission of the author and Wesleyan University Press.

Eric Baus: "Tuned Droves" and "The Song of Stunted Hawks" previously appeared in *Tuned Droves* (Octopus, 2008). Reprinted by permission of the author and Octopus Books. "Who King Tree Is" and "How King Tree Sleeps" previously appeared in the chapbook *Bee-Stung Aviary* (Further Adventures, 2010). Reprinted by permission of the author.

Dan Beachy-Quick: "Fess-Charm" and "Said Charm" previously appeared in *North True South Bright*. Copyright © 2003 by Dan Beachy-Quick. Reprinted with the permission of The Permissions Company, Inc., on behalf of Alice James Books, www.alicejamesbooks .org. Excerpt from *This Nest, Swift Passerine* previously appeared in *This Nest, Swift Passerine* (Tupelo Press, 2009). Reprinted by permission of the author and Tupelo Press.

John Beer: excerpt from "Lucinda: A Revision" is previously unpublished and appears here by permission of the author.

Mei-Mei Berssenbrugge: "Glitter" previously appeared in the journal *Conjunctions* (2007), and "Green" in the journal *Ecopoetics* (2006–2009). Reprinted by permission of the author.

Sherwin Bitsui: excerpt from *Flood Song* copyright © 2009 by Sherwin Bitsui. Reprinted with the permission of The Permissions Company, Inc., on behalf of Copper Canyon Press, www.coppercanyonpress.org.

Kamau Brathwaite: "Day at Devizes (2)" & "fflute(s)" previously appeared in *Elegguas* (Wesleyan, 2010). Reprinted by permission of Wesleyan University Press.

Susan Briante: "The End of Another Creature" and "A Photograph from Nature" previously appeared in *Utopia Minus* (Ahsahta, 2011). Reprinted by permission of the author and Ahsahta Press.

Oni Buchanan: "No Blue Morpho" previously appeared in *Must a Violence* (University of Iowa Press, 2012). Reprinted by permission of the author and University of Iowa Press.

Heather Christle: "Acorn Duly Crushed" previously appeared in *The Difficult Farm* (Octopus Books, 2009). Reprinted by permission of the author and Octopus Books.

Stephen Collis: "Blackberries" previously appeared in *The Commons* (Talonbooks, 2008). Reprinted by permission of the author and Talonbooks.

Jack Collom: "Ruddy Duck," "Bittern," and "Red-Shouldered Hawks" previously appeared in *Exchanges of Earth and Sky* (Fish Drum, 2005). Reprinted by permission of the author and Fish Drum.

Phil Cordelli: "Liquidambar (Sweetgum)" is previously unpublished and appears here by permission of the author.

T. Zachary Cotler: "Ångström Zion" is previously unpublished and appears here by permission of the author.

Brent Cunningham: "Principle of the Forest," "Principle of the Bird," and "Notes on the Two Principles" previously appeared in *Bird & Forest* (Ugly Duckling Presse, 2005). Reprinted by permission of the author and Ugly Duckling Presse.

Christopher Dewdney: Excerpt from "Concordat Proviso Ascendant" in *Signal Fires* by Christopher Dewdney. Copyright © 2000. Published by McClelland & Stewart. Reprinted by permission of the author and the publisher. "Grid Erectile" previously appeared in *The Natural History* (ECW Press, 2002). Reprinted by permission of the author and ECW Press.

Timothy Donnelly: "In His Tree" previously appeared in *The Cloud Corporation* (Wave Books, 2010). Reprinted by permission of the author and Wave Books.

Michael Dumanis: "The Woods Are Burning" previously appeared in *My Soviet Union* (University of Massachusetts Press, 2007). Reprinted by permission of the author and the University of Massachusetts Press.

Camille Dungy: "Her mother sings warning of the new world" previously appeared in *Smith Blue* (Southern Illinois University Press, 2011). *Smith Blue* © 2011 by Camille T. Dungy; reproduced by permission of the publisher.

Marcella Durand: "HPOME 1" and "HPOME 2" previously appeared in *Western Capital Rhapsodies* (Faux Press, 2001). Reprinted by permission of the author. "Remote Sensing" previously appeared in *Area* (Belladonna Books, 2008). Reprinted by permission of the author and Belladonna Books.

Lisa Fishman: "Field," "Creature," and "Request" previously appeared in the journal *Ecopoetics*. "Creature" and "Request" also appeared (as the opening, untitled sections of a longer poem entitled "Creature") in *The Happiness Experiment* (Ahsahta, 2007). Reprinted by permission of the author and Ahsahta Press.

Robert Fitterman: "LULU (Locally Unwanted Land Use")" and "Zoomburb" previously appeared in *Sprawl: Metropolis 30A* (Make Now, 2010). Reprinted by permission of the author and Make Now Press.

Forrest Gander: "Edge-Lit Scene" and "Escaped Trees of Lynchburg" are from *Science and Steepleflower*, copyright ©1997 by Forrest Gander. Reprinted by permission of New Directions Publishing Corp.

Merrill Gilfillan: Selections from "Ten Carbonated Warblers" previously appeared in *The Seasons* (Zephyr Press/Adventures in Poetry, 2002). Reprinted by permission of the author and Adventures in Poetry.

C. S. Giscombe: selections from "Inland" previously appeared in *Prairie Style* (Dalkey Archive, 2008). Reprinted by permission of the author and Dalkey Archive Press.

Peter Gizzi: "Some Values of Landscape and Weather" previously appeared in *Some Values of Landscape and Weather* (Wesleyan, 2003). Reprinted by permission of the author and Wesleyan University Press.

Jody Gladding: bark beetle translations first appeared in the journal *Ecopoetics*. Reprinted by permission of the author.

Johannes Göransson: "Nature Is Forbidden" is previously unpublished and appears here by permission of the author.

Chris Green: "A-Pastoral" and "Macbeth for Everyone" are previously unpublished and appear here by permission of the author.

Arielle Greenberg: "Tour of _____ Morning Farms" previously appeared in *Given* (Verse, 2002). Reprinted by permission of the author and Wave Books.

Richard Greenfield: "Eris" and "The Laws" previously appeared in *Tracer* (Omnidawn, 2009). Reprinted by permission of the author and Omnidawn.

Sarah Gridley: "Edifice" previously appeared in *Crazyhorse*. "Who is this" from the sequence "Half Sick of Shadows" previously appeared in *Columbia: a Journal of Literature and Art*. All are reprinted by permission of the author.

e. tracy grinnell: "36 / a tower is evident" and "45 / a lark, a wish-refrain (II)" originally appeared in *music or forgetting* (o books, 2001). Reprinted by permission of the author.

Gabriel Gudding: "ILLINOVORNEVERIVERNOIS—Ivne—MMX" and "[congratulations on being here]" appeared, respectively, in the journals *Seneca Review* and *EOAGH: A Journal of the Arts*. Reprinted by permission of the author.

Joshua Harmon: "Inscape" previously appeared in *Scape* (Black Ocean, 2009). Reprinted by permission of the author and Black Ocean Press.

Nathan Hauke: "A Surface. A Shore or Semi-transparency of Glass" first appeared in the journal *Intersection(s)*. "Deerfield" first appeared in the journal *26*, as well as in the chapbook *In the Living Room* (Lame House Press, 2010). Both reprinted by permission of the author.

Lyn Hejinian & Jack Collom: "The Woods" previously appeared in *Situations, Sings* (Adventures in Poetry, 2008). Reprinted by permission of the authors and Adventures in Poetry.

Mary Hickman: "Totem" previously appeared in the journal *Action Yes* and in the chapbook *Ecce Animot* (Projective Industries, 2010). Reprinted by permission of the author.

Brenda Hillman: "The Vowels Pass by in English" previously appeared in the journal *Berkeley Poetry Review*. Reprinted by permission of the author. "Cascadia" previously appeared in *Cascadia* (Wesleyan, 2001). Reprinted by permission of the author and Wesleyan University Press.

Kevin Holden: "Fir" previously appeared in the journal *1913: a journal of forms*. Reprinted by permission of the author.

Paul Hoover: selections from *Edge and Fold* previously appeared in *Edge and Fold* (Apogee Press, 2006). Reprinted by permission of the author and Apogee Press.

Erika Howsare & Kate Schapira: "Florida" is previously unpublished and appears here by permission of the authors.

Brenda Iijima: "Panthering Φ" previously appeared in *If Not Metamorphic* (Ahsahta, 2010). Reprinted by permission of the author and Ahsahta Press.

Sally Keith: "The Action of a Man," by Sally Keith, from *The Fact of the Matter* (Minneapolis: Milkweed Editions, 2012). Copyright © 2012 by Sally Keith. Reprinted with permission from Milkweed Editions (www.milkweed.org).

Karla Kelsey: an early version of "Vantage of Landscape & Soft Motion" appeared in the journal *Octopus*. Reprinted by permission of the author.

Amy King: "A Geography of Pleasure" previously appeared in the journal *Octopus*. Reprinted by permission of the author.

Melissa Kwasny: "Talk to the Golden Birches," "Talk to the Water Dipper," and "The Butterfly Conservatory," by Melissa Kwasny, from *The Nine Senses* (Minneapolis: Milkweed Editions, 2011). Copyright © 2011 by Melissa Kwasny. Reprinted with permission from Milkweed Editions (www.milkweed.org).

Brian Laidlaw: "Terratactic (II)" previously appeared in the journal *VOLT*. Reprinted by permission of the author.

Maryrose Larkin: excerpt from "Late Winter 30" previously appeared in *The Name of This Intersection Is Frost* (Shearsman, 2010). Reprinted by permission of the author.

Ann Lauterbach: "Still *No Still*" previously appeared in the journal *Conjunctions*. Reprinted by permission of the author.

Karen An-hwei Lee: "Dream of Inflation" and "Museum of Zona Radiata" are previously unpublished and appear here by permission of the author.

Paul Legault: "The You-Know-What" previously appeared in *The Other Poems* (Fence, 2011). "What One's Set One's Sights On" is previously unpublished. © 2012 by Paul Legault and printed here with his permission.

Sylvia Legris: "Almost Migration . . ." previously appeared in the journal *Conjunctions*. Reprinted by permission of the author.

Dana Levin: "Spring" previously appeared in *Sky Burial*. Copyright © 2009 by Dana Levin. Reprinted with the permission of The Permissions Company, Inc., on behalf of Copper Canyon Press, www.coppercanyonpress.org.

Eric Linsker: "The Bird Goes Behind You" and "Operative Spring" previously appeared in the journal *Conjunctions*. Reprinted by permission of the author.

Alessandra Lynch: "What the Meadow Said Afterwards" previously appeared in *Sails the Wind Left Behind* (Alice James Books, 2002). Reprinted by permission of the author and Alice James Books.

Aaron McCollough: "[*log*—a mild vision]" first appeared in *Double Venus* (Salt, 2003). Reprinted by permission of the author and Salt Publishing.

Joyelle McSweeney: "Arcadia, or, Anachronism: A Necropastoral Effigy" is previously unpublished and appears here by permission of the author.

J. Michael Martinez: "Water Poppies Open as the Mouth: The Body as Nature, History" and "The Sternum of Our Lady of Guadalupe" previously appeared in *Heredities* (Louisiana State University Press, 2010). Reprinted by permission of the author and Louisiana State University Press.

Nicole Mauro: "Three Pangrams" is previously unpublished and appears here by permission of the author.

K. Silem Mohammad: excerpts from "The Sonnagrams" appeared previously in the journals *Try* and *Boo,* respectively. They appear here by permission of the author.

Laura Moriarty: "Plumas" previously appeared in *A Semblance: Selected Poems, 1975–2007* (Omnidawn, 2007). Reprinted by permission of the author and Omnidawn.

Rusty Morrison: "Field Notes: 1–6," "Making Space," "Field Notes: 13–16" are reprinted from *Whethering*. Copyright © 2004 by Rusty Morrison. Used by permission of the Center for Literary Publishing.

Erín Moure: "Memory Penitence / Contamination Église" previously appeared in *Search Procedures* (House of Anansi, 1995). "14 Descriptions of Trees" previously appeared in *A Frame of the Book* (House of Anansi, 1999). Reprinted by permission of the author and House of Anansi Press.

Jennifer Moxley: "The Sense Record" previously appeared in *The Sense Record and Other Poems* (Washington, DC: Edge Books, 2002, and Cambridge, UK: Salt Publishing, 2003). Reprinted by permission of the author.

Laura Mullen: "The White Box of Mirror Dissolved Is Not Singular" and "Orographic" previously appeared in *Dark Archive* (University of California Press, 2011). Reprinted by permission of the author and University of California Press.

Melanie Noel: "The Lion Ant" and "Strangel Mine" are previously unpublished and appear here by permission of the author.

Kathryn Nuernberger: "U.S. EPA Reg. No. 524-474" previously appeared in *Rag & Bone* (Elixir, 2011). Reprinted by permission of the author and Elixir Press.

Peter O'Leary: "The Phosphorescence of Thought" is previously unpublished and appears here by permission of the author.

Craig Santos Perez: excerpt from "ta(la)ya" is previously unpublished. Printed here by permission of the author.

Patrick Pritchett: "The Dream of Open Space," "Forms of Disappearance," and "Twenty-First Century Ecology" first appeared in the journal *Interim*. Reprinted by permission of the author.

Bin Ramke: "A Measured Narrowness" previously appeared in *Aerial* (Omnidawn, 2012). Reprinted by permission of the author and Omnidawn.

Stephen Ratcliffe: selections from *CLOUD/RIDGE* previously appeared in *CLOUD/RIDGE* (BlazeVox, 2011). Selections from *Temporality* previously appeared on Ratcliffe's blog, http://stephenratcliffe.blogspot.com/; reprinted by permission of the author.

Matt Reeck: "Ode to /a/" and "Ode to /I/" previously appeared in the journal *Aufgabe*. Reprinted by permission of the author.

Marthe Reed: "Chandeleur Sound" first appeared on the website *Poets for Living Waters* (http://poetsgulfcoast.wordpress.com). Reprinted by permission of the author.

Evelyn Reilly: "BEAR.MEA(E)T.POLYSTYRENE" and "DAFFODIL.GONDOLA.POLYSTYRENE" previously appeared in *Styrofoam* (Roof Books, 2009). Reprinted by permission of the author. Photograph of "Garden" by Andrea Gardner is reprinted by permission of the artist.

Karen Rigby: "Autobiography as Panamanian Botanical Index" previously appeared in the journal *Mid-American Review*. Reprinted by permission of the author.

Ed Roberson: "City Eclogue: Words for It" and "*Sequoia sempervirens*" previously appeared in *City Eclogues* (Atelos, 2006). Reprinted by permission of the author.

Lisa Robertson: "Wednesday" previously appeared in *The Weather* (New Star Books, 2001). Reprinted by permission of the author and New Star Books.

Elizabeth Robinson: "Crossing" is previously unpublished and appears here by permission of the author.

Leslie Scalapino: "Meadow of dissociative disorder," "Soft Green (The notion of their being . . .)," "Soft Green (The soft green meadows . . .)," "Programmed death-center of the emerald dark," and "They see as if signing by hands" previously appeared in *The Dihedrons Gazelle—Dihedrals Zoom* (Post-Apollo Press, 2010). Reprinted by permission of Simone Fattal and Post-Apollo Press.

Standard Schaefer: "The L.A. River" previously appeared in *Water & Power* (Agincourt Press, 2005). Reprinted by permission of the author.

Brandon Shimoda: "[bulbs in the flash pillar]" from "Lake M" first appeared in the journal *Harp & Altar*. Reprinted by permission of the author.

Eleni Sikelianos: "ODE: To My Peoplery, Little Trees" and "The Most Beautiful Theorems of the Theory of Animals, Numbers" previously appeared in *Earliest Worlds*. Copyright © 2001 by Eleni Sikelianos. Reprinted with the permission of The Permissions Company, Inc., on behalf of Coffee House Press, www.coffeehousepress.org.

Jonathan Skinner: "Tope Prisms" previously appeared in *Political Cactus Poems* (Palm Press, 2005). Reprinted by permission of the author and Palm Press.

Gustaf Sobin: "Under the Bright Orchards" and "Pastoral" previously appeared in *Towards the Blanched Alphabets* (Talisman House, 1998) and subsequently in *Collected Poems* (Talisman House, 2010).

Juliana Spahr: "Gentle Now, Don't Add to Heartache" previously appeared in *Well Then There Now* (Black Sparrow Press, 2011). Reprinted by permission of the author.

Jane Sprague: "Politics of the Unread" previously appeared in *The Port of Los Angeles* (Chax, 2009). Reprinted by permission of the author. "White Footed Mouse" previously appeared in the journal *Ecopoetics*. Reprinted by permission of the author.

Fenn Stewart: "some grimy apple; or, my sequel's wiltshire parts" and "salt fish pan one" are previously unpublished and appear here by permission of the author.

Adam Strauss: "Others Necessary" first appeared in *Colorado Review;* "No Fathers without

Mothers" and "'The Wild Carrot Taking the Field by Force'" are previously unpublished. All appear here by permission of the author.

Mathias Svalina: "Metal" previously appeared in the journal *Trickhouse* and appears here by permission of the author.

Arthur Sze: "The Gingko Light" previously appeared in *The Gingko Light*. Copyright © 2009 by Arthur Sze. Reprinted with the permission of The Permissions Company, Inc., on behalf of Copper Canyon Press, www.coppercanyonpress.org.

John Taggart: "Slash" first appeared in the journal *VOLT*. Reprinted by permission of the author.

Michelle Taransky: "Barn Burning, An Eclogue" previously appeared in *Barn Burned, Then* (Omnidawn, 2009). Reprinted by permission of the author and Omnidawn.

Brian Teare: "Transcendental Grammar Crown" first appeared in its entirety as a chapbook by Woodland Editions in 2006. Individual poems first appeared in *Boston Review, Chronicle of Higher Education, Joyful Noise: An Anthology of American Spiritual Poetry,* and *VOLT*. The sequence is reprinted here by permission of the author.

Tony Tost: "Kept" previously appeared in the journal *Cannibal*. Reprinted by permission of the author.

Tony Trigilio: "Rainforests for Boneshakers" is previously unpublished and appears here by permission of the author.

Catherine Wagner: "Mercury Vector 1," "Pastoral Interlude," and "A Form for Verse" previously appeared in the journal *Verse*. Reprinted by permission of the author.

Jasmine Dreame Wagner: "Champion Mill" previously appeared in the journal *Aufgabe* and in the chapbook *Listening for Earthquakes* (Caketrain, 2012). Reprinted by permission of the author.

Elizabeth Willis: "The Similitude of This Great Flower," "The Oldest Part of the Earth," "Viewless Floods of Heat," and "Near and More Near" previously appeared in *Meteoric Flowers* (Wesleyan, 2007). Reprinted by permission of the author and Wesleyan University Press.

Jane Wong: excerpts from *Sea of Trees* first appeared in the journal *Versal*. Reprinted by permission of the author.

C. D. Wright: excerpt from *Deepstep Come Shining* copyright © 2010 by C. D. Wright. Reprinted with the permission of The Permissions Company, Inc., on behalf of Copper Canyon Press, www.coppercanyonpress.org.

AHSAHTA PRESS

SAWTOOTH POETRY PRIZE SERIES

2002: Aaron McCollough, *Welkin* (Brenda Hillman, judge)

2003: Graham Foust, *Leave the Room to Itself* (Joe Wenderoth, judge)

2004: Noah Eli Gordon, *The Area of Sound Called the Subtone* (Claudia Rankine, judge)

2005: Karla Kelsey, *Knowledge, Forms, The Aviary* (Carolyn Forché, judge)

2006: Paige Ackerson-Kiely, *In No One's Land* (D. A. Powell, judge)

2007: Rusty Morrison, *the true keeps calm biding its story* (Peter Gizzi, judge)

2008: Barbara Maloutas, *the whole Marie* (C. D. Wright, judge)

2009: Julie Carr, *100 Notes on Violence* (Rae Armantrout, judge)

2010: James Meetze, *Dayglo* (Terrance Hayes, judge)

2011: Karen Rigby, *Chinoiserie* (Paul Hoover, judge)

NEW SERIES

1. Lance Phillips, *Corpus Socius*

2. Heather Sellers, *Drinking Girls and Their Dresses*

3. Lisa Fishman, *Dear, Read*

4. Peggy Hamilton, *Forbidden City*

5. Dan Beachy-Quick, *Spell*

6. Liz Waldner, *Saving the Appearances*

7. Charles O. Hartman, *Island*

8. Lance Phillips, *Cur aliquid vidi*

9. Sandra Miller, *oriflamme.*

10. Brigitte Byrd, *Fence Above the Sea*

11. Ethan Paquin, *The Violence*

12. Ed Allen, *67 Mixed Messages*

13. Brian Henry, *Quarantine*

14. Kate Greenstreet, *case sensitive*

15. Aaron McCollough, *Little Ease*

16. Susan Tichy, *Bone Pagoda*

17. Susan Briante, *Pioneers in the Study of Motion*
18. Lisa Fishman, *The Happiness Experiment*
19. Heidi Lynn Staples, *Dog Girl*
20. David Mutschlecner, *Sign*
21. Kristi Maxwell, *Realm Sixty-four*
22. G. E. Patterson, *To and From*
23. Chris Vitiello, *Irresponsibility*
24. Stephanie Strickland, *Zone : Zero*
25. Charles O. Hartman, *New and Selected Poems*
26. Kathleen Jesme, *The Plum-Stone Game*
27. Ben Doller, *FAQ:*
28. Carrie Olivia Adams, *Intervening Absence*
29. Rachel Loden, *Dick of the Dead*
30. Brigitte Byrd, *Song of a Living Room*
31. Kate Greenstreet, *The Last 4 Things*
32. Brenda Iijima, *If Not Metamorphic*
33. Sandra Doller, *Chora.*
34. Susan Tichy, *Gallowglass*
35. Lance Phillips, *These Indicium Tales*
36. Karla Kelsey, *Iteration Nets*
37. Brian Teare, *Pleasure*
38. Kristen Kaschock, *A Beautiful Name for a Girl*
39. Susan Briante, *Utopia Minus*
40. Brian Henry, *Lessness*
41. Lisa Fishman, *FLOWER CART*
42. Aaron McCollough, *No Grave Can Hold My Body Down*
43. Kristi Maxwell, *Re-*
44. Andrew Grace, *Sancta*
45. Chris Vitiello, *Obedience*
46. Paige Ackerson-Kiely, *My Love Is a Dead Arctic Explorer*
47. David Mutschlecner, *Enigma and Light*
48. Joshua Corey and G. C. Waldrep, eds., *The Arcadia Project*

THIS BOOK IS DESIGNED AND SET IN
APOLLO AND HELVETICA TYPE BY QUEMADURA.
PRINTED IN CANADA.

Ahsahta Press

2012
JANET HOLMES, DIRECTOR

CHRISTOPHER CARUSO

JODI CHILSON

KYLE CRAWFORD

CHARLES GABEL

JESSICA HAMBLETON, INTERN

RYAN HOLMAN

MELISSA HUGHES, INTERN

TORIN JENSEN

ANNIE KNOWLES

STEPHA PETERS

JULIE STRAND